Tourism

Tourism
Between Place and Performance

Edited by

Simon Coleman

and

Mike Crang

Berghahn Books
New York • Oxford

First published in 2002 by **Berghahn Books**

www.BerghahnBooks.com

Library of Congress Cataloging-in-Publication Data

Tourism: between place and performance/edited by Simon Coleman &
Mike Crang..
    p. cm.
    Includes bibliographical references and index.
    ISBN 1-57181-745-X (cloth: alk. paper). -- ISBN 1-57181-746-8 (pbk. : alk.
paper)
    1. Tourism.   2. Tourism – Social aspects.   I. Coleman, Simon.
II. Crang, Mike.
G155.A1 T58953 2002
338.4791--dc21   2002018267

British Library Cataloging-in-Publication Data

A catalogue record for this book is available
from the British Library
Printed in the USA on acid-free paper

ISBN 1-57181-745-X (hardback)
ISBN 1-57181-746-8 (paperback)

Table of Contents

List of Illustrations

List of Tables

Acknowledgements

The editors would like to express their gratitude to The Dean's Fund of Durham University for supporting the conference at Durham, Collingwood College, on Practising Places and Tourist Performances in April 1998. The intellectual support and encouragement from the Tourism and Leisure Research Group at the University has been invaluable. We are grateful to the University of Minnesota Press for agreeing that this version of Mark Neumann's essay can be included in the collection. Thanks to Eli, Gabriel and Ferdy for their interest and providing reasons not to work on the book in their own inimitable fashions. Thanks to Leslie and Alex for putting up with obsessive chat and preoccupied partners.

List of Contributors

Jeremy Boissevain, *University of Amsterdam*
Simon Coleman, *University of Durham*
Mike Crang, *University of Durham*
Claudia Bell, *University of Auckland*
John Lyall, *installation artist in New Zealand*
Mark Neumann, *University of South Florida*
Fraser MacDonald, *University of Oxford*
Paola Filippucci, *New Hall Cambridge.*
Keith Ridler, *Massey University*
Penny Travlou, *University of Durham*
John Eade, *Roehampton Institute*
Hazel Tucker, *University of Otago*
Eve Meltzer, *University of California at Berkeley*
Charles Fruehling Springwood, *Illinois Wesleyan University*
Dick Chaney, *University of Durham*
David Crouch, *University of Derby* and *Karlstad University*

Preface

Jeremy Boissevain

This book is a welcome addition to a rapidly growing field of studies. Strangely, tourism, one of the world's major industries, was, until recently, all but ignored by most social scientists. A few sociologists – notably Eric Cohen (1972, 1979) and Dean MacCannell (1976) – and some anthropologists – many contributors to Valene Smith's *Hosts and Guests* (1977) – began to examine some of the social and cultural aspects of tourism in the 1970s. During most of the 1970s and 1980s, however, the interest in tourism remained feeble, until, suddenly, a decade ago, a spate of publications signalled its coming of age as a field of study. New editions of MacCannell's and Smith's seminal books appeared in 1989, as well as a review article on the study of tourism in the social sciences (Crick 1989), and 1990 saw the publication of sociologist John Urry's influential *The Tourist Gaze*. Since then, studies have proceeded apace. During the past three years no fewer than six new collections of case studies have been published (Boissevain 1996; Briguglio 1996; Selwyn 1996; Waldren 1996; Fsadni and Selwyn 1997; Abram, Waldren and Macleod 1997). The present volume reflects this renewed interest in tourism. Why, we may well ask, has interest in the field developed so slowly, and what accounts for its sudden take-off in the 1990s?

There are several reasons why some researchers – anthropologists for example – were reluctant to look at tourism. During the 1960s and 1970s, as mass tourism began to spread, most anthropologists were still engaged in studies of relatively isolated communities, which tourists seldom reached. Thus, they saw no tourists. Moreover, most were still examining 'their' communities as closed systems in which there was no theoretical place for tourists. If tourists were signalled, field workers tended to ignore their presence. Like Malinowski, who had disregarded the presence of white planters throughout his Trobriand fieldwork during the first World War, most anthropologists, until the 1970s, avoided facing up to the complex presence of 'outsiders'. Others, working with neomarxist theoretical models, regarded tourists as neocolonialists from the cosmopolitan centre, bent on exploiting the underdeveloped countries of the periphery. They dismissed them as furthering structural underdevelopment.

They, too, avoided tourism as distasteful. Yet others regarded it as a frivolous subject, unworthy of academic attention.

The current interest in tourism is, first of all, related to the fact that, by the end of the 1980s, tourism had become a massive and truly global industry. Tourists, in one form or another, now penetrate even the most remote communities. In many areas, like the Mediterranean coast, the Caribbean islands and the Alps, tourists vastly outnumber locals during the high season. Their presence can no longer be ignored. Also, in the 1980s, new theoretical questions began to influence research. Anthropologists started to look seriously 'beyond the community'. Neomarxist political-economists lost their following. Researchers have become progressively more concerned with the impact of steadily increasing urbanisation, the expansion of transnational corporations, industrial restructuring, the growing gap between rich and poor, progressive environmental degradation, new and expanding modes of communication and the growth of media leisure pursuits and the massification of popular culture. These developments are increasingly perceived as interrelated aspects of the overarching process of globalisation. At the dawn of the new millennium, globalisation has become the new academic buzz word.

Tourism, above all, and if nothing else, is emblematic of globalisation. Its transnational commercial and logistic infrastructure employs hundreds of thousands. The annual, and increasingly bi- and tri-annual, touristic exodus is fuelled by various impulses. Some seek authentic nature, culture, exotic others, amusement, or the discovery of self. The motives are legion. What is certain is that for all, being a tourist represents time-out-of-time, a liminal period removed from the constraints of normal, every day routine. Some researchers, sociologists by and large, probe for the motives that drive these masses to travel and gaze. They continue to uncover new ones and hotly debate their findings. Others, most often anthropologists and geographers, explore the impact of these leisured outsiders on those visited, euphemistically dubbed the 'hosts'. The impact is far-reaching, complex and raises many questions.

What is the nature and content of the interaction between tourists and those they visit? What do the different parties get out of the encounter? What does it mean to them? How are destination communities promoted and how do they promote themselves? How do locals react to the commodification of their culture, their lifeways, their landscape? What do rituals and events staged for outsiders mean to visitors and to locals who enact as well as watch them? How do locals cope with the expectations and demands of tourists and their commercial managers? What impact is the tourist gaze and globalised culture having on local identity and the perception of self?

The following chapters investigate these and other questions. Much of the analysis is innovative and the case material is certainly fascinating.

It is a truly stimulating exploration of a rapidly expanding field.

Grounded Tourists, Travelling Theory

Simon Coleman
Mike Crang

The authors of this collection examine how tourism shapes particular sites and how activities become scripted in certain locations. Our argument is that several theoretical stories about tourism have relied upon a number of assumptions about places and tourist practices which need to be recast. We suggest that, instead of seeing places as relatively fixed entities, to be juxtaposed in analytical terms with more dynamic flows of tourists, images and cultures, we need to see them as fluid and created through performance. By analysing a number of Western tourist locales in relation to the varied, often contested performances of 'visitors' and 'hosts', our intention is to highlight a dynamic sense of embodied and performed, as well as visualised and textualised, engagement with places and tourist activities.

Reinscribing the Local

Accounts of tourism frequently offer a declensionist narrative of a variegated world of myriad wonders and peoples gradually being brought within the ambit of the hegemonic tourist system. This approach posits a world of bounded cultures – national, ethnic or regional – all modelled as coherent and closed systems of meaning (Lury 1997). By introducing foreign values, altering local priorities or converting local customs into commodities, tourism appears to rupture and contaminate these systems. At worst, the process is perceived as producing interminable package resorts with thousands of identical hotels, offering private pools and reducing locals to servants.

The scenario presented above creates a vision of tourism as generative of the non-places of hypermodernity, eroding the innate and specific values of places (Relph 1976). Tourism is seen as of a piece with the shopping mall, the suburb and fast food outlets. These places all seemingly entail the production of standardised experiences for consumers, targeting a mass market and homogenising the world to produce a generic experience. Tourism is thus associated with the McDonaldisation of travel (Ritzer 1993). Explore the world and the same burger chain will serve products warranted to be of the same standard. Some tourism creates enclaves of 'tourist only' space, insulating tourists rather than expanding their experience, cosseting them inside the air-conditioned bus, moving them from airliner to hotel (Edensor 1998, Prato and Trivero 1985). This mode of tourism is about expanding the space of home rather than visiting the other. Marc Augé (1995) revisited Relph's critique of placeless and alienating environments to dissect a hypermodern landscape of non-places – that is, places where people do not belong but engage instrumentally in scripted performances. Relph maintained a Heideggerian concern with the idea of dwelling in place, whereas Augé emphasises how these non-places are offered at an 'occurrent' level, as intended and designed environments made available for a particular and limited use.

If one observes the sprawl of concrete along the Mediterranean coast with its assorted 'authentic English pubs', the vision of tourism as homogenising and destroying local particularity might seem to have some credibility, but clearly this view does not exhaust the range of tourist places. We might take the historical-geographical pattern of touristic development as a guide. It always seems to be the case that what were once fashionable, exotic and elite locations have gradually become popular and mass resorts, made more accessible and democratised by cheap travel and the increasing wealth of working people. There is, it appears, a game of élite and mass; in short, a matter of taste and distinction (Bourdieu 1984), entangled in this process. One consequence is the development of learnt practices and value judgements concerning what it is to be a good tourist. As one of Edensor's (1998: 126) interviewees (Linda, thirty-three, financial consultant from London, on a three week package tour with a friend) put it:

> I think Indians are really crap tourists. They just don't know how to be tourists, rushing around, talking all the time and never stopping to look at anything – even here at the Taj Mahal!

Urry [1990] draws out the distinctions between tourists in terms of desired experiences as 'romantic' and 'mass', where the romantic vision seeks uniquely framed contact with the place and the mass tourist seeks more of the same. The élite must always find new locations, uncontaminated by the mass – places which will thus still carry a high level of symbolic capital and which are guaranteed as different by the difficulty in getting there, hardships or cost. Modern tourism is therefore an inherently expansive economy, constantly appropriating and constructing new experiences and places. Yet such activity bears with it the ironic seeds of its own destruction, as the very presence of the tourist corrupts the idea of reaching an authentic and totally different culture. Paradoxically, a nostalgic semiotic economy is produced, one that is always mourning the loss of that which it itself has ruined (Rosaldo 1989, Frow 1988). The really authentic unspoiled place is always displaced in space or time – it is spatially located over the next hill, or temporally existed just a generation ago.

Faced with these challenges, workers in the travel business have attempted to reinscribe difference in places. In a global market, where tourists have a wide choice of similar destinations, it has become vital to make a distinctive pitch. Rather as cities compete to attract footloose capital, so places have to market their specificity (Harvey 1989). Destination regions do not simply exist nor naturally happen, and one can chart the creation of regions as linked and themed areas, excluding some places and highlighting others. Features and regions have a historical evolution and political and economic investments in their creation (Saarinen 1997). What results is not globalisation so much as glocalisation (Swyngedouw 1988), where the local has to be recovered, packaged and sold. This strategy has been applied not just to conventional resorts but also to formerly industrial cities in the marketing of short breaks or conference resources, as well as in the accentuated preservation of historic urban sites (Ashworth and Tunbridge 1990, Meethan 1996). Of course, many developments, trading on urban heritage, have risked forming a pattern all their own, where the specificities of the city are lost in the generic signifiers of yet another waterfront development, where the investment in sympathetic conservation and development serves merely to bring in a range of ubiquitous historic 'street furniture' that is no more local than anything else (Hayden 1996). The packaging of places, and especially the marketing of their 'heritage', has become almost unifying in many parts of the West, bringing together disparate sites and activities in the promotion of a place (but see Macdonald 1997). The commodification of the past almost provides a unity in diversity, or similarity at a higher level by making all these sites equivalent as potential places to visit.

It does not require a great leap of imagination to move from such urban reconstruction to the fabrication of places. Preserving local heritage can shade into a recreation of what might (or, from the perspective of the present, should) have been, blurring into straight make-believe (Fowler 1989, 1992). This is the world of hyperreality and theme parks (Eco 1987). The extremes dissected by Jean Baudrillard under the rubric of simulacra seem pertinent here. The simulacrum is the copy without an original, simulating what never existed in the first place. Thus, Disneyland's main street is a pastiche of what an archetypal north American main street might have been like. The logic of the theme park can also expand to other urban and tourist locations, such as the created environments of shopping malls (Simon 1992, Sorkin 1993). This logic is apparently about the loss of 'authentic' place – disappearing entirely in Baudrillard's most cata-clysmic moments. However, it would be wrong to say these environments are placeless – rather, they expend effort on creating ideas of places. Indeed, Moscardo and Pearce (1986) argue that it is perverse to claim that such places as historic theme parks are inauthentic when so much effort goes into realism and so many of their audience find them realistic. In saying this they rather miss the point: that so much energy has to be invested expresses something of an anxiety and desire, while the realism or otherwise is often judged in terms of other mediatised environments (such as other parks, malls or museums) and represen-tations (such as film and TV). These latter sites work to create a sense of locatedness and authenticity by deploying representations of places – both near and far in time and space. For instance, Simon (1993) takes a brief walk through a mall and points out how the stores play upon our knowledge of, or associations with, Viennese café culture, colonial adventure, Victorian Britain and the American West. These sites are not placeless, but are perhaps better seen as what Shields (1989) called 'elsewhere' – displaced and connected to images of other places in a global circulation. In the end it is not just the tourists who are circulating but also the place-images themselves. Lury (1997: 79–83) points to the objects between culture, which vary from trav-eller objects with immanent meanings, to tripper objects with mean-ings inscribed by the travel and to objects of travel that dwell – i.e., refer to another place. In this sense we need to be aware of the places that are created through technologies, and the construction of places of culture through mediating objects.

Globalised Knowledges and Practices

The arguments we have explored above may have a certain coherence to them, yet they seem to retain a distinction between places as either authentically experienced by locals or simulated and staged for visiting consumers. In fact, this very distinction has been argued to be an inte-gral presupposition of tourism practices themselves. Over twenty years ago, Dean MacCannell's (1976) pioneering work outlined tourism as an existential quest for 'authentic' experiences. He argued that, as modern life offered more and more reproductions, so the desire for the original would increase. An alternative outcome would be for the authentic, when found, to seem rather dowdy and indeed compare unfavourably with the sophisticated experiences that can be created (see Eco 1987). Alternatively, the postmodern tourist may well not care, but be prepared for the ironic interplay of constructed experiences. MacCannell's model, however, presupposes a particular structure and performative pattern. He refers to a dramatic space divided between Goffman's front and back regions (Hughes-Freeland 1998a: 3), where the front is the staged show while the back regions contain the authentic experience. The logic of MacCannell's argument is that, increasingly, the back regions become put on show and staged. In this sense, tourism is a genre error where the quotidian of one group is staged for the entertainment of another (Kirshenblatt-Gimblett 1991). Such translation from back to front is expected to change and perhaps threaten the very authenticity sought in the first place.

We argue that these views of the performative representation of authenticity rely upon a particular idea of place and its relationship to culture. This idea sees cultures as not merely located but circumscribed and rooted. Firstly, we might question the idea that people and cultures are, or still need to be, rooted in places (Meyrowitz 1985, Augé 1995) or more fundamentally that this ever was a necessary link (Olwig and Hastrup 1997: 1). We need to recognise that the intellectual vision of these territorially monopolistic, bounded and coherent cultures has been inflected by nationalist interpretation at home (Dundes 1985, Handler and Linnekin 1989) and by the creation of a spectacle of diversity for imperial (and later tourist) consumption (Mitchell 1994). In each case we might note that the idea of a whole and coherent (and with that, localised and discrete) culture often entails a good deal of retrospective logic. As Theodor Adorno once remarked, to pose the question 'What makes a German?' presupposes the existence of an essential Germanness (cited Morley and Robins 1993: 6).

Secondly, this vision operates through a dualistic model whereby cultures and belonging work in terms of a/not-a, inside and outside categories (Massey 1992). That is, the logic of belonging becomes one of either/or rather than allowing both/and. It is now common for commentators to point to the multicultural composition of nations and peoples, to the globalised movements of peoples and goods (of which tourism is a part), which have broken down any idea of the singularity of place and culture (eg., Hannerz 1996, Bhabha 1994). Distinctions between producers and consumers, hosts and tourists are also challenged in contexts where audiences can be both local and distant, and where hosts are themselves tourists in other places (Boissevain 1996: 1). While tourists and other temporary visitors might conventionally have been seen as extraneous to 'local' culture, undermining the autonomy of places, they can alternatively be regarded as helping to reconstitute it by adding a relational dimension to local performances and perceptions of the distinctiveness of place (Abram et al. 1997: 3–4).

More radical critiques have suggested that what is being described is not just a 'problem' of contemporary society, but one that has long historical roots. Any study of the history of empire – which is the shared history of three-quarters of humanity – suggests stories of cultures in contact, of one culture shaping the ideas and notions about another. Indeed, many commentators have pointed to notions of hybrid cultures and creolisation or mutual entanglement instead of seeing Western and non-Western cultures as confronting each other like two pre-formed blocks (Wolf 1982, Gilroy 1994). These criticisms are relatively well known, though their implications are less often drawn out in literature about tourism. The third point that we wish to stress is that this model has quite often mobilised a series of dualisms around notions of Being versus Becoming. Very often the toured are marked out as possessing a culture defined as an organic totality, fixed in a place. The local culture is seen as evolving through collective activity, production and reproduction. Local tradition is disrupted by outside forces. Indigenous culture, and especially folk culture, is thus framed as a non-modern activity. Most forcefully, this orientation has been applied to aboriginal peoples whose modern life is seen as antithetical to authentic life. We have seen the model of 'disappearing worlds' where anthropologists can only salvage the remnants of 'pre-contact' cultures. So we are left with Hopi handicrafts being authenticated as traditional by outside anthropologists. Or, in the case of English folk culture from the turn of the century, ethnologists and collectors saw themselves salvaging the remnants of folklore from people who were themselves unworthy guardians of such culture (Boyes 1995). Notably in this last case, the collectors actually took the fragments of performances and intellectually reconstructed a version of a unified past culture that had somehow been lost (cf. Hobsbawm and Ranger 1983). The only role for present performance was to repeat and replicate; innovation could only degrade. Instead, we want to stress how much of the performance of local cultures has always been conscious and reflexive, even if such reflexivity may not exactly have corresponded to that evident in Western contexts. Indeed, the construction of an unchanging, holistic view may be very much a product of modern encounters.

Richard Handler has neatly problematised the issue of authentic originary culture where, in his studies of Quebecois culture, he points out that folklore study and preservation have been carried out for so long that they themselves are almost traditional occupations and concerns (1988). Many local customs and traditions are indeed self-conscious and evolving performances. So we want to move the field away from a model that sees an authentic culture as singular and local, and thus as necessarily degraded through tourism. Indeed, in some cases we will suggest that tourism and global connections produce particular local configurations. However, we are equally aware that, while in analytical terms local cultures are evolving products created through the connections between and mutual constitutions of apparently different systems of meaning, many people are still struggling to create viable cultures based on models of local holistic containers (cf. Rojek and Urry 1997: 11). Indeed, if we accept that the contemporary world is marked by ever more prominent global flows (Appadurai 1990), one reaction is precisely that of nostalgic and defensive creation of seemingly more fixed and stable entities. We readily acknowledge the insight of Slavoj Žižek (1991, 1992) when he suggests that one of the tendencies at work is the (fetishised) inversion of Causes and Effects. Multiple cultural practices are assembled and given a collective identity, he argues; however, this practice is experienced as though the hidden collective identity causes those practices, as though it were an essence behind the surface phenomenon. He states further that such a process makes the collective function, in psychoanalytic terms, as though it were a Thing, as though it had actual substance. And, as a corollary, it is a Thing that can be imperilled or damaged and may need defending. In this way, identity becomes something that could be lost.

It is important to note, then, that although we see local cultures constructing themselves through performances, this process in no way makes them less 'real', or 'merely' discursive entities. They have an ontological depth that both animates practitioners and affects debate. Furthermore, care is needed not to simply celebrate defences of the local which can be exclusionary and defensive. Neither do we wish to slip into a morass whereby we theoretically free people from a notion of undynamic tradition only to deny them the possibility of rejecting threatening 'outside' initiatives in the name of their cultural identity. We must instead perceive a dynamic field where the very idea of authenticity is part of a reflexive poetic and political field – a term to be contested and used.

Knowing Looks

Through providing variations on the approach we have outlined, the papers in this collection play around the difficult positions often produced in tourism. Much productive work has analysed the conversion of the world, and places and people in it, into something that can be aesthetically consumed – often through visual means (Stallabras 1996, Debord 1984, Urry 1990). The conversion of the world into an exhibition is a recurring theme in this volume. However, the collection highlights a more dynamic sense of embodied and performed as well as visualised engagement with places and tourist activities. The ubiquitous idea of the gaze has proved useful in tourism studies, but is also limited by its static, auratic quality (see Chaney, this volume) and the fact that it does not take into account the answering 'gaze' of those being viewed (cf. Tucker in Abram et al. 1997: 8). Thus, the dynamics of who is looking at whom, and what is being staged, need to be unpacked. O'Rourke's (MacCannell 1993) film of 'Cannibal Tours' opens a significant angle of this critique. Here we follow the tourists being taken up river in Papua New Guinea. The tourists have come to see the 'cannibals', and that is what they get – the locals playing that role to earn money. Meanwhile the film suggests that those who are most voraciously consuming other people's worlds are the modern tourists (MacCannell 1992). The locals themselves are not untouched and are knowing participants in the process.

Meanwhile, the technologies of staging 'realistic' events are themselves very often part of the marketing of the experience (Slater 1995). The methods of staging realistic dioramas or events for tourists need not be hidden in the back stage, but can be part of the warranting of authenticity in a reflexive manner (Chaney 1993). Thus, recreations of past sites often put alongside the recreated scene the information and technologies of scholarship that went into their production. An appreciation of this point is important if we are to move from an impression that analysis works through what Morris called 'good and bad mirrors' (1992: 269). The visual metaphor often suggests tourism is producing inauthentic images that cloak and mask 'real' world processes. Tourists are bedazzled and allured by promotional images and fobbed off with manufactured and superficial images. Now, we might critique this argument in part through reiterating the activity and performances of tourists themselves in using and manipulating images more creatively than simply as dupes. However, we are also sceptical of the assumption that critical analysis operates like a good mirror, enabling the social commentator to see clearly the machinations of (usually) capital. In this argument, social images and optics are deceptive and alluring, while theory is unproblematically revealing. Instead, we would highlight analyses that point rather more at theory itself as akin to tourism. At one level it has become fashionable to note that theory tends to be about travel, to be developed through travel and the movement of people and things (Helms 1984, Clifford 1989, van den Abbeele 1992). Moreover, it is not a case of narrative being opposed to imagistic forms of knowledge (as Harvey [1989] implies), for tourism is not just about images, but also narration as a form of travel writing (de Certeau 1986, Stewart 1984). Tourism as a practice is not just gazing and viewing; Edensor (1998) points out how, despite its iconicity and importance to visitors, many people spend but a few minutes of a fortnight actually at the Taj Mahal. Tourism is also about storytelling, chatting, swapping anecdotes, competitive tales (either of success or fortitude), where the travel serves to organise what Hutnyk (1996: 145) called the 'endless flow of Indo-babble' among South Asian back-packers. Thus we might look at how symbolic sites are foci around which the mnemonic devices of travel narratives and photography are structured (Edensor 1998: 141). We see tourists fashioning stories about their travels – not in an academic idiom, but through the collection, editing and sorting of photographs, travel diaries and memorabilia. We also note then that those who are tourists one week, may well be the toured the next.

It has been argued that anthropologists themselves are sometimes better seen as a variant of tourists (Redfoot 1984). Both are seeking to create symbolic capital from travel and both work by translating foreign experience into domestic categories. Of course that is not to say they are identical, but the ideological structure whereby academic travel is seen as good and tourist travel as inauthentic still remains within a game of taste and distinction internal to the field of tourism. The differentiation of those who 'really' know places is surely still part of a game of authenticity and claims of backstage knowledge. Indeed, one might say that MacCannell's idea of the Tourist as a modern figure questing for authentic knowledge fits academics rather better than empirical tourists. In terms of the earlier mention of distinctions, it becomes important to note the diversity of motives and practices of tourism. While a typology of actual practices is not an adequate response to a theory of modernity (Selwyn 1996) it does offer the possibility of authentic hedonism. These possibilities, opened up, highlight the point that the thirst to be seen uncovering (not making or telling) the real stories of authentic people in real places is part of and not separate from the economy of taste in tourism. Alternatively, we might follow Trinh (1989) where she classifies anthropology as translation and gossip. As Hutnyk (1996: 32) points out, there is a journalistic and tourism apparatus producing endless 'rumours' of places, but there is also a theoretical machine that shares a similar will to representation. Hutnyk's own example is the positioning of the Modern Lodge in Calcutta as a base for 'independent travellers', which he characterises as making the classical 'view from the veranda' of anthropology open to mass tourism (ibid.: 49).

The turn to thinking about performance offers some ways to develop this debate. For a start, it does not reduce tourism to images that cover or obscure, but allows us to be sensitive to the practices through which tourism occurs. It also resonates with the field, where authors have noted the rise of performance as a genre and as a focus of self-understanding of actors and managers about working under the tourist gaze (Crang P. 1997: 153). Thus, Snow (1992) looks at the rise of performance as a modality of experiencing and making history present while Cantwell (1993) looks at performing identity as part of a current idiom of ethnomimesis that transposes the vertical hierarchies of taste into a more horizontal confrontation with difference. We have to see the performance of local identity not simply as repetition of a given form, but opening up the possibility (though not the inevitability) of an 'emergent authenticity' where, say, an artisan producing tourist art develops an aesthetic that satisfies their own cultural identity (Hoelscher 1998: 381).

Performing Place

The idea of performance is important to us partly because it is embodied; it involves all the senses, including, but not confined to, sight. While we wish to suggest that tourism as an activity implies a series of performances within places, we are certainly not arguing that such 'staging' inherently carries with it a narrative of lost authenticity, a decline from a purer, truer reality (Crang P. 1997: 149). We also want to introduce a sense of performativity as effecting something desired (Hughes-Freeland 1998a: 21) – the creation of places through tourism.

Our concern is therefore with tourism as, and indeed with places as, events. Too often, dramaturgical metaphors suggest performance occurs in a place – reduced to a fixed, if ambient, container. We should instead see places from the perspective of a performance that takes them up and transforms them, redeploys them and connects them through metonymic relationships, or what de Certeau called spatial stories (1984). However, it seems a simple next step to suggest that the places themselves are part and parcel of events, not separate from them. We might draw on the literary theorist J. Hillis Miller's idea of the 'atopical', where space 'is less the already existing setting for such stories, than the production of space through that taking place, through the act of narration' (Donald 1997: 183), where space is an eventful and unique happening, more to do with doing rather than knowing, less a matter of 'how accurate is this?', than 'what happens if I do it?' In this sense we want to open up the possibilities of understanding tourism as an event that is about mobilising and reconfiguring spaces and places, bringing them into new constellations and therefore transforming them. We are not telling a story of wholes brought into contact or of alien presences but more one of a fragmentary process. The models of place and performance generally deployed still seem to rely on a buried notion of self-presence. The actors are singular and holistic, as are the places, where instead we would argue that tourist places and performances are about admitting the incompleteness of experience and places. We want a sense of performativity of place rather than just performance in place. As Kirshenblatt-Gimblett (1998: 294–6) notes, we should look at the theorisation of performativity where the self is contingently and performatively produced, as opposed to the performance studies emphasis on performance in the sense of speech acts as derived from Austin's theory of language.

Our approach acknowledges the processual elements of identity formation (Hirsch and O'Hanlon 1995) or perhaps better focuses upon identification as process rather than identity as category. The spaces of tourism do not comprise a Euclidean grid around which self-present actors move, but rather a crumpled space (Hetherington 1998) where people and places are in process. The statement that we need to attend to events then goes further than may appear at first thought. Tourism study has been bedevilled by an event ontology – an analytic approach that sees only events. Typically it sees these as occurring in fixed locations between discrete actors – transactions, visits, 'bums on seats'. Instead, this collection moves us to look more closely at the ontology of events. Steering away from the taken-for-granted groundings of territorially rooted communities, we take some inspiration from Lury's (1997: 75) critique of tourism considered as 'people travelling to places seen as cultures mapped in space'. There is in this approach a presumption of not only a unity of place and culture, but also of the immobility of both in relation to a fixed carto-graphically coordinated space, with the tourist as one of those wandering figures whose travels, paradoxically, fix places and cultures in this ordered space. This we argue is a view which depends on the erasure of cosmopolitan intermediaries, and complex linkages of peoples, places and objects. Rather than the circulation of people amid fixed places we need to notice the mobilisation of places through objects – be they souvenirs (Gordon 1986), tourist commodities, folk products, or the material images circulating in postcards, brochures and cameras. In other words, we look at the dissemination of place. Alongside this instability there goes an instability in the tourist in a regime of pathic, part-objects and knowledges rather than totalisable, symbolisable systems. It is not that place is eroded through tourism, but rather that the roles it performs in subjectification can no longer be equated with stability.

Pathways

While we have presented one possible pathway through these issues by grouping contributions into subsections in terms of their substantive content, other perspectives are possible. For instance, a central theme in a number of papers is the idea of going beyond the visual to performance. Forms of movement and relationship to spatiality vary in the appropriation of place. Some of our authors concentrate on the views of 'hosts', some on 'tourists'. Some focus on specific media such as texts while others take a multidimensional view of performances 'in place'. Some look at how guides provide scripts for the traveller while others look at how such travellers do not always stick to the script, for instance producing 'glances' that are not 'gazes' (Chaney). All are united, however, in presenting a picture of tourism where place cannot be taken for granted either by people studied or by analysts.

At one level, Bell and Lyall tell a simple, linear story of accelerating movement changing tourism. However, their chapter shows the refiguring of places, as they also demonstrate a complex relationship between accelerated movement to a place and cultivation of movement at a tourist destination. They show a shift from static to dynamic landscape, with nature tourism as a unique kinaesthetic experience. This experience of nature contrasts with the framing of nature discussed in Neumann's essay, which deals with the development of tourism at the Grand Canyon. He emphasises the role of visual media in providing ways of experiencing the place. The two essays share, however, a concern with the technologies of motion and viewing and their role in shaping places and tourist performances. We have already noted that tourism has been one of the technologies converting the world into an exhibition, but we need to add more subtlety to this perspective. For instance, panoramas are linked to modalities of travel, where the leisurely steam boat trip was paralleled by the diorama, some of which extended to miles in length, that were unfurled before the stationary viewer (Sears 1989: 57). While one school of analysis has tended to see these technologies as allowing a virtual mobility for an actually immobilised spectator (Friedberg 1993), the chapters here reinstate the embodied nature of tourism. Bell and Lyall illustrate the production of the (active) tourist body in the expanding market of adventure tourism (Cloke 1997). However, this position does not repeat the distinction Prato and Trivero (1985) make between technologies of travel that are body expanding and those that are insulating containers. As with Crouch's discussion of the multisensuous experience of tourism, we have to think about the embodied experience of place, perhaps at its starkest in contrasts between the ordered enclave spaces of resort tourism in India and the diversity of the chowk offering a heterotopian space (Edensor 1998).

However, heterotopic spaces of multiple orders and stimulations are also actively produced through tourism, as is shown in the two papers on the revival of ritualised forms in Italy: both become essays on the relationship between memory in the body and memory inscribed in place. Bell and Lyall focus on experiencing the new in a new place; Fillippucci and Ridler are about evoking the old in a familiar place. Filippucci's paper looks at two forms of reenactment of past practices, both displaying and constituting 'the local' not simply discursively, but also through lived practice. The old town of Bassano is reinscribed with sensuous, bodily experiences that are to be viewed but also felt: they construct personal links with the past even as they enact it for onlookers. The work at bodily memory constructs senses of authentic engagement with the past. One issue that is raised is the extent to which the authentic link with former times is created through the cultivation of experience as opposed to a historically validated link with former times. We might reflect on this issue in the light of Snow's (1993: 198) argument that historical reenactments parallel rites that bring the myths and historical memories into play for contemporary members of a group. More relevant for our book, however, is the fact that Filippucci's urban Italians construct a perspective that looks at least two ways: enacting the local also means awareness of and negotiation of position in relation to the global gaze.

Ridler's paper is also about the construction of local identity through performances which may also be viewed by outsiders. It draws out the important point, implicit in Filippucci's chapter, that ethnomimesis can embrace ritual, but also extends to nonrepetitive, spontaneous acts of expression that fall within a performative idiom. Unlike Filippucci, though, what is stressed here is not so much the form of movements and their performance, but rather the ways in which rituals are claims on a past that is contested in relation to ambivalent relations in the present. Thus, the performance is also an assertion. It maps local identity in collective mode whilst struggling to define the social field of local identities in an ambiguous cultural space triangulated between identities of the town/village, tourist performances and the centrifugal politics of regionalism in the New Europe. In this sense, both these chapters focus on ethnomimesis and performance as doing, not just showing (Kirshenblatt-Gimblett 1998: 6; Snow 1993: 144).

However, the relationship of performances to audiences and how they are framed needs careful consideration. Looking at the US festival of folklife, Bauman et al. (1992) reported the conflicts produced for folk performers who maintained different conceptions of their own work from those of organisers. The performers drew upon previous experiences of recontextualising their work (Sheehy 1992), to develop performances designed for audiences. So they might see themselves as exhibiting their work, demonstrating it, instructing people in it or just doing it, or more complexly, they saw their performance as the exhibition of a demonstration of their work. Performers complained forcibly when their transport was still prominently labelled 'Zoo Bus' (Cantwell 1993: 143, Bauman et al. 1992: 43). Conversely, some performers made a deliberate play of becoming objects of study – constructing ironic games by telling audiences untruths before saying that they had to stop lying to the folklorists. Such action suggests power through deception for the performer, and by making it a knowing game makes them an equal player with the scholar. This sense of complicated framings is compounded by the histories of representations and performances. Thus, folk festivals may claim to present 'folk' performances located in some unchanging folk time, but there are connections and entanglements with already – and previously – circulating representations (Cantwell 1992: 270). Following these reflexive angles, Tucker's paper presents a local orientation that is altogether more ironic. Again, the issue is place construction with a double view in mind – for 'local' and external consumption, but here the hosts are learning very self-consciously to play themselves as hosts, reflexive representatives of place, with self-knowledge informed by new knowledge of the places from which tourists have come. A Flintstones theme plays to postmodern tourists' desire to meet the other in a form that is fun. Intriguing avenues are opened where the ludic space/time of tourism can be exploited by hosts as well as tourists. Indeed, they are all playing on a stage under the inflection of Turkish tourist-marketing of the country as 'the world's largest open air museum' (Kirshenblatt-Gimblett 1998: 131). The locals performing themselves as Flintstones are complicit in tourist stereotypes, but also resisting, or perhaps deflecting, them through self-irony. Performance here is not ritual or formal *per se*, but a representation of self for others' consumption that is also a way to rescue the self from that consumption.

Tucker's paper is similar to many others in its demonstration of the way performing place is also a contestation of and reappropriation of place. Irony is a form of passive resistance in Goreme. Fraser Macdonald offers a starker drawing of a spectacularised idea of the Western Isles and forms of local activity that disrupt the tourist image. Rather than being scenic stewards, the locals offer alternative interpretations of their landscapes and thus their role within it. The refusal of locals to play the parts scripted for them is seen as part of an attempt to claim a local identity that is not dependent on tourism for its legitimacy. Local crofting identities resist both the tourist industry and the complicity in that of romanticised clan mythology: portraying themselves as members of consumer society upsets stereotypes. Sharon Macdonald's (1997) study of Skye saw, by contrast, a deliberate opening of a heritage centre as a kind of autoethnography of the people, using all the representational tools of multinational tourist business to create a Skye story under the control of Gaelic revivalists. Here, it was this linking of Gaelic and commercial enterprise that was antithetical to the romantic myth of the Island. The presence of such conflicts perhaps encourages us to follow a model not of dualistic inside and outside, but involution (rather than dilution) of local identity. As Oakes (1999: 124) has noted of a tourist development in China, we need;

> A more culturally complex rendering of tourism's 'consumption' of places, one that sees not merely a globalising force bearing down upon

a once isolated community, but also the dynamic ways local cultural meanings – which are themselves a product of a dialogue between local and extra-local cultural systems – wrap the tourism experience in an envelope of local meanings. Rather than an alien force, tourism . . . [is] a phenomenon that must be rendered in the language of the people in whose places it developed.'

These multiple registers and framings may suggest we need to think not simply of semiosis but also the poetics of how these are strung together in the practices of visitors and performers – where neither side monopolises the right to define legitimate performances (Cantwell 1993: 284; Karp and Lavine 1991).

The creation of contradictory local and global places reaches perhaps its apotheosis in two essays by Meltzer and Springwood. Meltzer presents the case where a small town in the US develops its sense of hereness, a presence through vastly overstated and self-referential advertising campaigns. It is the signs that perform the place – almost. Certainly, Wall drug store is not known for its pharmacy. Amid the global inscription of its presence, this store develops a life of its own. It is not arriving there that really counts, but the getting there. Place is, as it were, disseminated through these signs. Meltzer's paper illustrates that such dissemination does not dematerialise place, but leads to mixed up, imbricated relationships between objects, imagination, signs and technologies of apprehension. As Hutnyk (1996: 52) remarks of a different context, the experience of India is 'hybrid, multiple, mixed-up and simulated all at the same time'. The relationships of the backpackers he studied both to home and to India were mediated by images and texts – of what a traveller should be, as well as what the places might mean. His study of Calcutta suggests that we might look at the mediated dispersion of a city, not as erosion, but as creating a recombinant, fragmented communicative city where, in Deleuze and Guattari's terms, an urban rhizome links different orders of experience and multiplies the places possible (Hutnyk 1996: 122). A contrasting case that picks up on these themes is Springwood's account of the 'field of dreams'. His essay raises issues that deal not so much with local culture, but with how national cultures are carried and instantiated. The Japanese baseball diamond he discusses is not only imitative of Americana generally, but a copy of a field created for a Hollywood movie, which itself used the diamond to symbolise American values. Springwood's paper again locates performance in the context of the global economy of signs, where everything has the potential to be commodified: the task to be accomplished is not reenactment of the past as a way of establishing contact with locality (Filippucci and Ridler) but rather the appropriation and reinscription of a 'foreign', commodified form. As with other papers, this is a negotiation rather than a completed act. Place is created and incorporated into 'local' practice as America is performed in a way that does not imply self-alienation: rather, performance of baseball in a field in rural Japan is a 'play' on ideas of what it means to be American and also an expression of ideas of what it means to be Japanese. Here the idea of place becomes both fragmented and globalised through mediation, yet it also comes into being through that very mediation. As Kirshenblatt-Gimblett (1998: 169) puts it, 'The production of hereness in the absence of actualities depends increasingly on virtualities'. This is true of many places where interpreters locate authenticity and the significance of sites in what cannot be seen.

The chapters by Travlou and Eade look at how audiences are led into reading the urban landscape through tourist literature and guides, which provide scripted performances for consumers. In both cases they suggest the complex interplay of previous readings, circulating texts and visitor practice. Travlou traces how guide books inscribe a very particular vision of Athens. A subtractive landscape is evident, which removes the contemporary city to offer a past Greece. In this way current locals become exoticised while historic locals are domesticated and possessed by the tourist. Tourist Athens is not the modern city, and the role of guidebooks in regulating the spatial practices of tourism brings us round to the inscription of tourist enclaves in the urban environment. The conventions of this landscape have been established for many years, and the routinisation and persistence of this representation remind us that performativity does not necessarily mean fluidity and change. Equally, when dealing with iconic sites, Travlou raises the question of prior knowledge and expectation almost swamping the actuality. While many writers about Athens have tried to depopulate it of its modern inhabitants in order to stage an imagined confrontation with its past ones, we can also think of Freud's famous visit, where he could not believe he was actually seeing the Acropolis. As a boy, it had been to him a thing of books, and it had only lived in his imagination (Rojek 1997: 56). Of course, widely circulated images now prefigure many an encounter, but still we may need to consider these imagined places lurking behind the disappointment many feel on reaching sites.

Eade, by way of contrast, examines a comparatively under-toured area of London: Spitalfields. He deconstructs attempts to uncover its 'essential' character – seeing it as a moving and contested space and subject to flows of people, information and images that visit but do not stop; shifting boundaries and alliances in terms of class, ethnicity, religion, generation and neighbourhood are evident. Eade's London, like Springwood's Japan, is a place of the global flow of culture as a form of resource in self-definition. However, while Springwood looks at literal place-construction, much of Eade's paper is on the role of texts in the representation of place for outsiders. In common with

Travlou, he is interested in the idea of place as trope for continuing stereotypes. While Travlou's focus is located in analysis that looks to ideas of orientalism/colonialism continuing in the new colonialism of travel, Eade looks at an old colonial centre that has itself become an arena for new populations.

Several authors raise questions over who constitutes the audience and who the performers. For Bell and Lyall, the audience are part of the performance, but much of their paper is about the creation of experience for those taking part. For Ridler and Filippucci audience is both self and implicit onlooker, who may or may not be part of the locality. For Eade and Travlou, the audience are the readers of an urban landscape and its texts. For Springwood, the main protagonist, Hori Haruyoshi, is the audience of a globally dispersed piece of Americana, which also inspired a US tourist site, but he turned his viewing into his own product – one that is both mimetic and transformative, though with few viewers. While Neumann's essay focuses on the techniques and scripts of visualising a canonical site/sight, the last two chapters by Chaney and Crouch take a less ethnographic and more exploratory look at the practices of viewing and experiencing places. Chaney wants to replace the idea of the gaze with that of the glance. His approach robs the site of aura as the ephemerality of appearance is celebrated. Haphazard consumption of tourists becomes a form of play in public spaces; glancing is carried out by mobile citizens who increasingly inhabit mobile spaces. The paper serves to remind us of the warnings Meaghan Morris (1988) gave about 'cruising grammarians' reading the semiotics of landscapes. We know that many accounts have risked offering an implied reader of the landscape, an assumed tourist – who tends to be male, white and travelling alone (Squire 1998: 85). Indeed, much analysis has been based on the finished texts about places rather than the perhaps more chaotic and provisional performances within them. Handler and Gable's (1997: 9) comment on museums may well apply more widely, 'Most research on museums has proceeded by ignoring what happens in them . . . very little of it focuses on the museum as a social arena in which many people of differing backgrounds continuously and routinely interact to produce, consume and exchange messages'. This point is brought out in Crouch's essay, which takes up the theme of embodiment and sociality. It asks us to think of tourism in the round, and as rather less instrumental and planned than either academic or management accounts tend to imply. He is not describing a case of the accidental tourist, but rather the accidents of tourism. The wayside café, the insect bites, the plumbing may all form part of the memoried texture of a visit when it is recalled. Crouch asks us to think of place as immersive, where not everything can be controlled, because it is experienced in all dimensions.

THE PLACE OF NATURE

The Accelerated Sublime

Thrill-Seeking Adventure Heroes in the Commodified Landscape

Claudia Bell and John Lyall

Introduction

Natural landscape is the overwhelming imagery of many tourist destinations: towering snow-capped mountain peaks, softly waving palm trees and turquoise lagoons, dark rugged forests reflected in mirror lakes. Meanwhile, the study of landscape has gone through two major shifts this century. First, and essentially modernist, the history of landscape as basically the history of landscape photography, following the nineteenth-century tradition of landscape painting. Second, in postmodernist terms, landscape has been decentralised in favour of the semiotic and hermeneutic approaches that treat landscape as an allegory of psychological and ideological themes, which may be decoded as a body of determinate signs. In these terms, 'reading' landscape works as a cultural practice. This latter approach leads to the analysis within this chapter.

In this discussion we locate landscape as a dynamic arena; not static. Ecotourism and adventure tourism are practices that (re)activate the sublime. The participants, descendants of grand tourists viewing the 'sublime' landscape, no longer meander, but accelerate through an increasingly compressed and hyperinscribed space. The passive viewing of nature has evolved to kinetic experiences within this accelerated nature. Contemporary technologies (personal video cameras in particular) inspire and promote these new forms of visitor consumption of the reified kinaesthetically enhanced landscape. Only a moving image device can adequately encode the white water, bungee, paragliding experience.

Tourists are important to national identity and imagery of place in countries/ regions dependent on the commodification of landscape as a consumer item/experience for tourism. Inventive entrepreneurs within the domain of travel capitalism seek or create new thrills for the intrepid traveller. Bungee jumping, white water rafting and paragliding are exemplars of this tendency. It is not by accident that these activities take place in stunningly beautiful, dramatic natural environments. They are a postmodern recapitulation of the high Victorian pleasure at gazing upon landscape. Nature provides a site in which tourists indulge their dreams of mastery over the earth; of being adventure heroes starring in their own movies. In this way, they are showing not only their adventurous and indomitable spirit in the face of (supervised, safe, tourist-orientated) daring experiences; they are also showing off their skills and talents as sophisticated consumers of travel, the major leisure commodity of the late twentieth century. These adventures within nature will become part of their own travel narratives, their own self-constructed illustrated autobiographies.

The Inverted Sublime

In the eighteenth century and earlier, one stood at the bottom of a sublime landscape and looked up at the uninhabited and dangerous abode of the Gods (such as the regard for Mt Athos by the Greeks). Avalanches, floods and lahars reminded one of the mountain's awesome nature. The peaks, often shrouded by sudden storms, or blurred to insubstantiality by mist, remained untracked. Early European travellers, benighted in the high passes, trembled in fear of wolves and worse unknown perils. Eventually, the world's mountains were climbed. This construction of an ascending vertical sublime finally has its epitaph uttered by a New Zealander: 'We knocked the bastard off!': the death of the Kantian sublime. The moment the tallest peak in the globe has been stood on, the uninhabited montaine, abode of the gods, can no longer be constructed.

The sublime had already moved on, however. In the eighteenth and nineteenth centuries the sublime fell on its side. It became a phenomenon of great distance. The landscape boiled away into the heat and dust and bushfire haze of the vast horizontal vistas of North American and Australian landscape paintings. Railways speeded access across space. In the nineteenth century we gained the built sublime: the railway cuttings, tunnels and viaducts that heroically conquered the mountains. This horizontality can also be illustrated by the famous story of Queen Victoria, who sat for some hours and viewed a mile and a half long painting unrolling before her, depicting the shores along the Mississippi river.

The notion of the sublime migrated to the Antipodes. The southern hemisphere was a sublimity mine of virgin peaks, as yet undepicted. On Cook's second voyage to New Zealand, all the gentlemen on board were unanimous in their opinion that voyage artist William Hodges had chosen the correct genre, sublimity, to represent the landscape here. Though we can date this arrival to 1773, in popular culture the concept arrives in the twentieth century by a more convoluted route.

When the sublime is picked up in twentieth-century landscape painting in New Zealand and Australia, it deals with the waterfall and the gorges and chasms. Thomas Mann claimed that modernity is in love with the abyss, and certainly the still unknown places on the planet are the deep potholes and the trenches and abyssal plains of the ocean. In adventure tourism, the current state of the sublime is to stand at the top of the vista (on top of the picture frame) and to leap into this codified, reified, aesthetic arena, with bungee rubber wings attached to heels, and accelerate into the beloved abyss (down past the face of the painting), courtesy of A. J. Hackett Bungee.

Marketing Destinations Using Nature Imagery

The commodification of natural attractions and experiences in nature is a fundamental process within travel capitalism. Many places are promoted to tourists who want to escape from urban cultural environments to marvellous nature: for instance, the Grand Canyon, Serengeti National Park, Igauco Falls. In New Zealand, we can track nature promotion back to the relatively recent colonial period. New Zealand, the last and most remote outpost of the British Empire, was promoted to potential immigrants as a highly desirable Arcadia, a fertile land with splendid scenery (Fairburn 1989, Belich 1996). The earliest tourist brochures included images still commonly replicated today: great mountains reflected in green and blue lakes, rivers racing though steep rocky chasms, lush farmland.

In discourses on identity, representations of nature are a way of accounting for distinctiveness. In countries dependant on tourism, the relationship between topography, culture, identity and the economy has become pivotal. Indeed, for some countries the natural environment may provide one of the few bases on which favourable comparisons can be made with other nations. Tourism reorganises the perceptions of nature and our place in it, explains Wilson, redefining the land in terms of leisure at a time when most of the population is urban, with little direct connection with the land. 'It is no coincidence', he writes, 'that industrial agriculture, the spread of suburbs, and the growth of mass tourism all coincided in the mid-twentieth century' (Wilson 1992: 220). In choosing New Zealand as destination, tourists submit to processes that deliver packaged concepts of the country's natural beauty.

In the early twenty-first century, millions of people live and even travel widely without necessarily having any physical contact with wild country. As Clark tells us, 'where once the European explorer arduously traversed the globe in search of otherness, now the codified signs of the wild and the exotic make their own way around the planet. In this new universe of circulating signs, we are all simultaneously strangers and familiars' (Clark 1994: 65). How then can individuality stand out? Tourists seek experiences not just of exotic places, but places where they can state their own uniqueness.

MacCannell points out that tourism is not just a commercial enterprise, but an 'ideological framing of history, nature and tradition, a framing that has the power to reshape culture and nature to its own ends' (MacCannell 1992: 11). We remember that national and cultural identity are also implicitly tied up with the beginnings of nineteenth-century tourist destinations. Thus, for the English tourist, there was a strong link between the fashionable subjects of literature, poetry and painting and what later became tourist attractions, such as sublime landscape. If we look, in New Zealand, at artistic depictions of particular sites in the nineteenth century, we can see that these same highly celebrated vistas became the icons of cultural and national identity. The tourist postcard worked in the same way to valorise these landscapes. Commercial travel brochures then subsumed these images.

The Tradition of Nature as Aesthetic

Wilderness as a concept in Western thought has deep resonances. As Nash explains, historically 'it was instinctively understood to be something alien to man – an insecure and uncomfortable environment against which civilisation had waged an unceasing struggle' (Nash 1968: 8). With the flowering of Romanticism in the eighteenth and early nineteenth centuries, untamed country lost much of the fearful repulsion ascribed to it in the Middle Ages and in Judeo-Christian tradition. A new intellectual assessment arrived: notions of wild places were reconceptualised. In Burke's manifesto of the sublime (1757) we see a profound terror, an overwhelming admiration for the powerful forces of nature. As Soper explains, 'the abyss . . . the mountain range, the unbounded celestial space may have proved fearsome to earlier cultures, but it is only in the age of modernity that they begin to be celebrated as the source of peculiar pleasure' (Soper 1995: 222).

Early painters brought to the Antipodes European ideas about landscape, depicting local mountains as Kant's and Ruskin's Alps. Within tourism discourse this interpretation persists: they are established as the local sacred version of the European sublime, free of local politics, ecological issues, history and contested land rights. Size and difficult access makes these special sites for recreational pleasure. New Zealand art historian Pound explains that 'the very idea of landscape is a European import . . . The Maori did not paint landscape, nor feel the need to. Landscape, the pictorial attitude to the land, stopping still just to look at it, to see it as a picture, is purely an imported convention' (Pound 1983: 11–12). He explains that landscape painting, for the first settlers of New Zealand as for us, was a way of inventing the land we live in, of modifying and reconstructing it in pictorial terms, in terms of the codes of the genres. Subsequent visual experiences of nature are denied a fresh view: appreciation of the view has already been pre-scribed.

Contemporary Western cultures have experienced their power over nature as severance from it. Wilson suggests that appreciation of nature 'flourishes best in cultures with highly developed technologies, for nature is the one place we can both indulge our dreams of mastery over the earth and seek some kind of contact with the origins of life – an experience we don't usually allow urban settings to provide . . . the natural world is 'other' to an urban industrial civilisation' (Wilson 1992: 25). Nature has become an aesthetic 'luxury' for individuals who live in cultures that value, as consumer commodities, access to travel and adventure. Soper (1995: 227) suggests that 'it is only . . . a culture that has commenced, in some way, to experience its alienation from nature as the negative consequence of its industrial achievement that will be inclined to "return" to the wilderness'. Our suggestion is that a culture that is physically surrounded by the reminder of extinctions and forest denudation takes 'holidays' from this to psychically green its conscience; not so much a 'return', as Soper suggests, but a flying visit. In addition, the nature we have engaged with has been coded by the entrepreneur for the visitor, not the local; hence it automatically serves as this 'greening' of conscience because it has been recast as a fantasy nature constructed to do exactly that.

Mitchell explains that the study of landscape has gone through two major shifts this century. In the first, associated with modernism, the history of landscape is essentially the history of landscape painting, a site for contemplation. In the second, associated with postmodern-ism, landscape is decentralised in favour of the semiotic and hermeneutic approaches that treat landscape as an allegory of psycho-logical and allegorical themes, which may be decoded as a body of determinate signs. This decoding of landscape as a set of textual sys-tems places landscape in the arena of cultural practice. In order for the values ascribed to the particular landscape to be consumed by tourists, they must be reified or commodified. Tourism requires spectacle. Gigantic natural features such as the Grand Canyon are reproduced as titillation to the tourist gaze, motifs of enticement in the commercial urban milieu. The places become familiar, even if never visited, and excite us as desirable destinations. A visit is still necessary because in glossy books or in National Geographic magazine, on television or in movies, in those vehicles with their physical page or screen-edged borders, the representation can never be as big as the real thing. The mass of reproduced images means exclusivity and authority can only be achieved if one has actually been in its physical presence (and become the author of a similar document oneself). A sense of overwhelming size can only be experienced by being physically present with it. Sometimes the visitor is disappointed: 'but its not as big as I expected!' This is because often the sum total of the reified, commodified spectacle dwarfs the real thing, a canyon flooded to overflowing with its reproduced images. There is dispensed about the world an ever growing 'mountain' of depictions, books about, films of, famous mountain ranges; this grows as the feet of the authors erode the mountain.

From Static to Dynamic Landscape

To achieve commercial success, merely taking visitors to look at magnificent nature may be insufficient. Imaginative entrepreneurs devise novel forms of physical participation in the landscape. For instance, anyone can go and look at Fox Glacier, New Zealand, with no fee to pay. This experience is now mediated for some tourists by converting the placid (paying) traveller into an alpine adventurer, provided with cleated glacier boots, parka, sou'wester and ice axe. By augmenting (artificially) the scale and danger, the costumed tourists in effect become participants in a recapitulation of a nineteenth-century experience of the vast and sublime. The fifteen minute walk has been transformed into a half day 'expedition'. The actual contact between visitor and attraction remains uncommercial. The expenses are involved in getting there, and payment for accommodation, maps, souvenirs, guides, suitable clothing, film etc. Tourists themselves become promoters, taking home 'advertisements' for places they have visited: souvenirs and photographs that they bought to represent attractions that are not for sale. For the promoter, the actual attraction instils no fee; and the Glacier expedition can be offered to different demographic groups: any nationality, any language, any age group (Bell, 1996: 41–43).

Local people will not pay for the same experience. They know enough about the landscape to deflate the inflated claims of height, danger, and rarity. Besides, it is 'ours', why should we pay? This is, of course, at the expense of possibly having our landscape re-enchanted, but when we go elsewhere and our experience of that new landscape is ungrounded we are consumers of the culturally constructed hyper-sublime – not authors of our own unmediated interrogation of that new topography.

This 'added value' is taken a lot further in adventure tourism and extreme sports. Both use sublime landscape as context for its powerful aura as an element of human desire. These activities present an invitation to engage with the landscape on an heroic scale: to be daring, to be reckless. Where once commodification was of the vista, or the view translated into a painting or photograph to sell, people now expect to interact with nature in exciting new ways. Nature, for many tourist consumers, has evolved from something to look at, to something to leap into, jet boat through, or turn completely upside down in: the 'inverted sublime!' (bungee jumping). Novel, daring sports in glorious landscape settings are invented every year.

At some locations, these activities capture two sorts of participants, for instance, those who bungee jump, and those who watch. The jumpers become performers and entertainment for other tourists. The viewers provide an audience for the heroic jumpers, thus valorising the experience and adding exclusivity. Rationally, these activities could take in almost any environment with suitable physical features (something tall to leap off; a river wide enough for rafts), but the mystification and glorification of the experience depends greatly on the environment in which it takes place. Nature tourism as kinaesthetic experience – paddled through, jumped into, trekked across – is still dependent on the glorious vista. This means particular activities can be promoted as unique to New Zealand, for taking place in the unique landscape.

Consuming the Sublime

Most local people do not participate in these activities. They relate to the landscape in quite a different way. For instance, in New Zealand, Maori oral history contains recitations of both human and spiritual ancestors and their relationship with land features. Pakeha (White) New Zealanders enjoy an occasional drive through 'postcard' landscapes, affirming belief in a national image of 'clean, green and beautiful'. They might have some vague knowledge that last century this was perhaps a gold mining area, or that there was an earthquake here, or that a dam gave us this now picturesque lake.

The tourist does not have these readings. Sheer beauty by itself may even be boring. A hilly walk may be just hard slow effort simply to achieve more uncoded vista. The new extreme sports add the frisson of danger. Adventure activities stimulate the senses to a pitch beyond everyday experience; tourists feel the landscape rushing towards them

faster than ever before. Being an adventure tourist involves acceleration through sublimity. Placing oneself in the unmediated locale – not
merely seen through a bus or plane window, but by actually jumping
into it – is tourist consumption at the most extreme. The (apparent)
danger is important for consumers seeking a far more dangerous and
rare experience than their competitors (other tourists).

Walle (1997) writes of adventure tourists seeking peak experiences
for self actualisation and fulfilment. In his 'insight model', subjects
engage in these activities as a way of seeking spiritual insight and as a
form of higher learning, with risk and danger as side effects. We maintain that commercial adventure tourism activities may seem risky, but
are merely ways of packaging safe experiences to look risky. For
instance, no one has ever been seriously injured at an A. J. Hackett
Bungee venue (the world's first, and still major, commercial bungy
operation). The company practically guarantees safety (you can
change your mind about jumping; no, the bungy rope cannot break;
yes, they will immediately retrieve you from the river). This is quite
different from the against-the-elements real danger of, for instance,
mountaineering or cave diving. The forms of adventure of interest in
this paper are those consumed quickly, perhaps just a few exhilarating
hours as part of one's holiday – which may, or may not, include other
adventure activities. The adrenaline rush comes from the speed, the
novelty, the sense of personal daring in undertaking such activity.

The Accelerated Sublime: nine forms of acceleration

Getting there quicker, and from horizontality to verticality

The journey to the site of consumption of the sublime over the past
200 years has speeded up. For centuries, walking, riding an animal or
travelling in a horse-drawn vehicle were the only forms of transport.
Later, railway tracks across the landscape marked the extension of
frontiers, and increased the democratisation of movement across
physical space. For the first time in human history, travellers could
move faster than a galloping horse. Far greater access to vista was
opened up, the steam train imposing a horizontal quality on the landscape. New features appeared on the landscape, including great spans
of sublime railway viaducts, with the landscape boiling away to insubstantiality in the steam, smoke and sheer speed of the train. The private motor car extended this access. Over the century, cars were
designed to go faster; new road surfaces accommodated this, and, as
Crary puts it, 'the car defined a socioeconomic mapping' (Crary 1984:
290). Wilson (1992: 33) notes that, the faster we travel the flatter the
earth looks: overpasses and cloverleaf interchanges are almost two

dimensional when seen from a car window. He also points out that the advent of air-conditioning in cars meant that nature was further appreciated by the eyes alone: one did not have to feel the chill blasts of a snowy landscape, or tropical humidity; nature was comfortably accessible all the year around. 'The other senses were pushed further to the margins of human experience as nature came to play a role in human culture that was at once more restricted and infinitely expanded' (1992: 37).

Hunger for spectacle stimulated the aircraft passenger industry. With the development of commercial air travel, greater goals could be realised – not just extending reach to distant countries, but including excursions to and over remote mountain regions. This shortcut to otherwise inaccessible sites, and the small numbers present on each excursion, makes these exclusive experiences. The impression of speed, the ground rush from flying at low altitudes (previously available only to fighter pilots) is now used as the final accelerant in the rush to the venue. The helicopter ride is marketed as one of the Big Four thrills. Unlike cars and trains the vehicle is accelerating and decelerating both laterally and vertically, taking the viewer, the view point and the camera into three dimensional space.

Accelerating the opening of windows on the world

In the late nineteenth century new visual media – mostly print-based – took on unprecedented importance. The increasing investment in design and promotion of industrial products, and the development of chromolithography, gave rise to trade marking, specialised packaging and advertising. Visual representation appeared on all manner of consumer objects. As Clark observes, 'in retrospect it can be argued that the men and women of the late nineteenth century were immersed in a transformation of one of the most basic components of their daily lives: the signifying object' (Clark, 1994a: 173).

Eventually, television arrived in every household. Television, like car windshields, writes Crary, 'seemed to open onto a visual pyramid of extensive space in which autonomous movement might be possible.' The two, car and television, became 'the dominant machinery of capitalist representation' (1984: 289). By the late twentieth century visual audiences could see most of the world in very fine detail – more detail than if they were physically present; from exotic insects mating, to slow replays of crucial moments in sport and crime and exotic peoples in remote places. It seemed that the viewer, like the TV film maker, could go practically anywhere, and be present with and cast their eyes upon almost anything, especially if they carried one or a selection of little plastic credit cards. The televisual eye implies an unprecedented emancipation of access. More recent visual technology has increased this access, and added virtual spaces as well.

Speeding up the documentation

Simultaneously, there has been an ever increasing acceleration of the recording and documenting of the sublime experience. Nineteenth-century travellers made annotated sketches on site, often translating these later in the studio to paintings (with the written journal of the whole tour), a body of work over some months. This process gradually accelerated to the more direct modes of painting *en plein air*, directly on the canvas, in the mid-nineteenth century, the depiction completed in maybe an afternoon (facilitated by the portability of pre-mixed paint in tubes, rather than having to use loose pigments).

The speed of sublime image-taking then accelerates into the wet plate view cameras of the nineteenth century. However, while the image may have been gathered in the camera in perhaps three minutes (faster than painting the observed view), the physical effort entailed in getting the camera there and processing the print was time consuming. Photography accelerated to film in still cameras 10 × 8, 4 × 5, 35mm, the famous instamatic, and automatic multi-exposure mode cameras, zoom lenses (an acceleration in its own right) and to modern lenses and shorter exposures ($^1/_{400}$ of a second). We now have tough outdoor waterproof cameras, with all the rapid picture-taking virtues of other 35mm cameras, but also capable of being taken into the sublime experience and even immersed in it. The new disposable panoramic or underwater cameras can safely be taken river rafting, or be hurled into the experience with you on your jump. Underwater cameras and video recorders are no longer technology for specialists, and a panoramic 35mm camera the size of a credit card can fit into one's lycra mountain-bike pants' pockets. The tiny camera can fully document the great sweep of the mountain range, with the trusty mountain bike, and its rider in lycra gear, dominantly placed in the foreground. The time delay function and ultra-wide off the camera makes the rider/adventurer/explorer the tallest item in the panorama. The consumer of the sublime experience can carry documentation devices far off the beaten track to get a more extreme, unmediated depiction. Amateur photographers can document the onrushing scenery of the wild river ride and the bungee jump. New digital camera technology means that the jumpers can instantly send the stills of themselves jumping via laptop and modem to the folks back home on the other side of the world.

As we go from static viewing of the vista to a rapidly accelerating high speed kinaesthetic interrogation of a landscape, the documentor of the experience uses a video camera, a standard tourist accessory by the 1990s. At A.J. Hackett Bungee this acceleration means digital still from the video of oneself bungee jumping can be printed onto a T-shirt and sold to the visitor just minutes after the jump. The jumper becomes an instant walking hoarding for their own action video. At the end of the white water rafting, riders collect photographs of themselves swirling about midstream, kindly provided by the raft business's photographers, who shoot from strategic spots along the river's edge.

Acceleration of the designated spot

In some popular tourist locations, Kodak offers little signposts urging the amateur photographer to 'shoot from here'. With these prescriptions, Kodak is reinforcing conventional notions of just what constitutes aesthetic beauty in landscape. The 'here' that the adventurous photographer shoots from is now much further up the mountain, or under the sea, and much wetter and much colder, and/or possibly moving much more rapidly. It also demands a whole new level of technical performance from the equipment being used to record the interactions in low light, water, chill temperatures, actual immersion, violent movement and the G-forces of extreme turns. A bungee jump from a cable car over a huge bush-filled gully near Cairns, Australia, may include photographers in both the cable car and the helicopter itself, and cameras attached to the helmet and feet of the jumper, to gather images of both the person jumping, what they see as they jump, and close-ups of one's facial expressions while jumping. Television documentaries of extreme sports (generally sponsored by airlines, travel agents and resorts) use these sequences to simulate the drama and 'rush' of the experience of the jumper – convincing others that this is indeed the ultimately exhilarating experience. For the person who jumps, this experience is indeed well documented, as permanent tangible evidence of those few minutes of extreme daring.

The viewing platform itself has accelerated. The fact that the landscape which is the site of what was the sublime ascent (mountain climbing) and descent (base jump point) is static has been overwritten. Now sky-surfing requires a fellow surfer who is also a photographer to jump alongside, to film the moves. One brochure promises that 'our skydive photographer will freefall beside you recording your entire experience.'

Accelerated experiences: from trip of a lifetime, to frequent flyer

Adventurers can now cram the maximum amount of these activities into the shortest possible time. Activities that may have once been the highlight of a 'trip of a lifetime' have accelerated to be crammed into annual options, as more individuals spend discretionary income, or credit, on travel. In Queenstown, Adventure Capital of the World, combinations of thrilling activities can be concentrated into a single day. The day is now so event-rich (so folded) that it is endlessly unpicked (retold – unfolded) because it has been over-documented with the high speed motor driven camera and the video camera. The effect is that in the telling and retelling (or re-showing on videos) the thirty second bungee jump now takes far longer than the actual event.

The accelerating body

The sheer physical enormity of nature transformed the human body into something miniature, downscaled and not in control of the earth. It left space for reflection on human insignificance in the face of gigantic forces and formations of nature, and in Victorian times it left space for reflection on new knowledge about the age of the earth, which added a whole new grandeur.

Susan Stewart observes that:

> we move through the landscape; it does not move through us. This relation to the landscape is expressed most often through an abstract projection of the body upon the natural world . . . our words for the landscape are often projections of an enormous body upon it: the mouth of the river, the foot-hills . . . the heartlands . . . the gigantic (presents) an analytical mode of thought, (a) selection of elements that will be transformed and displayed in an exaggerated relation to the social construction of reality (1994: 71).

The touristic body can literally hurtle through physical space. In adventure tourism the most adrenaline filled experiences are those where the body leaps or falls from a great height, or plunges down a steep slope or surging river. With little applied muscle power, the body becomes a high speed hurtling object, darting with gravity down the landscape. We note the rapid and voluntary increase in the speed of the body of the participant: from languid or leisurely over-clothed aesthetes surveying and depicting the nineteenth-century vista, to lycra and neoprene clad sublimity junkies hurtling into the next extreme panorama. While the skydive tandem claims to be 'the highest, fastest most spectacular adventure of them all', new sports keep appearing. The latest include vertigo canyoning, river surfing and parapenting.

Acceleration of self gratification and heroism

During the summer of 1997–98 in New Zealand there was a brief craze for jumping over waterfalls. While some people survived – sufficient numbers, apparently, to encourage others that this act was not necessarily inevitable suicide – five young men were killed in just a few weeks. There was widespread publicity for their jumps. The activity had the great caché of proven danger. The practice was banned, with security guards placed to guard the falls. These were not tourists; these were local people apparently needing new excitement. More recently, three New Zealanders successfully retraced Shackleton's journey across South Georgia. Their three week effort included battling with icy mountains and glaciers in seventy-five knot winds, poor visibility, rain, sleet and extreme cold – including five nights tent-bound during a storm. This was not a front page item, and did not include a photograph of the team. If one wants to achieve heroism in one's spare time, then clearly there are quick ways of doing this. A publicity-gaining leap over a waterfall does not require arduous physical training to peak fitness, sustained determination during extreme weather conditions, or long absences from the comfort of home.

Current television programmes feature so-called celebrities engaged in activities in which someone less famous is expert. Viewers are assumed to be less interested in the experts and their expertise than in these 'personalities'. The underlying premise is that if they can do it, the viewer can, too. Meanwhile, in 1998, two young New Zealand men rowed across the Atlantic, taking an extraordinary thirty days off the previous world record. They have not become household names, and are still trying to pay for an event that attracted little sponsorship.

Participation in paid adventure and extreme activities is a way of achieving instant gratification as self-acclaimed hero. For extreme adrenaline junkies (or tourists pushed for time) the all-in-one-day sets of events may be satisfactory. The Helijet Double Deal, Triple Thriller, or Awesome Foursome (bungee jump, raft trip, jet boat and helicopter rides) all taking place in stunningly beautiful, potentially treacherous surroundings.

The accelerating autobiography of the tourist

The tourist experience may be recollected at will. Evidence is present in photographs, videos, saved ephemera (such as entry tickets) and personalised souvenirs, such as the A. J. Hackett's Bungee video and T-shirt. Exotic adventures become stories in which the teller owns the experience: the story is their property, an abstract currency of social exchange. Lowenthal writes that 'indeed, some prize their personal past as they would a valuable antique. They congratulate themselves on having the experience they recall, treasuring memories that enhance self-regard' (1985: 195). The experiences now stand for the character of the teller: casually daring, adventurous, and well-travelled. By trawling the globe for adventure they have acquired worldiness, heroism and a substantial stock of experiences. Been there, done that! The tale is viable currency to outbid other adventurers from around the globe who exchange anecdotes in backpackers' hostels. For the individual this is a way 'to puff himself [sic] up into selfness', as Adorno put it (Roemer 1995). It is the ability to consume different signs that establishes social distinctions. The social emphasis on citizens as producers within the capitalist milieu has shifted, as people mobilise as consumers. Finding a way of serving their leisure needs has become as essential a status symbol as their labour role. Each person starts life with various givens: genetic inheritances of race, gender, physical features and intellectual potentials. As adults 'I am' is increasingly expressed as 'I own, or I can pay to experience . . .'. Barbara Kruger highlights this in her famous text 'I shop therefore I am'. The teller of travel stories is affirming that 'I am special – because I have had these experiences'. If one's life is bereft of thrilling experiences that 'just happened', well, these may be bought through tourism.

Accelerating family history

Exotic experiences contribute to the quest to fulfil the need to collect narratives for one's own (future) nostalgia, just as one takes photographs of the children, the house, the happy family times. In the current climate of individualism and consumption, rivalry can be acted out through travel consumption, and the previous generation outdone by glorious twenty-first century consumers. Travel through life and across space: this is the fundamental sequential litany of family history. Indeed, the story of family settlement in the Antipodes necessarily begins with a travel adventure story.

This is a generational issue. Our colonial forebears were well equipped with 'pioneering spirit', hand tools and a savagely persistent Protestant ethic that did not give priority to leisure, pleasure and material consumption. Parents of the present middle-aged – the most affluent travel consumers – tell of growing up in large families, surviving the depression, then going to war. They did not talk about racing camels in Mongolia, or whale watching, or taking a guided tour up Everest. The next young adults enjoy the thrills of skate-boarding and sky-surfing, and the 'rush' of extreme sports. Family experiences of travel have speeded up: our great grandparents boarded sailing ships and took weeks to travel half way around the globe, and told this sole travel narrative over and again (museums in the Antipodes display debris of these journeys). Our parents may have had perhaps one hard-earned overseas trip by boat via Suez. The post-war baby-boomers refer to their first big trip which started in London. The new generation see themselves as global citizens, casually comparing conditions and experiences in various countries.

The intrepid postmodern tourist

Our discussion illustrates the continuum that tracks the route to post-modernity. When those positioned at one point (modernity) can view the authentic environment and cultural practices of those placed at the other (tradition) the gap between the two narrows. Indeed, those at the modern end leap further along the continuum, to postmodernity: viewing the innovative ways of commodifying what was once simply 'landscape' becomes a feature peculiar to postmodern society. In this postmodern period, remote, difficult or dangerous landscapes are richly – and commercially – romanticised.

The tourists' monologue is not about political correctness. Like the travel articles in newspapers and magazines (usually sponsored by airlines or holiday resorts) there is seldom observation of anything other than that which they set out to see. Little is said about recolonisation of indigenous peoples and their employment in subservient roles to please the needs of visitors. Nor is there much comment on environmental destruction (for instance in Nepal where one hot shower taken by a weary, grubby visitor means the destruction of three trees) or distorted development in Third World countries, or the power of global corporations to commodify otherwise untouched small places, or visitors' own personal impact as tourists. Recalling and recounting personalised places and events: this is how humans construct the sequence of events in their lives, and 'progress' from where they were before (for example, before travel) to where and who they are now (worldly, sophisticated global consumers). Continuity depends on memory of past experiences. One's life history, much of it deliberately constructed, forms one's identity. Adventure tourism via global travel is a tactic that helps fulfil this aspect of the self.

Promoting the Nation

In 1953 a young New Zealand man and a Nepalese sherpa together slogged their way to be first to stand on the top of the world's tallest mountain. They became internationally renowned heroes. The mountain was far from New Zealand, but the achievement reinforced notions of New Zealand male prowess – already successfully tested on battlefields and in sport (Phillips 1996). It does not take much of an imaginative leap to establish New Zealand, a mountainous country, as a place for heroic adventures: a place in which the stunning scenery provides an enchanting backdrop for daring adventure activities. Each year about five million adventure experiences are sold; over half of all tourists visit conservation sites. They take away memories and documentation of vistas of New Zealand, views of dramatic landscape; the version of New Zealand they have been promised and have had realised. Other elements of New Zealand culture are marginalised, as the viewer obtains that which is paid for.

The accelerated sublime; this is a way that New Zealand packages landscape for consumption. Entrepreneurs are brokers of versions of landscape whose by-products – the reification of the values which can become commodity – are validated by the weight of officially sanctioned mediators of that landscape, such as the Department of Conservation. When tourists want something daring and adventurous in their itineraries, local entrepreneurs are not just complicit, they actively manufacture these experiences, then offer them as unique because of their placement in this particular grand environment. This pervasive interweaving of accelerating strands, which come together in the complicit construction of the sublime by the tourist consumer and entrepreneur (producer), is obviously a wilful and temporary mindset. The moral, ecological and political impacts of adopting this mindset can be readily critiqued, because in any one ecotourist's transit through New Zealand they are equally complicit in other constructions of nature at other nodes of consumption of nature. At Kaikoura the indigenous people mediate a low impact participation in indigenous ecology: whale watching, diving with the dolphins, snorkling with the seals. The Department of Conservation, through its signs, huts and tracks, allows a walk through an annotated New Zealand nature, and farm stays on working sheep and dairy farms sell the rural way of life.

Accelerating the sublime is not the only possible consumption of mountains. Alternatives might include ecotours, similar to New Zealand's major bush walks at Milford and Routeburn Tracks, and other locations. Or there could be engagement with the indigenous people's historic and mythological construction of this landscape (Rotorua is partly 'packaged' in this way). Specialised treks through this landscape, for instance to follow *pounamu* (New Zealand jade or greenstone) or Chinese and Pakeha old gold-mining sites could also be possible. However, the location can be milked for more dollars if constructed as an adventure or extreme sports site. Entrepreneurs construct an economically viable 'tourist space' within the nation, particularly designated for these forms of consumption. Serving the tourists' gaze and activity creates a profitable hyper sublime: a space that is effectively an indigene-free, ecology-free hyper-resort, overlaid seamlessly onto the terrain of the fragile mountain environment.

Images of these constructed spaces are also used as packages of imagery about national identity. For instance, at New Zealand Expo displays, images of adventure activities show an exciting place with exhilarating outdoor life. At the new Museum of New Zealand, *Te Papa* in Wellington, visitors may pay for a virtual bungee jumping experience, indoors, far away from an actual vista. As repository of symbols and representations of this country Te Papa has shifted style from traditional storehouse of national treasures to a space in which visitors virtually participate with representations of New Zealand.

Adventure tourism and extreme sports; these are 'our' commercial response to globalisation. New Zealand asserts distinctiveness to tourists by promoting uniqueness through nature as a commodity, simultaneously reiterating nature for citizens as a dominant positive feature of national identity. However, that uniqueness is the landscape in which commercially profitable activities take place as well as the activities themselves, not the truly unique biodiversity. This commercial repositioning maps a northern-hemisphere construct of the sublime onto the indigenous substrate, thereby obliterating any of the genuine biological differences.

Through investigating the acceleration and inversion of the sublime, we hope we have conveyed ideas of landscape as a social construct, the way in which relations to the nonhuman world are always historically mediated, and some of the ideological functions of the appeal to 'nature'. In the case of New Zealand, the processes of both incidentally and deliberately accelerating the sublime have helped re-energise identity, while the landscape is being economically rationalised. In short, the acceleration of the sublime functions as a New Right exemplar in the attempt to accelerate the progress of a commercially struggling nation.

Making The Scene

The Poetics and Performances of Displacement at the Grand Canyon

Mark Neumann

The city is redundant: it repeats itself so that something will stick in the mind . . . Memory is redundant: it repeats signs so that . . . [t]he city can begin to exist.

Calvino (1974)

Setting the Scene

Along the trail on the Grand Canyon's South Rim, I have been watching and listening to the tourists confront the world famous scenic wonder. This afternoon, not far from the national park visitor centre, I listen to Joe and Kaye, a semi-retired couple from Massachusetts, tell me about their vacation. They are pulling a camping trailer around the United States, and seeing the American West for the first time in their lives. Along the way, they have purchased a video travelogue of Yellowstone and Yosemite national parks, and they are considering buying a video about the Grand Canyon as well. 'We want to show our children what we've been seeing', Kaye tells me as we sit on the edge of the chasm. 'It gets to the point where the only way to understand it is to show them. You just can't find the words to say what you see, so we bought those videos and they can get an idea of where we've been.' This afternoon, the couple is walking along the rim of the canyon, but for the past few days, they have been looking at the scene from a variety of viewpoints.

'Have you been on the plane?' Kaye asks me. 'We took the plane and it was marvellous. It was a six-seater so each person had their own window, and they flew us all around the canyon', she says, tracing a loopy flight path through the sky with her finger. 'It was just short of an hour', adds Joe, 'but you really should see it. I mean this is nice seeing it from here, but you really get a different sense of the grandeur from the air. It's just stupendous. This is nice, though. Have you seen the IMAX?'

Joe was referring to the IMAX Grand Canyon Theatre in Tusayan, a gateway tourist community six miles south of the canyon's edge where we stand talking. The 525-seat theatre holds thirteen daily showings of *Grand Canyon – The Hidden Secrets*, a thirty-four minute film projected on a seventy-foot-high screen with six-track Dolby stereo sound. 'You should've seen that before you came here', Joe continues. 'It's really an experience. For one thing, they go back to pre-historic times, well, not *pre*-historic. But they tell the history of the first people living here. It's all done with modern photography, of course.' Kaye nods in agreement with everything Joe says. 'They go back to when the first people were here and they were all nude and running around on the rocks . . . and that was nice', he grins and winks at me. 'Then, they've got you up in a plane and going down through the canyon on the river in a raft. Really exciting.' Kaye says the whole film made her feel a 'little queasy' because of its intense images of flying through the canyon and white water rafting. 'You shouldn't miss the IMAX, and the plane, too', says Joe. 'I mean it doesn't matter if you take the flight for half an hour, an hour, or two hours. Once you get up there, you really see the grandeur of the canyon.'

'That's what they told us to do when we got here', says Kaye. She tells me the people at the KOA campground told them to first go to the IMAX, then take the plane, then go to the canyon. 'They've been around here a few years, so they knew the best way to do it', she says, 'but we took the plane first, then went to the IMAX, then here. That's what you should have done before you came here. I mean this is nice, but it's really different. I don't know, I guess it's better from the air. It's just different to see it like this.' Kaye suddenly stops speaking and the three of us stand in silent anticipation as we watch the colours and contours of the Grand Canyon slowly appear between the borders of a Polaroid snapshot Joe has snapped while we have been talking.

Outline

Tourists like Joe and Kaye sometimes raise a chuckle because they seem like pawns of an enormous system that keeps them from seeing the 'real thing'. Tourists are strangers in the landscape. They are carried by technologies of vision, and carry cameras – machines of memory – as an automatic response to their present. They are the audience for preformulated views, commercial tours, and they often appear as passive consumers of lifestyle models packaged for their fantasies. Perhaps more than any of these images, tourists are often targets of disparagement and humour that stems from a fear of becoming lost in the crowd, of being resigned to the anonymous commercial landscape drawn by marketers and entrepreneurs. Such views of the tourist beckon back to many critics, but was most concisely summarised by Daniel Boorstin (1961) who said the tourist is a 'shallow' figure, superficially satisfied with 'diluted' and manufactured 'pseudo-events'.

Some may laugh at Joe and Kaye for their lack of discrimination when choosing among a spectrum of canyon views. Those who yearn for an 'authentic' experience of nature may find Joe and Kaye's adventures a pitiful story of loss or alienation. Behind such assessments, there is often an idealised image of the solitary spectator who can get away from it all and take in the sublime spectacle of nature. I think this is roughly a popular view of our hopes about nature, and they have been with us since the last century. It is an ideal that leads many to express a sense of regret for all those caught up in the canyon's tourist machinery, people like Joe and Kaye who come to the rim and take a seat as their last stop. Yet, the truth of the matter is that those seats in the scenic plane, the IMAX Theater, and on the fallen log at the canyon's rim have been long in the making.

This chapter examines how the Grand Canyon is a landscape where modern forces of cultural mobility materialise through concrete discursive and spatial practices. While the Grand Canyon is an enduring icon, symbolic of nature and the West, it has also been a 'theatre' or 'stage' dramatising an American pursuit of national culture and identity. Here, I suggest, the Grand Canyon is a complex geography of fantasy that historically reappears at an intersection of places, both real and imagined. It is a landscape of a cultural poetics erupting from a vast chasm of desires for location and presence in a modern world of discontinuities, a landscape where people stage dramas of culture, themselves, and others.

Drawing from a variety of texts that imagine the canyon and the observer, and by making observations of tourists vacationing at the canyon, I describe how travellers have arrived at the edge of its spectacular, divided landscape to figuratively embody what James Clifford (1989: 9) suggests is a broader predicament of modern life: 'a pervasive condition of offcentredness in a world of distinct meaning systems, a state of being in culture while looking at culture, [and] a form of personal and collective self-fashioning.' Since the end of the last century, the Grand Canyon has been a geography of fantasy for numerous observers. Considering how the canyon first appeared to the American public, and how observers and writers interpreted the scenery in popular accounts, the idea of an 'authentic' Grand Canyon quickly dissolves into a stage where fantasy and reality become inseparable. Instead, the canyon's landscape has historically been a place of performances, aspirations and a politics of identity in modern American culture. Since the beginning of its days as a tourist shrine, it has been a space of invention and internal landscapes, a space where modern questions of location, continuity and identity are lived, imagined and remembered in a place of leisure escape, and a cultural landscape where spectacle and observer are integrated through narratives and performances that mutually energise each other.

Painting the Canyon

Atchison, Topeka and Santa Fe Railway (hereafter, the Santa Fe Railway) trains first began hauling tourists to the Grand Canyon's South Rim in 1901. Yet, many who walked up the hill from the canyon depot to stand on the rim had already seen the canyon. By the early part of the 1890s, most Americans who came to the Grand Canyon were likely to have first gazed upon the abyss through the eyes of Thomas Moran. Moran went to the Grand Canyon in the 1870s as part of John Wesley Powell's government funded survey of the Colorado Plateau. His trip provided a starting point for a canvas called *The Chasm of the Colorado*. Unveiled in 1874, *The Chasm* fetched the thirty-six year-old artist a ten thousand dollar commission, and hung in public view at the Capitol building opposite an earlier canvas of Yellowstone's scenic landscape. By 1875, a woodcut version of Moran's *Chasm of the Colorado*, along with twenty-eight other wood engravings of the canyon region, had appeared in a three-part article written by Powell for *Scribner's Monthly*. They also illustrated Powell's official report of his expedition down the Colorado.

Nonetheless, it was the Santa Fe Railway, whose trains would carry visitors to the South Rim by 1901, that most forcefully seized on the idea of the canyon as an aesthetic experience. In the last decades of the nineteenth century, the railroad began heavily promoting the canyon through art. For the railroad's advertising department, what made the canyon worth seeing heavily depended on framing it as a site of culture rather than on the geological interests that first drew observers to the region. They saw the value of a landscape reflected in the eyes of writers and painters who claimed the canyon for an observer of great art. In 1892, the Santa Fe Railway secured rights to another canvas by Moran – *The Grand Canyon of the Colorado* – and put it into chromolithographic reproduction. These it mounted in handsome gilt frames and then sent out, first by the hundreds and then by the thousands. The Santa Fe 'placed them in offices, in hotels, in schools, even in homes – almost anywhere that there was a fair chance of the picture bringing in business' (Hungerford 1923: 44). Moran agreed to give the railroad the copyright for his canvas in 1892 after the Santa Fe subsidised a summer trip through the West for the artist, Moran's son Paul, and photographer William Henry Jackson. In fact, the railroad quickly became a patron for Moran and other artists such as Louis Akin, Oscar Berninghaus, William Leigh, Elliot Daingerfield, Gunnar Widforss and Carl Borg. They would spend weeks at the canyon and the Santa Fe would underwrite their travel, accommodations, and even provide some with studio space. In return, the artists either sold or exchanged their canvases to the railroad for advertising and promotional purposes.

More than any other artist, however, Moran revealed the conflation of the canyon with the painter's canvas. In the early decades of the twentieth century, visitors could look at the canyon from 'Moran Point' near Grand View, or venture to 'Artists View' off the Rim Road, and at night, they might see Moran chatting with fellow artists at the canyon's El Tovar hotel in a spot known as 'Moran's Corner'. For the painter who had first seen the canyon on the North Rim with the Powell Survey in the 1870s, the early twentieth century canyon had become a resource for launching a career and cementing a vision of the landscape in American culture. Moran was as fervent about his romantic idealisations of nature as he was about the American artist's role in creating a national culture. 'That there is a nationalism in art needs no proof', wrote a sixty-four year-old Moran.

> Before America can pretend to a position in the world of art it will have to prove it through a characteristic nationality in its art. . . On a recent visit to the Grand Canyon of Arizona I was more than ever convinced that the future of American art lies in being true to our own country, in the interpretation of that beautiful and glorious scenery which nature has so lavishly endowed our land . . . [The Grand Canyon] offers a new and comparatively untrodden field for pictorial interpretation, and only awaits the men of original thoughts and ideas to prove to their countrymen that we possess a land of beauty and grandeur with which no other can compare. (1902: 86–7)

Moran's 'manifesto' reflected a sense of anti-European nationalism that could boost Americans' pride in their scenic monuments. Investors and tourism promoters enthusiastically supported Moran's pursuit of national cultural symbols and parlayed American cultural anxieties toward an economic advantage. The Santa Fe Railway saw this truth early on. Picking up the tab for artists at the canyon and collecting their paintings not only provided an ample supply of advertising images for promoting the canyon, but symbolically forged a relationship between the observer and the landscape as an experience endowed with artistic vision. The colours of the painter's palette blended on the canvas in images of a landscape that reflected in the eyes of Americans who hungered for cultural security and ideas of unity, and who would also spend money to possess the experience for themselves.

Given the accounts of early visitors, it is unlikely anyone was disappointed with the view from the rim, but no matter how they tried to see the canyon from the vantage point of Moran, they would have failed. In fact, there was no such place to view the canyon on the rim and see Moran's 'Chasm of the Colorado'. His painting had been an invention, a composite of sketches made at different places along the North Rim rather than the South Rim where the train tracks went. Moran had also drawn from various photographs supplied to him by Powell's survey photographer, Jack Hillers. Moran painted the "Chasm of the Colorado" in Philadelphia, the cradle of liberty, and home to other American icons that rang of freedom despite the crack in its surface. 'My personal scope is not realistic; all my tendencies are toward idealization', said Moran. 'The motive or incentive for my Grand Canyon was the gorgeous display of color that impressed itself on me . . . and while I desired to tell truly of nature, I did not wish to realize the scene literally but to preserve and convey its true impression' (in Sheldon 1881: 125). Moran apologised to no one for moving scenery around to suit his purposes. Art, he argued, was an emotional expression of the individual who looked upon the scene, and this was equally true for both the artist and those who looked at the space in the frame.

While Moran provided Americans with an idealised image of Grand Canyon in the 1870s, Clarence Dutton – a geologist and government surveyor for Powell – instructed them in how to approach the canyon as an aesthetic experience. The Grand Canyon is 'a great innovation in modern ideas of scenery', claimed Dutton in his 1882 survey report for the United States Goverment. 'Great innovations, whether in art or literature, in science or in nature, seldom take the world by storm . . . They must be understood before they can be estimated, and must be cultivated before they can be understood' (in Sheldon 1881: 142). In part cultivating the canyon as a 'great innovation', Dutton called upon familiar images of civilisation and culture to orient observers to the landscape. His pen decorated the canyon as a vast and magnificent display of Eastern architecture. 'Hindoo Amphitheater', 'Ottoman Amphitheater', 'Brahma Temple', 'Vishnu's Temple', and 'Shiva's Temple' are only some of the names he gave to canyon buttes and towers spread out before him, and he set an example others would follow for naming the landmarks at the Grand Canyon and other national parks such as Bryce Canyon and Zion in Utah (Stegner 1937).

'The study and slow mastery of the influences of that class of scenery and its full appreciation is a special culture', he wrote, 'requiring time, patience, and long familiarity for its consummation' (Dutton 1881: 141). Expressing a desire to cultivate an understanding of the 'innovative scenery', Dutton's instructions to canyon observers fit well with dominant aesthetic propensities of many nineteenth century artists and elites. Noting the 'class of scenery' and the 'special culture' which could most appreciate its meaning, Dutton's gaze into the abyss looked into the heart and mind of an ideal observer who contemplated the canyon like a great landscape painting for a revelation of Nature's power, magnificence and beauty. In many ways, the observer Dutton envisioned was nothing less than the ideal spectator who looked at the canyon landscape paintings of Thomas Moran.

For both men, the truth of the canyon lay in the aesthetic and spiritual experience of the individual. As Dutton argued for a slow and careful study of the canyon's landscape, he provided not so much an image of the canyon but an outline for how the viewer should locate himself or herself in the scene. Dutton clung tightly to an idea that the true canyon rested somewhere inside the patient man or woman standing on the rim. His advice appeared later in guidebooks which quoted him directly: 'A visitor to the chasm . . . must necessarily come there (for so is the human mind constituted) with a picture of it created by his own imagination', said Dutton in a 1901 guide. 'He reaches the spot, the conjured picture vanishes in an instant, and the place of it must be filled anew. Surely no imagination can construct out of its own material any picture having the remotest resemblance to the Grand Canyon. In truth, the first step in attempting a description is to beg the reader to dismiss from his mind, so far as practicable, any preconceived notion of it' (in James 1900: 86).

Surely, not even Dutton could live up to this ideal. When he stared over the rim, he reported cities of architectural beauty that Ruskin would have appreciated. Dutton reinforced the ideas and practices of an individual observer – particularly one who understood the terms of the 'special culture' the canyon symbolised – to remake the scene in his or her own contemplative efforts. Naming a promontory 'Point Sublime' was, perhaps, an auspicious starting place – whether at the canyon or in the mind – for later writers who would aspire to Dutton's eloquence and aesthetic sensibilities when they described their own view. Dutton placed the canyon within the scope and vocabulary of a nineteenth-century aesthetic that attracted many other visitors prone toward public displays of their individualism, morality and the power of culture to recognise both.

For instance, Charles Dudley Warner, an essayist, editor and novelist from Hartford, Connecticut, devoted two chapters to the Grand Canyon in *Our Italy*. 'I was continually likening this to a vast city rather than a landscape', wrote Warner, 'a city of no man's creation nor of any man's conception. . . . yet everything reminds us of man's work' (1891: 195–6). Finding a city in the depths of the canyon was more than an act of literary imagination or hallucination. In his own way, Warner recapitulated Dutton's desire for a cultivated understanding of the canyon. 'There was a castle, terraced up with columns, plain enough, and below it a parade-ground; at any moment the knights in armor and with banners might emerge from red gates and deploy there, while the ladies looked down from balconies. But there were many castles and fortresses and barracks and noble mansions', he wrote. 'In time I began to see queer details: a Richardson house, with low portals and round arches, surmounted by a Nuremberg gable; perfect panels, 600 feet high, for the setting of pictures' (Warner 1891: 195–6).

Nearly everyone who described the canyon to the public seemed to wind up in the same imaginary city, effusively conveying images of magnificent architecture and testifying to the 'soul-shocks' that ran through them on the rim. 'Instead of being filled with air, the vast space between the walls is crowded with Nature's grandest buildings, a sublime city of them, painted in every color, and adorned with richly fretted cornice and battlement spire and tower', John Muir told *Atlantic Monthly* readers. 'Every architectural invention of man has been anticipated, and far more, in this grandest of God's terrestrial cities' (1898: 28). Nearly two years later, Harriet Monroe, also writing in *Atlantic Monthly*, said 'the souls of the great architects must find their dreams fulfilled … the proud young world had commanded architecture to build for her' (1899: 818–9).

To a Protestant nation steeped in a rhetorical legacy of Biblical imagery, Warner, Muir and Monroe sounded like visionaries seeing a landscape of divine providence. Their voices carried strains of John Bunyan's Christian in *Pilgrim's Progress* who dreamed of fleeing to the 'Celestial City', and Puritan leader John Winthrop, who told his company in exodus across the Atlantic, 'we shall be a City Upon a Hill, the eyes of all people are upon us'. By the late nineteenth century, imagining a perfect and heavenly city in the canyon's depths could appeal to deeply inscribed American visions of social harmony and divine order that had yet to materialise in the New World. For many, nature not only offered a retreat from the harsh realities of city life, but also a place to reimagine its uncorrupted possibility. Assigning such images to the canyon's landscape, writers simultaneously preserved the ideal of God's City in America and bore witness to their own idealised inner landscape. However, if the canyon was viewed as holy ground, it was not only because Americans felt a godly presence stirring their hearts, but also because many felt a need to push something monumental, and distinctively American, before European eyes.

Wandering along the edges of this imaginary city, their accounts were maps of their desires for a civilised culture. The Grand Canyon 'flashes instant communication of all that architecture and painting and music for a thousand years have gropingly striven to express', boasted Charles Higgins in an early 1892 Santa Fe guidebook. 'It is the soul of Michael Angelo and of Beethoven' (Higgins et al. 1892). Recording their spiritual reveries from the rim, writers also suggested the canyon possessed an historical and cultural depth comparable or superior to any work of human civilisation. Although many drew comparisons with antiquities of the Old World, each sought to affirm the canyon as a symbol of culture and heritage in the New World, a distinctively *American* cultural shrine that was superior to any ruin, museum, or symphony on European soil. The Grand Canyon could help fill what many Americans feared was a void of American culture and offer another shrine of national pride to help soothe those Americans haunted by feelings of cultural impoverishment.

As writers and promoters elevated the Grand Canyon into a national shrine and a scenic wonder for all Americans, their accounts, guidebooks and brochures staked out the terrain as cultural property not everyone could appreciate in the same ways. Writers feared tourist crowds would infringe on the sanctity of their personal experience with Nature as Culture, and offered a set of instructions that marked the scenery with lines of taste, propriety and social decorum. Looking into the canyon for an artistic masterpiece or an internal Celestial City required a civilised man or woman, who possessed the intelligence and sophistication to claim the view.

The canyon offers 'dreamy landscapes quite beyond the most exquisite fancies of Claude and of Turner', Charles Warner claimed, and 'when it becomes accessible to the tourist it will offer an endless field for the delight of those *whose minds can rise to the heights of the sublime and the beautiful*' (1891: 178, original emphasis). Warner's estimation of the canyon's scenery over the canvases of renowned French and English landscape painters surely expressed a desire for American cultural superiority. Yet, he did more than refract the canyon's beauty through a seemingly unshakeable élite aesthetic sensibility. While anticipating the tourist crowds who would arrive on the rim, he recognised that the power of sublime experience had long been reserved for a select group.

'The power of scenery to affect men is, in a large way, proportionate to the degree of their civilization and the degree in which their taste has been cultivated', wrote landscape architect Frederick Law Olmsted (1865: 117). 'This is only one of the many channels in which a similar distinction between civilised and savage men is to be generally observed. The whole body of the susceptibilities of civilized men and with their susceptibilities their powers, are on the whole enlarged.' Olmsted prepared these remarks for the California legislature to advocate the preservation of Yosemite for the benefit of 'the great mass of society'. Those who did not appreciate beautiful scenery, he said, were 'either in a diseased condition from excessive devotion of the mind to a limited range of interests, or their whole minds are in a savage state; that is, in a state of low development' and 'need to be drawn out generally'. Olmsted merely expressed a view many early observers would repeat in their accounts: scenic areas offered a moral and didactic landscape – a nineteenth-century 'outreach' programme – for building the character of the 'vulgar' and 'uneducated' American masses (Levine 1988: 186, Weyeneth 1984). Ideally, scenery, like art and literature, could educate the American public in matters of taste and proper social conduct.

Among nineteenth-century American aristocrats, reformers, and members of a rising middle class, the term 'culture' became 'synonymous with the Eurocentric products of the symphonic hall, the opera house, the museum, and the library', argues Lawrence Levine, 'all of which, the American people were taught, must be approached with a disciplined, knowledgeable seriousness of purpose, and – most important of all – with a feeling of reverance' (1988: 145 – 6). The same divisions of class, hierarchy and public order developing in America's eastern cities soon became applicable to the scenic vistas of Grand Canyon and other preserved landscapes. Employing metaphors of high culture to characterise the canyon's cultural magnificence, writers elevated themselves as being able to fully experience and comprehend the scenery and its potential to enrich one's soul.

'We know that in order to appreciate the best music the ear must be trained to distinguish musical harmonies, the rhythm appeals to us naturally, but the soul of music comes to us through musical training as well as natural endowment', wrote Mrs. M. Burton Williamson, 'The eye must be educated in order to appreciate art in its highest sense. I was reminded of this when viewing the canyon. Each view of it only enhanced my admiration of it' (1899: 203). Admiring the scenery equals an encounter with an *objet d'art*. For Williamson, it is also a way of honouring and displaying her own *naturally endowed* qualities of perception and aesthetic education. However, aesthetic appreciation was more than a matter of training the ear or eye. It also meant a properly educated visitor should approach the wilderness the same way they approached the symphony, opera, or art museum – by practising the rules of appropriate social conduct, and self-restraint.

Like the well-mannered museum or opera patron, some guides suggested that properly 'attending' the canyon involved an ability to control the emotions in an environment best comprehended through silent contemplation. 'Speech is inadequate and uncalled for, at least until the scene familiarises itself; and the nervous haste with which at first one is prone to glance from object to object gives place to a calmer and more critical mood', noted P. C. Bicknell's (1901) canyon guidebook. 'A chattering man or woman would have ruined our pleasure in that brilliant panorama, just as such empty-headed creatures mar the rendering of an opera for those who are there to enjoy the music.'

Comparing a canyon visit to the social etiquette of the opera hall offered a means of constituting social order, framing and controlling the experience through self-observation and self-discipline. Assuming a silent public posture conveyed an aesthetic disposition that Pierre Bourdieu (1984: 56–7) describes as 'a distant, self-assured relation to the world and to others which presupposes objective assurance and distance... Like every sort of taste, it unites and separates.' For Bourdieu, the contemplative posture of artistic appreciation is one of 'aesthetic distance' and indicative of a privileged class. It is a product of educational and social conditioning that inevitably serves to distinguish them from others who do not possess a strong relationship with 'cultural capital.' They see 'the world and other people through literary reminiscences and pictorial references', he argues, 'the 'pure' and purely aesthetic judgements of the artist and the aesthete spring from the disposition of an ethos' that becomes 'a sort of absolute reference point in the necessarily endless play of mutually self-relativizing tastes'.

If a visitor on the rim in Arizona demanded contemplative quiet, it was in part because the Grand Canyon described in the pages of popular texts seemed noisy with directions for silence. Even as their articles helped popularise the canyon to an American public, they were often reluctant to welcome the masses who then came looking for the scenes framed on their pages. From the 1890s to the 1930s, tourism promoters and preservationists invited everyone to witness the natural wonder for themselves, yet continually exalted an eighteenth century vision of a solitary encounter with Nature's sublime. Enthusiasm for a divine city conjured in the canyon's depths was, after all, a play of the literary imagination, and silently *reading* travel accounts best seemed to encapsulate the experience of canyon solitude authors described. As writers mocked tourists and constantly opted to slip away from the swelling crowds in order to 'really see' the canyon, the exclusion and debasement of tourists served to uphold a sanctified image of the canyon and the culturally (and 'naturally') endowed observer who could truly appreciate the view.

Technology and Representing Nature

For all the disparagement 'common' tourists may have suffered in the pages of popular texts, everyone looked through some figurative or literal device for their vision of the canyon. Painted landscapes, guidebooks, advertising, travel articles and stereographs not only shaped the canyon into a marvellous spectacle and distributed it to the public, their pages and images traced a path for the spectator's retreat into the interiors of a subjective landscape where image and experience became powerfully entwined. The empty space of the Grand Canyon became absorbed in the metaphors of Art, Spirituality, History and Science that anxious visitors had carried to the edge of the abyss and into the pages of their accounts. These accounts located the canyon visitor in a vast landscape of intertextualised references where the conflation of geographical terrain with images, names, codes of conduct and experiential narratives energised the dislocated and mobilised practices of modern observation. As various textual portraits of the canyon celebrated an individual observer's capacity (or lack of one) to possess the scene, that observer disappeared into a series of established and legitimated viewpoints.

Jonathan Crary (1990: 150) argues that, by 1840, modern forms of institutional and discursive power had also redefined the status of an observing subject. While railroads collapsed temporal and spatial distances, visual technologies – from the stereoscope of the 1850s to early forms of cinema in the 1890s – had relocated vision from a material site of observation, which depended on the bodily presence of the viewer, to the subjectivity of the observer 'that depended on the abstraction and formalization of vision'. Nineteenth-century visual technologies dislocated, extended, reassembled and mobilised images and knowledge and aimed toward 'multiple affirmations of the sovereignty and autonomy of vision', argues Crary. At the same time, the autonomous viewing subject engendered by this shift became inseparable from 'the increasing standardization and regulation of the observer'.

Commodifying, regulating and standardising tourist experience was an inevitable feature of the Grand Canyon by the first years of the twentieth century. Yet, as the landscape became a place of mass produced visions and experiences, it continually manufactured images of an *autonomous and sovereign observer* – an individual figure who surveyed a geography dislodged from time and space, but who also served as its point of coherence. By the last decades of the nineteenth century 'any significant qualitative difference between a *biosphere* and a *mechanosphere* began to evaporate', notes Crary. 'This disintegration of an indisputable distinction between interior and exterior became a condition for the emergence of spectacular modernizing culture' (1995: 47). The tourist world on canyon's rim was a place where *bio-* and *mechano-* spheres converged in the space between the observer's eyes.

For instance, John McCutcheon (1909: 5) reported the pleasures of willingly suspending himself in a canyon of fantasy. 'The sense of unreality is so strong that one imagines himself standing in the middle of a cyclorama building looking at a painting of highly colored mountains and mysterious gorges', he wrote in his *Doing the Grand Canyon*. 'The silence aids in this delusion, and one half expects to go down some steps out into the noise and reality of a street again.' Like so many others, McCutcheon's view of the canyon was an inside job. Its enjoyment issued from a sense of 'unreality' comparable to the technological illusion of the cyclorama, a city building where he could recede from the flow of everyday life and 'imagine himself' at the centre of a spectacle designed for his consumption.

Indeed, visitors to Chicago's 1893 World Columbian Exposition might have sensed something similar as they stood in the middle of the Cyclorama of the Grand Canyon painted by Walter Burrage. Seven years later, Bicknell's 1900 guidebook would direct tourists to Cyclorama Point at the canyon – a rocky extremity on West Rim near Monument Creek where Burrage had framed the view for his Chicago exhibit. With scenery surrounding his party like a curved painted canvas, Bicknell (1901: 55–6) both recalls what his tourists saw and directs the reader who may stand on similar ground. 'Very striking, too, is the scene spread out below us', he writes. 'Studying the prostrate landscape with our fieldglasses we were enabled to pick out some of the monuments that give the stream its name.' Standing at this observation point – named after a mechanical representation of the Grand Canyon – becomes a circular search for points of reference that serve to remake the view. Binoculars study geological formations to identify specific *monumentalised* landscape features that, in turn, bestow a name to Monument Creek which can be seen from Cyclorama Point – a point of observation found in both Arizona and Chicago.

Technologies of vision not only suspended the coordinates of a lived time and space, they equally implicated the spectator in a real and fictional landscape of successive images effortlessly moving across their eyes. For instance, the Hermit Rim Road advertised by the Santa Fe (1915) was more than a surface for transportation. It was a monument to enhanced and unconstrained vision. 'No other roadway in the world is built along the brink of such a tremendous abyss. While whirling along in an El Tovar yellow coach, or standing on one of the 'points', you have some of the sensations of an eagle winging the abyss unafraid', claimed a Santa Fe brochure, 'in places there is a sheer drop of 2,000 feet within a rod of the rim. Yet you are as safe as in an easy chair at home. Along the entire route the gigantic panorama of the Grand Canyon unfolds for miles and miles'. Visiting the canyon promised a cinematic spectacle for a spectator whose vision reached the heights of an eagle from the perch of a comfortable chair. In cars or on horseback, field-glasses hanging from their necks, visitors could see the canyon as if sitting at home or in a theatre.

In fact, long before the IMAX theatre was built six miles south of the canyon's rim, early twentieth century tourists found an equivalent to the IMAX experience hanging from the canyon's edge. Ellsworth and Emery Kolb, two brothers from Pennsylvania who came to the Grand Canyon in 1901 – 2, began operating a make-shift photography studio in a tent on the South Rim in 1903. They used an abandoned prospecting hole below the rim as their darkroom. Where mineral claims had largely failed at the canyon, the Kolbs developed a good business of mining the tourist population for images of themselves. In 1911, the brothers made a motion picture of a harrowing journey in a wooden boat down the Colorado River. By 1915, they had added an auditorium to the east end of their photography studio which hung over the rim of the canyon. On the front of the building, they hung a sign that read: 'Kolb Bros: Shooting the Rapids of the Colorado River Canyons in Motion Pictures'. As the studio stood next to the trail-head, tourists could opt against going down the trail and instead climb down the stairs into the studio's auditorium. Once inside and seated, they would listen to Emery Kolb give a lecture about his adventures exploring the canyon before he darkened the room and projected his movie of the Colorado River (Suran 1991). With canyon and river just beyond the screen wall, the Grand Canyon appeared silently before each seated tourist in a flow of black and white images chattering through the sprockets of a projector.

Even before the Kolb's movie screen collapsed the arduous hiking distance from the rim to the river, people at home were told that gazing at stereographic images of the canyon carried a freedom of vision that surpassed an actual visit. 'Tourists often lose half the meaning and half the pleasure of a journey because of their nervous way of scampering from one sight to another without stopping to think about what they see', suggests the guide, *The Grand Canyon of Arizona: Through the Stereoscope* (published in New York by Underwood and Underwood, 1904: 7). 'But when you are looking at the country through stereographs, you can take your time about it. You can linger long enough in any one spot so that the beauty and meaning of what you see may be mentally digested.' Finding the canyon through the device was nothing less than an exercise in monasticism, a retreat into a solitary space of studious contemplation. Here are the guide's methods for using the device:

> Hold the hood of the stereoscope close against the forehead, shutting out all sight of your immediate surroundings. . . Read what is said of each place in this book. Refer to the map and know exactly where you are in each case. Read the explanatory comments printed on the back of each stereograph mount. Go slowly. Do not hurry. Go again – and yet again. Think it over. Read all the first-class books and magazine articles that you can find bearing on the subject of the Canyon.

Following these instructions, the viewer could, ideally, become seduced by their intensity. After locating themselves on maps and perusing expert testimony in books and magazines, they focused the cards to find the hypnotic drama of a mechanically reproduced Grand Canyon. The whole affair, the guide suggested, would lodge them in a fiction of *realism*: 'Does it not make you almost draw back with a shock of surprise? You feel the dizzy space below that perilously overhanging shelf from which the men are looking off; you almost hold your breath as you peer down towards the invisible bottom of the gorge.' For home viewers looking at an image of men looking into the canyon, perhaps there was no place where the Grand Canyon hit bottom. Instead, the canyon revealed itself and found comprehension through a repetitive, interiorised orientation to a larger realm of reference points and disjointed images. As the canyon receded into this discourse, so too did the viewer.

'The stereoscope signals an eradication of "the point of view" around which, for centuries, meanings had been assigned reciprocally to an observer and the object of his or her vision', argues Crary. Although parlour stereoscopes were a popular leisure pastime since the 1850s, they engaged their users in a tangible production of 'forms of verisimilitude' (Crary 1990: 124–32) '[W]hat the observer produced, again and again, was the effortless transformation of the dreary parallel images of flat stereo cards into a tantalizing apparition of depth. . . And each time, the mass-produced and monotonous cards are transubstantiated into a cumpulsory and seductive vision of the "real".'

As an early visual technology that dispersed Grand Canyon scenery into a series of views and voices, the stereoscope is an emblem of a broader approach to seeing the landscape where exterior and interior images and discourse converge in the spectator. In the stereo cards accompanying the 1904 Grand Canyon guide, home viewers may have found a pleasure and promise as they pressed the hood of the scope against their forehead. Inside the chamber placed over their eyes, they shut out everything that surrounded them. In this space, the dual images of the card appeared as a single picture of reality that became joined in the mind of the viewer. On more than one card, they found pictures of a visitor or a couple – like themselves – alone, gazing into the abyss. It was a view that reimagined a fantasy of the canyon and nature before tourists began arriving on the scene, and an image that found its antithesis in the crowds of noisy and contemptible tourists who became a source of managed vision since the turn of the century. Stationed behind a metal shroud and focused on the surface of the reproduced photographs, they could silently contemplate a place they held in their minds and controlled with their hands. It was a place shut off from the crowds, a place of depth and dimension. And although some of the cards showed the Colorado River rolling through the canyon, the stereograph, like images of the canyon since that time, proposed to the viewer that there was no bottom in sight.

Notes

This chapter is based largely on excerpts from an extensive study of the tourism practices, landscape, culture and history at the Grand Canyon titled *On The Rim: Looking for the Grand Canyon*, (Minneapolis: University of Minnesota Press, 2000).

The Scottish Highlands as Spectacle

Fraser MacDonald

Since the early explorations of Scotland in the late eighteenth century, debates over tourism and tourist representation have been prominent in the cultural politics of the Scottish Highlands. From Samuel Johnson's search for the 'noble savage' in 1773 to more contemporary tourist encounters via theme parks and multimedia, Highland places have been transformed in accordance with the tourist imagination and the logic of capitalism. Although tourism is increasingly dominant in strategic economic plans for the region, local dissent is evident in the social practices of crofting, the prevailing mode of agricultural life. Curiously, much of this local dissent is manifestly anticapitalist in nature and, in complex and contradictory ways, resonates with other Left critiques of tourism and its relation to place. This chapter is therefore concerned with local responses to a particular suite of Highland imagery which projects notions of wilderness, primitive virtue and 'natural heritage'. These visual ideologies are identified as being an important vehicle of capital accumulation, the images being bought and sold all over the world as part of a global imagining of Scotland as a commodity. Guy Debord's critique of advanced capitalism, *Society of the Spectacle* (Debord 1977), is used to critically unpack the commodification and banalisation of Highland culture, motifs which are further examined with reference to other texts such as Henri Lefebvre's *The Production of Space* (Lefebvre 1991). These urbanist projects are translated into a rural context in order to explore the politics of tourism, nature and the picturesque in Highland Scotland. Tourist performance and the meaning(s) of place also feature among the core themes of the chapter, with particular attention given to the ways in which the scripted dialogue and practices anticipated by tourists are subverted by 'locals'. The final sections consider various responses to tourism and tourist representation in the form of abandoned trash, Calvinist

Presbyterianism and the work of the prominent Gaelic writer, Iain Crichton Smith. With such disparate material, the style of the chapter – being neither closely argued or particularly coherent – should be considered as something of a discursive experiment; an experiment which draws attention to the epistemological problematic of combining ethnography with radical critique.

In the present academic climate, any association of tourism with capitalist alienation is something of an embarrassment. This is evident in a recent collection of essays entitled *Tourists and Tourism*, in which we are told on page one that 'mass tourism is tainted with the imagery of a totalising modernity that tarnishes all that it touches, destroying "authentic cultures" and polluting earthly "paradises"' (Abram et al. 1997). 'However', the introduction continues, 'the very pervasiveness of tourism, as a way of thinking and of living in a "post-"modern/structural/colonial world has yet to be related to contemporary discussions of the finer issues in social anthropology'. It is not surprising then, that throughout that book issues of tourist identity predominate, a preoccupation which is entirely in keeping with the claim that the collection 'challenges received wisdom about the "commoditisation" of culture assumed in tourism'. Against such a background (of a book that has index entries for 'backpackers' and 'bodily experiences' but not 'capital' and 'class'), it is necessary to re-emphasise an emancipatory approach to tourism studies. After all, it is not as if anyone has disproved either the necessity or the validity of Marxist analysis; as Eagleton has written, 'it is less disproved than discredited, out of the question rather than out of the arguments' (Eagleton, 1998:247). Perhaps, in reacting against the fetish of consumer identity within tourist anthropology, I have drawn from what some might consider to be needlessly extreme currents in the Marxist tradition. In the theoretical detour that follows, I hope to demonstrate their applicability and efficacy.

Situating the Spectacle

The *Situationist International* (SI), formed in 1956 out of a union of surrealist-inspired revolutionary groups, produced a clutch of radical critiques of postwar consumption, representing a theoretically important and often overlooked strand of Marxist thought. Although Guy Debord's *Society of the Spectacle* is perhaps the best known, other texts by Henri Lefebvre and Raoul Vaneigem share (with minor differences) the common aim of providing 'a total critique of the world as it exists, that is, of every aspect of modern capitalism and its generalised system of illusions'. Debord's work is particularly helpful in this context, emphasising the relationship between capital and the image, and at the same time providing a critical edge and dialectical flexibility that both prefigures and undermines postmodernism. The situationist preoccupation with an emancipatory analysis of consumption and alienation – which is followed in this chapter – places them firmly in the Marxist tradition. Indeed, in order to properly understand the SI one would have to excavate the intellectual history of Marx and Hegel, from whom they repeatedly draw. However, given the limited space available here, it is only possible to deal with a small and unrepresentative selection of situationist ideas and not with their development and practice (see Plant 1992 or Bonnett 1989 for a fuller discussion).

Despite my claim that Situationist ideas are often overlooked, I am also conscious that it is respectable for writers on the Left to make a cap-tipping reference to *Society of the Spectacle* that, being casual rather than systematic, tends to dissipate its critical force. John Urry's *The Tourist Gaze* (1990), a book which invokes a situationist-style critique, regrettably contains the citation in the most predictable context: the consideration of theme parks and shopping malls. This reduction of Debord to a figure who attacked the most stupefying manifestations of capitalism was also in evidence at the time of his death, when the news agency report of his suicide labelled him as merely 'an avant-garde essayist who denounced the show-biz society' (Imrie 1994). Not wanting to make the same mistake, I must first reiterate that the theory of the Spectacle is all-encompassing, and to isolate particular theses for consideration is deeply problematic. This said, I shall *partially* examine *Society of the Spectacle,* focusing on our present interest in tourism, capital and place.

Society of the Spectacle and other stories

First published in 1967, *La Société du Spectacle* consists of 221 'theses', short aphorisms on social life that render 'all men and women, even those who staged the play, passive spectators and consumers of their estrangement from their own words, gestures, acts and desires' (Marcus 1995). The theory in its most basic form is contained on the first two pages of the book, the remaining theses just repeating and elaborating the same formula:

> In societies where modern conditions of production prevail, all of life presents itself as an immense accumulation of *spectacles*. Everything that was once directly lived has moved away into a representation. (Debord 1977:#1)

> The spectacle is not a collection of images, but a social relation among people, mediated by images. (Debord 1977:#4)

> Understood in its totality, the spectacle is both the outcome and the goal

of the dominant mode of production. It is not something *added* to the world – not a decorative element so to speak. On the contrary, it is the very heart of society's real unreality. In all its specific manifestations – news or propaganda, advertising or the actual consumption of entertainment – the spectacle epitomizes the prevailing model of social life. It is the omnipresent celebration of a choice *already made* in the sphere of production, and the consummate result of that choice. In form as in content the spectacle serves as total justification for the conditions and aims of the existing system. It further ensures the *permanent presence* of that justification, for it governs almost all the time spent outside the production process itself. (Debord, 1994:#6)[1]

At a general level we can consider the spectacle to be nothing less than the 'vast technical and intellectual apparatus of late-capitalism' (Best and Kellner 1991), which extends beyond the familiar archetypes of television and tourism, to include all aspects of economy, society and culture. One of the principal methods of *Society of the Spectacle* is what Debord calls *detournement*, the incorporation of other texts (principally Marx and Hegel) into a new assimilated form, since he believed that 'the literary and artistic heritage of humanity should be used for partisan propaganda purposes' (Debord and Wolman 1981). Clearly the ghost of Marx hangs heavy over the whole situationist project. Similarly, the influence of Lukács is also evident, particularly the theory presented in *History and Class Consciousness*, 'that in capitalist society the commodity form permeates every aspect of social life, taking the shape of a pervasive mechanisation, quantification and dehumanisation of human experience' (Eagleton 1991:98). It caused Debord a certain haughty displeasure that subsequent theorists were to draw from him in this same way, only without the 'partisan propaganda' justification of detournement. Foremost amongst these was Jean Baudrillard who, although deeply influenced by situationism, later abandoned the idea of any critical relation to the spectacle in his writing on hyperreality and simulation. Debord, of course, always resisted such a position, jealously guarding a revolutionary theory grounded in the concrete *reality* of people and place. For contemporary analyses, *Society of the Spectacle* therefore has a radical utility that is unavailable in the bleak rhetoric of hyperreality so often favoured by cultural theorists. There is also a lyrical fluidity and yet icy precision to Debord's work, which further commends it to those lost in the diffuse language (not to mention political vacuum) of postmodernism. One must be careful, however, to avoid being seduced by the captivating style of the book whilst being unaware of its explosive potential. As Debord reminds us in the preface, 'this book should be read bearing in mind it was written with the deliberate intention of doing harm to spectacular society' (Debord, 1992). To use it for any other purpose is futile. It is necessary to say something of *how* the writing of Debord can be used in this context. There can be little doubt that he violently opposed its appropriation by those who did not share his own revolutionary fervour. With characteristic foresight he went to considerable lengths to ensure that the legacy of the SI could not be easily consumed by an anodyne academia. This fate, however, was inevitable. His response in '*The Veritable Split in the International*' certainly hits a raw nerve:

> Submissive intellectuals who are presently at the beginning of their career see themselves as obliged for their part to disguise themselves as moderate situationists or semi-situationists, only to show that they are able to understand the last moment of the system which employs them (Debord and Sanguinetti 1974).

So how can a situationist critique be used in contemporary academic discourse? I would describe what follows as 'playing' with Debord's writing. That is to say that in a spirit of *detournement*, I reproduce various excerpts from *Society of the Spectacle* with a minimum of explanation. The style of his text is so compact that further elaboration appears clumsy in comparison; nevertheless I make some attempt to relate it to the rest of the discussion. This results in a rather disordered narrative that should be read without any expectation of order and causation, and with an awareness that it contains discursive elements that may not be easily reconciled. As to whether my extensive use of quotation is acceptable, Debord himself agreed that quotation was 'useful in periods of ignorance or obscurantist beliefs' (Imrie 1994). His first (anti-)book, *Memoires,* consisted solely of quotations, bound in rough sandpaper so that it would shred its shelf neighbours. Before proceeding to the dialectic between tourism and place in spectacular society, it is worth mentioning that Debord's work should be seen as located as much within the broad tradition of Marxist theory as constituting a heretical departure from it.

Tourism, spectacle and place

Tourism is mentioned in only one thesis of *Society of the Spectacle* (#168) in a chapter which deals with the production of space under capitalism. entitled 'The Organisation of Territory' or in another translation, 'Environmental Planning'. In this chapter, tourism, like urbanism, is considered to be one symptom of the unification of space under modern conditions of production. Indeed, space is the fundamental category here. The 'economic organisation of visits' involves transformations of space which facilitate capital accumulation, a theme which is later traced in the case of the Scottish Highlands. These transformed spaces may take the form of place creation or recreation which, according to Debord, will be necessarily banal given that the 'corporative restrictions' which preserved the quality of craft and place have been superseded by the market.

Capitalist production has unified space, which is no longer bounded by external societies. This unification is at the same time an extensive and intensive process of *banalization*. The accumulation of commodities produced in mass for the abstract space of the market, which had to break down all regional and legal barriers and all the corporative restrictions of the Middle Ages that preserved the *quality* of craft production, also had to destroy the autonomy and quality of places. (Debord 1977:#165)

The society which eliminates geographical distance reproduces distance internally as spectacular separation. (Debord 1977:#167)

Tourism, human circulation considered as consumption, a by-product of the circulation of commodities, is fundamentally nothing more than the leisure of what is going to see what has become banal. The economic organisation of visits to different places is already in itself the guarantee of their equivalence. The same modernisation that removed time from the voyage also removed it from the reality of space. (Debord 1977:#168)

The language of the critique is consciously totalising, a deliberate rhetorical device which aims to reflect the universal triumph of the spectacle and the impossibility of escape from its social relations. Adorno has suggested that 'a totalizing critique, while being a form of untruth, is a necessary consequence of and response to a totalizing system' (Stallabrass 1996:184). Eagleton also considers that 'not looking for totality is just code for not looking at capitalism' (Eagleton 1996:11). Thesis 168 of *Society of the Spectacle* (above) summarises an interesting dialectic, that the production of difference through inter-place competition actually reproduces *similar* places and thereby acts as 'the guarantee of their equivalence'. Harvey (1989:295) also observes that:

heightened inter-place competition should lead to the production of more variegated spaces within the increasing homogeneity of international exchange. But to the degree that this competition opens up cities to systems of accumulation, it ends up producing . . . a 'recursive' and 'serial' monotony.

Of primary interest here is the marketing and representation of place. Tourist-orientated products or services are given meaning – such as 'quality', 'uniqueness', 'authenticity' or 'prestige' – by association with a particular place. Marketing strategies frequently rely on past histories of social struggle, but paradoxically, contemporary protest is usually perceived as a threat to the meaning of the commodity, presenting unwelcome connotations of instability, disharmony and resentment. There is, too, the possibility that certain histories present a barrier to capital accumulation and must therefore be transformed to facilitate tourism and other inward investment. The 'Red Clydeside' history of Glasgow, for instance, was systematically written out of the '1990 European City of Culture' campaign in favour of a more 'high culture' emphasis and has since been considered a complete success (Boyle and Hughes 1991). Marketing place in this way – whether it be a city, region or nation – is often undertaken by the state, most firms deciding that if the campaign is privately financed the leakage of benefits to rivals is too high (Britton 1991). Thus, in the sphere of representation, the state ('the bureaucratic spectacle') exercises an additional power over place, using the desirable associations so favoured by capital as the motor of economic 'revival'. Lefebvre (1991:160) identifies the danger of *over-signification*:

> Are there spaces which fail to signify anything? Yes – some because they are neutral or empty, others because they are overburdened with meaning. The former fall short of signification; the latter overshoot it. Some 'over-signifying' spaces serve to scramble all messages and make any decoding impossible. Thus certain spaces produced by capitalist promoters are so laden with signs . . . that not only is their primary meaning (that of profitability) effaced but meaning disappears altogether.

The visual consumption of the picturesque is an obvious mechanism of over-signification, particularly through photography which reinforces a specific cultural aesthetic associated with purity of form and freedom from visual pollution (Urry 1995: 176). Amidst the fluid and dynamic process of place construction, there is no sense in which tourism scrambles some 'true' or static meaning. Rather, I am suggesting that over-signification by the commodity-spectacle has important political consequences, particularly with regard to spaces of current or historical social struggle. The production and maintenance of the picturesque very often has a naturalising effect on social relations and may overwrite concerns about social justice; 'denaturalising' tourist landscapes – uncovering their latent values – therefore becomes an essential and neglected task of academic research (Duncan and Duncan 1988). In *America*, Baudrillard has also observed the stupefying impact of a 'surplus of meaning':

> Elsewhere, sites of natural beauty are heavy with meaning, with nostalgia, and the culture itself is unbearable in its seriousness . . . strong cultures reflect back to us the image of our degraded one, and the image of our profound guilt. The surplus of meaning in a strong, ritual, territorial culture turns us into gringos, zombies, tourists kept under house arrest in the country's natural beauty spots. (1988)

Images of the picturesque, centring on 'strong cultures' and 'natural beauty spots', unite an otherwise disparate coalition of interests in the form of Scottish tourism, conservation and the sporting (deer stalking) estate. In the discussion that follows I attempt to apply theories of the commodity-spectacle to the particularity of the Scottish Highlands, reflecting on the appropriation by capital of meaning and place; the politics of tourism, nature and the picturesque; and dissent from their social relations. Before this can be done it is necessary to mention, albeit briefly, that the use of this 'urban' theory requires 'translation' into a 'rural' context, noting at the same time that the rural/urban dualism is itself politicised and problematic. The historical imagining of the Highlands as a playground and its use as a receptacle of urban fantasy has already been well documented (Womack 1989; Withers 1992). There is a sense in which the Highland landscape represents the material embodiment of predominantly urban ideas about wilderness, tradition, primitive virtue and (Scottish) national identity (Withers 1992). Under the unified space of capitalism, where the rural is an extension of the urban and tradition is a function of modernity, the material landscape of the Highlands must be subject to the same interrogation as that of the city. The emphasis of many critical works, such as David Harvey's *The Condition of Postmodernity*, has been predominantly urban in nature and yet its principal theses translate very well into the rural.[2] Similarly, Debord and the situationists were totally dedicated to the city – it was the spatial category of both their revolutionary theory and practice, a suitable panegyric for Debord being '*in difficillimis Republicae temporibus, urbem non deserui*' ('in bad times, I did not abandon the city') (Debord 1991:19). So in ignoring Marx's personal disdain for the countryside, I believe that many of the urban social struggles have their parallel inscription in rural space and any revolutionary theory or project must incorporate both.

The Spectacular Highlands

Tourism is in no sense the first agency of spatio-economic restructuring in the Highlands. The region has been repeatedly transformed to facilitate capital, leaving a distinctive geography of uneven development. Any glance at Highland economic history situates tourism amid a variety of spatial transformations, the most famous of which, the Highland Clearances, involved the appropriation of common lands and the dislocation of numerous communities to the marginal lands of the north and west coasts of Scotland during the late eighteenth and nineteenth centuries (Hunter 1976). Initially used for extensive sheep farming, the region was again transformed into sporting estates where 'the cult of the red deer', a vision of romantic nature and 'clan tradition', was acted out by royalty and the urban industrial élite. This was the age of 'Balmorality', the excesses of the Highland landlords being matched by the poverty of their tenants. On the coastal margins, tiny parcels of agricultural land, or crofts, were allocated to the clearance victims and, being too small to feed a family, created a captive and desperate labour force.[3] Throughout the social struggles that followed, Highland places – townships, districts or islands – became resonant with new meanings: repression, freedom, justice, loss, triumph, slavery. The subsequent history of the Highlands under the same pattern of land tenure has been one of continued economic marginality. Other industries that were once attracted by the availability of cheap, nonunionised labour are now thin on the ground, except of course those which, for reasons of political expediency, are ideally suited to northern Scotland, nuclear waste reprocessing for instance. With this background, the reorganisation of space around heritage and tourism is now the dominant strategy of economic revival, a recent survey indicating that the 'consumption' of 'Gaelic cultural activity' could be the engine of a tourist-orientated regeneration (MacKinnon, 1998). The current fashion for 'themed' multimedia tourism is another recent (and more obviously spectacular) model of economic activity which sells and modifies place. Tourism – particularly the techno-fetish variety – is now being hailed as the panacea of the Highland economy.

It is tempting to view the products of this information technology, those new places of leisure and new spaces of representation, as being characterised by an absence of meaning. However, it would be wrong to suggest that these techno-spaces are entirely meaning-less, given that on one level they may represent the internalisation of feudalism. The fulfilment of this is illustrated in the fact that both of the large-scale theme parks planned for the Highlands in 1997 embody the fantasies of the sporting 'wilderness' (McBeth, 1997). The ability to produce and reproduce images of the Highlands is now a key factor in inter-place competition. Innovation is then required to facilitate the unending search for 'new' images and as the reproduction quality improves, so the market for the improved image expands. The role of the image in the promotion of the Highlands is inevitably centred on the concept of the picturesque, and despite the growth in more interactive forms of spectacle, the 'scenic tour' remains the primary component of the tourist itinerary.

Performing the Picturesque

Travelling through the Scottish Highlands, the tourist is confronted with an ever-changing scene that variously conforms to and resists the anticipated delights of the picturesque. The experience is ephemeral. One cannot linger indefinitely in one place; it is necessary to submit to the narrative of travel, taking in new sights and leaving behind the old ones. Postcards and picture books are then required to reproduce each view as a momento of visual consumption, turning the tourist into a collector and reducing the experience to 'an administered and lifeless collection of images' (Stallabrass 1996: 27). The

psychology of the collector has materialised in the form of the 'viewing point', a walk-in postcard where 'the act of taking the picture is a
performance in itself', an inscription which says not merely 'I was
there', but 'I took this' (Stallabrass 1996: 26). Julian Stallabrass draws
attention to the innovations used in amateur photography which
make the landscape more compliant with the desire of the photographer, using filters and printing techniques which somehow allow the
subject 'to be truer to itself'. Amateur photography has developed in
tandem with tourism, in what has become a thoroughly modern sym-
biosis. As Susan Sontag observes, because 'the camera is a device which
makes real what one is experiencing . . . it seems positively unnatural
to travel for pleasure without taking a camera along. Photographs will
offer indisputable evidence that the trip was made, that the program
was carried out, that fun was had' (1979: 9). Sontag goes on to suggest
that, 'a way of certifying experience, taking photographs is also a way
of refusing it – by limiting experience to a search for the photogenic
. . . travel becomes a strategy of accumulating photographs' (ibid.: 9).
The centrality of the image, however, does not mean that tourist
experience is necessarily 'disembodied' or unidimensional; on the contrary, the practice of amateur photography – particularly video photography – implies a broader corporeal aesthetic (Crang 1997). This
endless search for the photogenic inevitably contributes to a process of
over-signification or, in the critique of Walter Benjamin, a loss of 'aura'
through the mechanical process of reproduction (Benjamin 1992:
217). For Lefebvre, truth is the casualty and illusion is triumphant:

> Take images for example: photographs, advertisements, films. Can
> images of this kind really be expected to expose errors concerning space?
> Hardly. Where there is error or illusion, the image is more likely to
> secrete it and reinforce it than to reveal it. No matter how 'beautiful'
> they may be, such images belong to an incriminated 'medium'. . . . As
> for error and illusion, they reside already in the artist's eye and gaze, in
> the photographer's lens . . . wherever there is illusion, the optical and
> visual world plays an integral and integrative, active and passive, part in
> it. It fetishizes abstraction and imposes it as the norm. (Lefebvre 1991:
> 97)

Lefebvre provides a radical antidote to those who rely on the
mimetic 'truth' of photography to legitimate the existing (or an imagined) visual order. One such example is the work of Robert Adam who
used landscape photography as part of a campaign for national parks
for Scotland in the 1940s (Scottish Council for National Parks, 1944).
A well known landscape photographer, Adam produced work for
many of the most popular travel books in the 1940s and 1950s, and
helped establish a canon of Scottish scenery linking urban nostalgia,
recreation and conservation in a visual way as yet unchallenged. This
tradition is currently upheld by the contemporary photographer

Colin Baxter whose postcard reputation has been used by the conservation agency, Scottish Natural Heritage, in a variety of books and publicity material (see Baxter and Thompson, 1995). In denial of history, these images loudly proclaim 'this is *the way it is* and the way it shall be':

> The glory of Scotland's natural heritage is superior to the limner's art, and photographs are but imperfect symbols of what they portray. As symbols, however, they serve to focus attention on *reality* . . . and provide some . . . indications of the type of scenery to be conserved either as national parks or as wildlife sanctuaries. (Adam and Kenneth 1944; my emphasis)

One characteristic of picturesque photography is that it has its own locational geography (Withers 1994). Not just any loch or glen will do. Particular places, having established a reputation in tourist iconography, are enduringly popular, the historical interest or meaning of the site having been displaced by the image itself. Many of these iconic images are the most questionable from a social justice perspective, the three favourite themes being the deserted or wilderness landscape; 'majestic' Scotland epitomised by 'kilts and castles'; and 'everyday' Scotland, which often focuses on incongruity or quaintness, like the postcard of cattle standing around a phone box in torrential rain (McRone et al. 1995). These pictures are highly naturalising, that is to say that they project a permanence and naturalness to the landscape that lies outside of its ideological context. This is particularly important when we consider the role of conservation agencies in presenting a specific visual and ecological order as being *the* 'natural heritage' of Scotland, without an awareness that ecological systems both instanciate and reflect the social systems that give rise to them (MacDonald 1998; Harvey 1996:185).

From History and Nature to Heritage and natural heritage
Walter Benjamin's idea that 'history breaks down into images, not into stories' (Gilloch 1996:112) makes apparent the 'historical' force with which notions of the picturesque are maintained, 'spectacular culture [having preserved] the old culture in congealed form, going as far as to recuperate and rediffuse even its negative manifestations' (Debord 1994: #192). Selling history or heritage is contingent on the commodity being free from any association that could hinder capital accumulation; there is little possibility of selling the local history of Calvinist Presbyterianism for instance, with its emphases on austerity, restraint and spiritual freedom. Selling heritage and place is therefore a highly selective business, which writes out or visually excludes anything that it cannot assimilate. Paradoxically, there are certain radical legacies which capital will confidently embrace as another way of

neutralising their revolutionary potential, in what Debord refers to as the 'spectacular critique of the spectacle'. The history of the Highland Clearances, which is currently invoked in protests about everything from inshore fishing restrictions to tolls on the Skye Bridge, is surely being neutralised by its saleability as heritage. Perhaps this is the ultimate victory of the Clearances, whereby a popular and radical history can be reduced to waxwork peasants and kilted landlords, just another ingredient in the postmodern Scotch broth of culture. The phases of capitalist transformation, which correspond to the title of John McGrath's play *The Cheviot, the Stag, and Black, Black Oil*, have passed into a new and more abstract condition of symbolic depletion. This is the logic of late capitalism made real in place; a process which, through over-signification, empties the Highlands of symbolic capital as it attempts to survive the increasingly competitive market of international tourism. Heritage need not necessarily be conservative, however, a theme taken up in Raphael Samuel's encyclopaedic work *Theatres of Memory*. He argues that 'it is one of the few areas of national life in which it is possible to invoke the common good without provoking suspicion of party interest' (Samuel 1994). There is, too, an element of literary or intellectual snobbery in the cultural criticism of Debord and Lefebvre, that the alienated masses cannot be trusted with pictures; 'that images seduce when the printed word engages the full intelligence' (Samuel 1994: 267).

The same forces that have turned history into heritage have also transformed nature into natural heritage. These constructs are embodied in the concept of national parks which, although never implemented in Scotland, has a distinctly Scottish pedigree, the Dunbar-born naturalist John Muir having played a key role as the architect of the first American parks. The rhetoric of 'despoliation' and 'desecration' – so prevalent at the time of Muir – remains part of the textual apparatus of national park proponents in Scotland and proves to be a reliable way of mobilising middle class interests around the picturesque (see Scottish Council for National Parks, 1993). In a Debordian critique, the prospect of national parks would statutorily legitimate the tourist gaze on Highland culture, simultaneously reinforcing the autonomous power of the state and its complicity with capital accumulation. Being thus tied to a visual order conducive to recreation, Lefebvre considered that national parks were areas earmarked 'for economic and social decline' (Lefebvre 1991). The most recent consultation paper suggests – with reassuring ambiguity – that they 'should be places which set an example of how to integrate the rural economy with the proper protection of the natural heritage' (Scottish Natural Heritage 1998). Crofters are less than enthusiastic; at a public meeting in Lochcarron, Wester Ross, earlier proposals met with a frosty reception, many predicting that such a designation would 'put our culture in a time capsule' (Macaulay 1990). Much of the grassroots concern relating to national parks anticipates inequitable social relations, particularly the element of performance which positions crofters as 'museum custodians ... scenic stewards for tourism' (Lowenthal 1991, cited in Urry 1995: 209).

Reflexivity and Dissent

One of the themes of this chapter is that crofting communities express dissent from tourism which, being spasmodically anticapitalist, can concur with critiques from the Left such as those of Debord and Lefebvre. This is surely a bizarre coalition, given that these groups are well known for their theological, if not political, conservatism. With such an unlikely thesis some qualification is therefore necessary. On the basis of ethnographic fieldwork both in Wester Ross and on the Hebridean island of North Uist, it is apparent that most crofters welcome the economic input of tourism. This situation is unsurprising given the marginal status of agriculture and the traditional pluri-activity pattern of crofting, which, in an area of high unemployment, demands additional sources of income. There is, however, an obvious ambivalence in their attitude, evident in the large repertoire of 'stupid tourist' jokes which invert the holiday brochure image of the Highlands and emphasise the wit, education and rationality of the crofter (Macdonald 1997:110). This humour not only shows an awareness of unflattering tourist representations, but also indicates a reflexive enquiry into the nature of representation itself. It would be unusual however, for a 'local' to give any public intimation of disdain; not so, the stereotypical tourist, who happily volunteers opinions on all aspects of Highland culture. The local newspaper, the *West Highland Free Press* (hereafter *Free Press*), regularly hosts a post-mortem of the tourist experience by some disappointed visitor, frustrated at the disparity between the realities of Highland life and their more romantic preconceptions.

Confirming the centrality of the picturesque to the tourist imagination, it is the presence of trash which forms the basis of the most common complaint. In order to explain this careless disregard for the tourist's vision, idiocy or laziness are ascribed to locals, prejudices that have precisely the same historical origins as the picturesque itself (Clyde 1995). Following a visit to Skye Woollen Mill, one tourist writes:

> Reading your paper and the broad news coverage of the Western Highlands, one receives the general impression that your readers consider that the rest of the United Kingdom owes them a living ... [Skye Woollen Mill] is dirty, untidy and neglected. A few sour faced operatives work the machines, pretending the visitors aren't there. Where is the guide? Where is the manager to take the parties round? I'm afraid a great deal of this is caused by laziness. (*Free Press*, Letter, 18.7.75)

Another example shows how a loyalty to the order of the picturesque results in a scripted ambience of community which anticipates 'natives' and *bona fide* 'tourists' but most certainly excludes other forms of travellers.

> when we did a pilgrimage to Tarskavaig bay . . . last week we were disgusted to see an old rusty car dumped on the land side of the rocks and what appeared to be a permanent caravan and tent site on the shore. Surely the car dump could be removed? As to the camp site, one sympathises with people enjoying camping but I should have thought that the 'powers' would contain that within certain areas. So I turn to you for help. Firstly to see what can be done about that dump. Secondly, if possible to tidy up that gypsy looking encampment. (*Free Press*, Letter, 1/8/75)

The Place of Trash

There is something uniquely offensive about trash; it is *out of place*, incongruous, absurd. In the rural environment the spent articles of modern life assume a different – even more insolent – character than their urban counterparts. The Outer Hebrides, the chain of islands off Scotland's north west coast, are awash with all manner of domestic and agricultural refuse. From beer cans and bicycles to crisp packets and coal sacks, it seems that everything has moved away into a roadside ditch, or onto the shore or maybe just abandoned outside the house, leaving tourists to cope uneasily with the burden of 'things'. Within this inadvertent collage of rubbish we can find grounds for critique; just as Walter Benjamin used the fragment to reconstruct the totality, Julian Stallabrass (1996) has opened up the allegorical aesthetic of waste to reveal the operations of the capitalist system. He forcefully argues that taking trash seriously highlights the true absurdity or 'real unreality' of the system that produced it (see also Debord 1994:#6). As with other aspects of the material landscape, unwanted household debris is replete with accidental meaning. 'Loosed from exchange and use value, it takes on an apparently more genuine aesthetic air', the 'redundant beauty' invoking a sense of embarrassment, 'a reminder of some vague promise unredeemed' (Stallabrass 1996:174).

Rubbish will always be the greatest means of subverting the tourist imagination in the Highlands and, indeed, one might even argue that litter could have a useful role in rural political practice in the same way that graffiti is used in the city. The washed up squeezy-bottle on the beach, the remains of a dead car or the wind-strewn wreckage of an ex-washing machine become inverted icons of modernity, reminders that Highland people have the same materialistic concerns as those from the tourist's city. The fact that islanders chose for themselves a new washing machine or a new car in the same way that the tourist chose a holiday disrupts the image of an other-worldly, childlike peasant. Negating the myth of 'primitive virtue', the peasant-turned-consumer demands to be situated 'in the centre of the world from which the tourist has come, with all the difficulties and treacheries that such a world contains' (Smith 1986: 14). Here in the midst of the picturesque lies the corpse of the commodity, one of capitalism's idiosyncratic contradictions where the built-in obsolescence of the 'white good' assaults the tourist imagination. However, fewer crofters can now enjoy the same untroubled conscience with regard to abandoned trash. The system *naturally* insists on the fig leaf of order to mask the barrenness of the spent commodity. 'Cleaning up' is therefore the priority of both local and central government despite the sadness expressed by many islanders at the sterilisation of their local history. Although this is most obviously directed at the removal of ruined houses it can also apply to vehicles and agricultural machinery. A walk along the coast of almost any crofting township on the island of North Uist will reveal the history of mechanised agriculture in a series of lichen-covered artefacts. It is interesting to note how the 'period' exhibits such as a cartwheel or a horse plough may be readily incorporated into the picturesque, satisfying the spectacular predilection for rural nostalgia. Half a Ford Capri, on the other hand, retains the label of trash. There is little intentionality in this use of waste to disrupt the visual landscape but there is, I believe, a waning disregard for appearances that originally stems from a dignified ignorance of the picturesque and its formal etiquette. The presence of litter and the offence it causes is also strangely resonant of the situationist project.

Dissenting Presbyterians

For tourists coming to the Highlands, whether they are from Lowland Scotland or further abroad, the exacting codes and minimal aesthetic of Calvinist Presbyterianism are, like abandoned trash, among the least appealing features of local custom. Both are so difficult to reconcile with the more romantic images of community and Celtic tradition (Macdonald 1997: 166; Chapman 1987: 25). For many Hebrideans, however, the tourist economy presents a threat to the moral and spiritual integrity of island life. Presbyterian dissent from tourism centres on the sanctity of the Sabbath, and prospect of moral degeneracy if urban values are adopted and the 'entertainment' provision for tourists enthusiastically shared by local people. Sabbatarianism, although slightly less evident in the Hebrides than twenty or even ten years ago, is still very much part of the temporal organisation of island life. Shops are closed, croft work is suspended and there is little activity other than the diurnal convoy to the services of the three Presbyterian churches. Tourists can find this Hebridean Sabbath a trying experience unless they have received prior warning. Until recently, there was no possibility of leaving North Uist, making it a day of enforced quietness, a time when many visitors had to reflect on whether 'getting away from it all' was really what they came for. 'If Skye wants a growth tourist industry, the traditional Sabbath and all the dreary old outworn shibboleths will have to be abandoned' moaned one tourist in the local paper (Free Press, 11.7.80). 'Why should Skye people adjust their lives and ways of life to suit the visitors?' came the defence (Free Press, 18.7.80a). 'Well, until you move to within 50 years behind the times, here is one tourist who won't be back' continued another (Free Press, 18.7.80b). These lively exchanges are less common now than in the 1980s, a testimony perhaps to the strengthening hand of tourist provision and the fading light of religious protest. The late Rev. James Morrison, a Free Church minister and local councillor on North Uist, was notoriously candid about tourism, which he viewed as a threat to the communitarian nature of crofting. Fiercely opposing a plan to allow private ownership of crofts, he wrote in dismay of the 'irresponsible sections of our present day society':

> When they get their crofts into their hands they will soon hand them over to the best buyer and the Crofters Commission will see to it that the buyer will be the man or the woman who will sponsor tourism – caravans, chalets etc. And the major destruction and overruling consequence of all this will be the desecration of the Lord's Day and all that represents. (Collins 1984: 33)

This last comment is revealing. The rigidity of Sabbath observance reflects more than a devotion to the Bible as the inerrant Word of God (although this surely is the principal motive). It also represents an expression of difference between 'home' and 'away'; the sacred and the secular; 'the church' and 'the world' (see Macdonald 1997). It is a way of emphasising the purity of island religion to a postreformation Scotland that has long since relinquished the Sabbath in favour of shopping and football. Such unwillingness to compromise religious observance for tourist comfort is, in a sense, a reaction against 'the present age, which prefers the sign to the thing signified, the copy to the original, representation to reality, the appearance to the essence . . . [where] *illusion* only is sacred, *truth* profane' (Feuerbach, cited in Debord, 1994:11).

Iain Crichton Smith and the Art of Dissent

The discursive elements of this chapter – disparate though they are – were conceptually wedded by the author after reading *Towards the Human,* a collection of essays by the Lewis-born author Iain Crichton Smith (1986).[4] It seems sensible, then, to introduce this material as a means of weaving together some of the more unlikely threads of my argument. One essay in particular provides us with a parallel critique to that of Debord, Lefebvre and the academic Left. Entitled *Real People in a Real Place*, it is critically reflexive in its assessment of the social relations of Hebridean tourism, the language sharing some of the characteristics of Debord: totalising, but dialectical; considered and yet angry. Smith's ire is directed at a specific genre of 'literature' epitomised by Lillian Beckwith, a writer who achieved considerable commercial success by portraying islanders as backward, comic and childlike, an unworldly race that struggles with modernity and the English language. Beckwith's writing style has its counterpart in the language and photography of the tourist brochure and, according to Smith, in tourist performance. Like Debord, he initially objects to the 'unreality' that is projected onto place, a mythology which binds together notions of the picturesque, primitive virtue and a (false) nostalgia for pre-capitalism:

> It is easy to assign the islander to this misty, rather beautiful world, and leave him there if one first of all succeeds in making that world unreal, and it's inhabitants unreal, off the edge of things, a noble savage with his stories and unmaterialistic concerns. (Smith 1986: 14)

In a masterstroke of reflexivity, Smith assumes the role of a tourist in order to parody their preconceptions:

> The islander is not a menace to us, he is the tame feed for our happy comedy, he makes no demands. Why should he? Does he not have after all a beautiful place in which to stay, that blue morning of the world in which he doesn't have to work too hard, in which he actually welcomes the slightly silly, but really superior tourist. . . The islander regards the tourist as one who lives on the surface of what he sees, and the tourist, on the other hand, while seeming to admit this, at the same time knows, really knows, that his world is more gritty, more real, and therefore he can afford to make fun of himself, as if he were in a wonderland (Smith 1986:14, 16).

The tourist imagination prescribes an unworldliness to the islander, evident in the distaste for trash and the disappointment at the extent of local integration into capitalism. These social relations are also manifest in the imperialism of language:

> The islanders must become little children who have no lust for possessions as corrupt that of the mainlanders, but are simply *enacting a play* for the benefit of the stranger. And this can be best done but inventing a language for him which will itself be as ludicrous as the language given to the Red Indians in Westerns. . . In this way the islander is labelled, surrounded by mythology, so that the meanest tourist can feel superior to the brightest islander (Smith 1986: 15, my emphasis)

Smith's concern is not merely for the crippling political effect of this language. He also recognises its suffocation of creativity amongst an island people accustomed to bardic innovation and poetic experiment. Moreover, tourism's introduction of a class distinction in what was a largely undifferentiated crofting population, brings with it a self-awareness in artistic expression. 'Behind this haze of falsity' continues Smith 'lies the broken-ness which will not allow [local] writers the confidence that others can have, who when they write do not feel their subject matter disappearing before their eyes' (Smith 1986).

Conclusion

Although this chapter has almost exclusively (and perhaps naively) focused on the depletion of symbolic capital from place, the discussion could easily be restructured to examine the more practical consequences of tourism in the Highlands. It is an economic sector characterised by intolerably low rates of pay (£1.80 an hour is not uncommon for hotel staff), highly concentrated profit, poor working conditions, a seasonal pattern of employment and little investment in training. My concern here, however, has been with the more abstract consequences of tourist-related capital: the process of over-signification; the naturalising effect of the picturesque; the politically neutralising impact of spectacular heritage. Other studies of tourism in the Highlands have focused on elements of local performance (Macdonald 1997) or on the flexibility of tourist identity (Kohn 1997), but the social justice implications of tourist iconography demand our critical attention, and 'denaturalising' tourist landscapes is, I believe, a neglected avenue of ethnographic enquiry. There has been a tendency to overemphasise the repertoire of tourist 'identities' without recognising that these reflect the intensification of economic competition, as much as any overarching cultural phenomena. As identity seems to be the dominant theme in much ethnographic writing on tourism (Abram et al. 1997), I have felt it necessary to reiterate a more critical stance. The dissolution of popular categories of investigation such as 'hosts' and 'guests' which is a feature of this recent work (for instance, Kohn 1997) can actually be taken a step further. 'In a world that *really* has been turned on its head' what were previously thought of as 'guests' do indeed become hosts in the landscape of spectacle (Debord 1994:#9); the tourist implores the islander to 'visit' and partake in the fantasy, to be the 'guest' star in this scripted Scottish Eden. This discussion then, is intended as a playful attempt to explore the interconnectivity of dissent and critique. Guy Debord's *Society of the Spectacle* does not willingly submit itself to this type of analysis, but rather demands a practical realisation of justice that goes beyond the realm of academic discourse.

Acknowledgements

I am grateful for the financial support of the Pirie-Read Scholarship for the University of Oxford and the Vaughan Cornish Bequest. It is only fair to admit that the latter fund was intended to assist research relating to 'the beauty of the countryside', a condition ironically satisfied by this eulogy for trash. I would also like to thank Mike Crang for his comments on an earlier draft of this paper.

Notes

1. I refer to two different translations of *Society of the Spectacle*. The first translation (1977) published by Black and Red, Detroit, has several errors but sticks closer to the original style. The second translation by Donald Nicolson-Smith (1994), while taking some liberties with the style, is easier to read.

2. Harvey has made it clear that 'the distinction between the built environments of cities and the humanly modified environments of rural and even remote regions . . . appears arbitrary except as a particular manifestation of a rather long-standing ideological distinction between the country and the city' (Harvey 1993).

3. As Marx wrote of the Sutherland Clearances, 'they [the landlords] conquered the field for capitalist agriculture, incorporated the soil into capital, and created for the urban industries the necessary supplies of free and rightless proletarians' (Marx 1976).

4. It is with great regret that I record the death of Iain Crichton Smith during the preparation of this book.

BACK TO THE CITY

Acting Local
Two Performances In Northern Italy
Paola Filippucci

Introduction

> So we said 'Come on, let's do Carnevale as they used to do it once' – and we went out in the square and jumped, laughed, and entertained all those who watched us. (Luisa, born 1950, about going to Carnevale with friends in 1988)

> Old ladies, grandmothers come to us and say 'I remember this, it was called such-and-such; I remember that, it was done in such-and-such a way'. (Gina, b. 1948, a member of the Arti per Via folklore group, speaking of her audiences)

Gina and Luisa live in Bassano, a small town in North-East Italy.[1] Both, in recent years, have periodically gone 'out in the square' wearing unusual clothes, acting in unusual ways in front of audiences. Gina has done so as a member of a folklore group called 'Arti per Via' (ApV) ('Trades on the Road'), performing traditional street-trades for audiences in Bassano and elsewhere. Gina has also, like Luisa, taken part in Carnevale (Carnival), a yearly festival when people go out wearing unusual costumes and masks and, ideally, behave outrageously.

In Bassano, both the ApV and Carnevale are presented as reenactments of past practices and as moments in which something essentially 'local' is displayed. I will focus on these performances in trying to understand what 'local' means in the early twenty-first century, in an industrialised, affluent, well-connected place within one of Italy's, and indeed Europe's, most prosperous regions. I will suggest that in these performances, people celebrate space and time as bodily, sensuous experiences. They imagine and enact an intersubjective field that they identify with locality, in turn cast as an absolute, self-contained and authentic, immediately experienced reality. This way of characterising the 'local' ostensibly isolates it from the 'global' context in which local lives now unfold. However, I will link this way of producing locality with the area's involvement in 'global' relations (Wilk 1995: 118; cf. Ekholm-Friedman and Friedman 1995).

Bassano

Bassano is a town of some 40,000 inhabitants at the Northern edge of the Po plain, in the Veneto region of North-East Italy. Since its tenth century origin, Bassano has been an urban centre, seat of local government bodies, of religious authorities, of a landed aristocracy, and of wealthy traders, entrepreneurs and artisans engaged, from the sixteenth century, in protoindustrial production (see StdB 1980; Berti 1993 for this section). Economic decline in the nineteenth century was followed by the appearance of modern industry in the early twentieth century. Neither industry nor farming could support the population, so emigration was great throughout the nineteenth and early twentieth century (Berengo 1963; Berti 1993; Franzina 1984). The flow was reversed from the late 1950s, when Bassano and its hinterland began to expand with the proliferation of light industry (ceramics, shoes, mechanical parts), in small-scale, kin-based productive units. The area is now one of the most prosperous in Europe, and Bassano is the service centre of a populated, busy hinterland (see e.g. Bagnasco and Trigilia 1984).

Conservation and revival

The physical form of Bassano reflects its history. Until the 1950s, the town was largely contained within the circle of its fifteenth-century walls, beyond which was largely open countryside. It was during the postwar economic boom that 'houses and factories covered the countryside', as one local put it. A haphazard spread of low-rise housing, factories, warehouses, large-scale service infrastructure, fields and busy roads surrounds the oldest urban nucleus that is now the centre of town, a dense fabric of pre-twentieth century buildings. Its narrow streets open onto three interconnected squares, graced by churches and palaces, the Civic Museum and the Town Hall, cafés and elegant shops. The squares (collectively known as *la piazza*) are considered to be the 'heart' of Bassano, where people come to see and be seen, to stroll and window-shop, to gossip and hang out. The piazza is also the location of the weekly market and the stage of civic ceremonies, and of open-air shows and festivals such as those I consider below.

While the piazza has never ceased to be the the town's spatial, social and functional core, during the years of economic expansion the centre became depopulated and run down as people moved out to modern housing in the outskirts (see Petoello and Rigon 1980). The 'valorisation' (valorizzazione) of the centre began in the 1980s, when private capital was invested in restoring historic buildings and converting them into luxury housing. This development was in line with a contemporary national, and indeed Europe-wide, trend of identifying 'historic' artefacts as marketable signs of social distinction (see e.g. Bourdieu 1984). This was followed by a programme of conservation of historic public buildings and urban features sponsored by the local administration. In the 1990s, this has come to include the partial banning of cars, and total pedestrianisation is under discussion (see Filippucci 1997). The stated aim of such 'valorisation' is to attract visitors by a blend of history, culture and high-quality shopping. The tourist promotion of Bassano's 'historic centre' includes the staging of open-air events, some of which (like fashion displays and concerts) bring to Bassano extra-local images, figures and personalities, and are aimed at lending the town a cosmopolitan aura. Other events, by contrast, stage images and activities described as 'local', celebrating what is purportedly unique and 'traditional' about Bassano. The most elaborate of these are a yearly festival, Carnevale, and a folklore performance, the Arti per Via. Both are associated with, and celebrate, 'the streets and squares' of 'old Bassano'. These are the focus of this paper.

Carnevale is the local version of an old yearly festival widespread in Catholic countries of Southern Europe that includes masquerading, dancing, excess in food and drink, sexual and social license (see Counihan 1985; Galt 1973; Poppi 1983; Caro Baroja 1979; Gilmore 1975, 1987). The festival climaxes in the week before Ash Wednesday, when costumes and face masks are worn to disguise one's identity and mock accepted social roles (e.g. by reversal), to mix sacred and profane and to indulge in transgressive behaviour (see e.g. Bakhtin 1968; Burke 1978; Ginzburg 1972). In Bassano, Carnevale is said to have been introduced in the seventeenth century by nobility from Venice, seat of a world-famous version of the festival (see Burke 1987; Muir 1980). Local sources[2] from the nineteenth century document indoor dancing for the wealthy and outdoor dancing for the lower classes (see Filippucci 1992). The current form, with parades of floats, masque groups and 'folklore' displays, emerged in the interwar period, in the context of a nationwide campaign of 'return to traditions' by the Fascist regime. [3] Carnevale continued in this form until 1950, when it declined into a low-key affair, mostly involving children. In 1979, in the wake of the recent revival of Carnevale in Venice,[4] Bassano's tourist bureau reintroduced a floats' parade, outdoor dancing and competitions for the best costumes in the two weeks preceding Ash Wednesday. This has been the pattern since.

At one Carnevale in the early 1980s, some some fifteen members of a local amateur drama group specialising in dialect plays formed a masque of 'old street trades'. The masque won the first prize and, when a 'Festival of Folklore' was held in Bassano,[5] it was reformed as a permanent folklore group to represent the town and 'carry its name' to other places. The group was named Arti per Via and performed 'traditional' craft activities and trades. By 1994, the group had performed locally, all over Italy and in Europe and Latin America. It counted some sixty members, men, women and children impersonating thirty-two kinds of 'artisans and peddlers of the beginning of the century' (ApV promotional leaflet, 1994).

Both Carnevale and the ApV claim to represent and to bring back to life something authentically local. The ApV is presented as a serious, near-scholarly enterprise: the 'perfect reconstruction of an epoch', 'a museum that comes alive' (promotional leaflet, 1994). Present-day Carnevale is cast as the continuation of an 'old tradition of the town', partly by characterising the contemporary version as a pale reflection of the past, when Bassano's was 'the second most famous Carnevale in Italy'[6] as older Bassanesi, some of whom are organisers of the contemporary festival, are fond of saying. In both cases, 'revival' means rein-scribing with 'old' gestures, motions and sounds the space of the 'historic centre' town. The ApV reenact 'street trades' so that 'the road becomes a museum and the museum becomes a performance' (promotional leaflet, 1994); while the organizers and participants of Carnevale aim at recreating the 'real' Carnevale that used to take place in 'the streets and squares' of town, thronged by 'the people' who could not afford to attend the sumptuous indoor balls of the rich (cf. Filippucci 1992). By thus referring to the physical space of the town, both performances command a space that is quite literally 'local' (cf. Tuan 1990: 238).

Carnevale

In the late 1980s,[7] Carnevale took place in the town centre. The most popular event was the floats' parade, followed by evening entertainment during 'Fat Week'. Among those who attended, mainly only children wore costumes (maschere), except on the day of the parade, when adult masque groups appeared. Maschere led the outdoor dancing, although 'plain clothes' bystanders might join in. While not wild, the atmosphere at outdoor venues was informal, the social and bodily boundaries of normal life somewhat relaxed: the maschere in particular would tease friends, acquaintances and strangers, throwing confetti, streamers, shaving foam, flour, and stink bombs. Everyone was noisier than usual, the town centre resonating with laughter, shouting and chanting late into the night.

The maschere

The maschere are the protagonists of Carnevale, a time for 'putting on a different face and doing what you want for one day' (Simona, b. 1966). In present-day Bassano, anything goes: people dress as animals, outsize vegetables, exotic, religious and political figures, TV and film stars, mythical creatures and so on.[8] The effect of some costumes rests on comic reversal (cf. Bakhtin 1968): men dressed as women,[9] children dressed as old people, adults as children of the same or the opposite sex. The wearer's real identity is sometimes concealed under a face mask, but eccentric make-up is more common. This may be because being recognised and praised for one's ingenuity and creativity in making the costume is a key part of the pleasure of going in maschera. Most are handmade and utilise cheap, everyday materials to simulate precious or striking textures. Mundane objects may be used to comic or grotesque effect (as when silver-coloured plastic funnels are used to make the breasts of a female robot). People also play with colour, juxtaposing bright hues in dramatic contrast; and with size, dressing as a giant pencil or donning an outsize papier-maché' head (see Babcock 1978; Stewart 1984; cf. Turner 1967). Many invest much care and effort in their costume, especially, but not only, to enter competitions for the maschera, masques and floats to show the greatest 'imagination, aesthetic value, liveliness, humour, ingenuity' (from the 1989 Carnevale regulations). By encouraging competitive display, the organisers seek to develop Carnevale as a spectacle and a tourist attraction (cf. Poppi 1983).[10] However, both organisers and participants also emphasise that Carnevale is not primarily about visual display.

Acting local

In the 1980s, Carnevale organisers began to promote floats that carry masque groups, which they contrast with inanimate papier-maché ones typical of other Italian Carnevali, 'that don't make you laugh nor cry' as Pino, president of Carnevale committee, put it. The masque groups are meant to 'enliven' the atmosphere in piazza, fostering 'the true spirit of Carnevale, that of drawing in the crowd, not of parading, of showing off' (a float leader). This is also the perceived function of music: 'you can't sustain a parade without music, it's useless to do a tour of the square without music – you must mess around some' (Pino). 'Messing around in the square' ('fare casin in piazza') is also how the maschere describe what they do at Carnevale. Members of a masque group I joined used this phrase to characterise their performance during the floats' parade as an entirely spontaneous moment. The same spirit pervaded their rehearsals for a 'Gypsy' masque at the 1989 Carnevale, when a dance instructors' attempts to teach them

'Gypsy' dancing were met by 'once we're there, with music and all, we'll manage something'. The session was spent instead exchanging loud banter, singing, teasing one another and running around. A friend who had introduced me to the group later asked 'did you enjoy messing around with us?' This kind of 'messing around' is what group members enjoy together, what they recollect after Carnevale outings and what makes time with the group 'fun', explicitly identified as their main aim: 'we do it for fun, not to show off to other people' (Gina, b. 1948, group member, commenting on the group's string of prizes).

The same idea is found in smaller, informal groups of friends who go out in maschera at Carnevale: 'the best costumes are simple ones, cheap and cheerful – rather than spending a bomb for a costume and then they all admire you, but that's not the fun of it' (Simona). For Simona and her friends, who every year prepare elaborate, striking, humorous costumes for Carnevale, 'the fun of it' is teasing strangers, dancing, running around, being loud and rude. This affects the nature of maschere. For Luisa (b. 1946), costumes must be 'jolly, humorous, light', 'allowing you to jump, to run and act crazy'. Luisa also drew a contrast with the 'static, melancholy' costumes typical of the revived Venetian Carnevale,[11] emulated by some Bassanesi. This was a common theme:

> Now people go to a shop and spend 200000 Lire [about £100] because it must be the best – no, [costumes should be] home-made, hand-sewn . . . not perfect – that's what's good about them. The maschera must be something different, it's no use if you go out looking like a mannequin. In Venice, for instance, [you see] beautiful maschere, wonderful to see, but [nothing like] home-made ones . . . [here] we used to find bits and pieces in the attic and we'd put something together with a bit of ingenuity (Lino, b. 1928, a newsagent who for nearly thirty years 'did' Carnevale dressed as a woman).

The aspects of the 'Venetian' costumes criticized locally are their cost and their physical stillness. At Carnevale, the visual is not enough: what is needed is motion and sound:

> once you came to Carnevale because you felt like having fun, you felt Carnevale . . . now they don't feel it . . . you see those maschere that walk up and down the square, without opening their mouth, without saying anything, statuesque stuff . . . if I wore a maschera now I would still mess around more than the maschere that there are now. (Giulio, b. 1920)

'Feeling' or 'living' Carnevale requires not only having a visually striking costume, but also acting it out. So Anna (b. 1940), who every year carefully plans and prepares a different costume, maintains that you must invent an appropriate comic routine for it: as 'Tarzan', for instance, she would approach men saying 'I Tarzan, you

Jane' and kiss them. 'True' Carnevale is a matter of doing rather than watching:

> You have had fun [this year] because you have thrown yourself right in, you have participated – had you stood by watching the floats, you would have got bored . . . nowadays it's hard even to teach children to partici-pate rather than look on, people are more used to watch than to act, they take Carnevale just as a spectacle. (Eleonora, b. 1927, Carnevale organiser)

As this quote suggests, the impulse to take an active part is seen as a thing of the past. Locals disregard the fact that, in the past, the point of Carnevale was not to be recognised,[12] making it a very different kind of event from that of the present day. Instead, the past is invoked as a blueprint for the present:

> then the piazza was thronged, everyone in maschera, everyone jolly, you heard laughing, shouting, and dancing . . . people jumping around you, taking your arm, telling you secrets . . . when you went to the piazza you had to jump, to dance – it's impossible to explain that atmosphere [it was] a universal euphoria: you didn't see a maschera who stood still, who was serious . . . so those of us who have lived the Carnevale must teach the young by drawing them in. (Luisa)

In Luisa's imagery, Carnevale happens between people, it is an urge that is transmitted by example and cannot easily be resisted. This is echoed by people who go in maschera in the present day: 'I told her I wasn't the right type, and now every year I tell myself that it's the last time I go in maschera, but then Carnevale comes and I can't resist' (Rosa, b. 1946). Going in maschera is now often described as a matter of nerve: 'you are blocked', you feel 'shy', so you must learn 'not to give a toss about anything'. This is partly attributed to individual tem-perament, but also to other people's influence:

> I grew up seeing my father and brothers going [to Carnevale], so of course I too did a lot of Carnevali . . . but if at home they don't do it, it's likely that you'll dress up with friends, because they tell you 'Come on, let's go, try it at least once', you are drawn in, you go . . . in Carnevale you are never alone – you can decide to go out alone, but soon enough you join up with others, you form a group – it's a thing of friendship. (Lino)

'A thing of friendship'

If friendship is central to local representations of the 'old' Carnevale, in the present too, masque groups define themselves as 'groups of friends', even though in order to join larger ones (of up to some ninety people) it is sufficient (but also necessary) to know just one or two members. The group I joined also included kin, especially nuclear families. However, in the group, family ties were played down:[13] children formed a gang, unsupervised by their parents, and couples mingled separately and even flirted with other group members: one woman complained of her husband that 'even here he'd like to rule me'. Conversely, while a stranger to most members, I was treated more familiarly and casually than in normal social contexts. In the masque groups, 'friendship' means diffuse sociability, mutual ease and playful openness (cf. Simmel 1950).

Friendship is locally considered an optional kind of social relationship, a matter of personal whim and inclination rather than obligation (associated with kinship) (cf. Eisenstadt and Roniger 1984: 18; Papataxiarchis 1991). There is a clear affinity between the whimsical spirit of friendship and that of Carnevale: 'improvisation – today I do this, I go there, I stay here, just because I feel like it . . . when you are in maschera, you feel a spirit inside you that you'd do what . . . you'd do anything, you don't give a toss' (Lino). As these words suggest, the maschera that covers the surface of the body brings out an unrestrained, haphazard and wilful 'spirit'. This spirit works between people, not against them: it is eminently sociable. The creativity and presence ideally expressed by a maschera is communicative, a subjective bid to reach towards others. It is in this sense that proper maschere are opposed to fashion, locally associated with competitive, socially divisive, individualistic display of social status through the manipulation of 'appearances'. In the context of Carnevale, the sociable spirit epitomised by the vivacious, noisy, cheap and cheerful maschere is also presented as eminently local, by contrast with the aestheticising, 'perfect' but silent and still 'Venetian' costumes. Thus, at Carnevale, even as they impersonate and so, quite literally, incorporate nonlocal (exotic, mythical, televisual) characters and images, local people claim to be capturing (or recapturing) 'locality' as an intersubjective experience that engulfs them immediately by reverberating from body to body (cf. Cantwell 1993).

The Arti per Via

The Arti per Via group, unlike Carnevale, includes a fixed set of well-defined 'characters', impersonating street traders of the past: washerwomen, straw-plaiters, potters, woodworkers, menders, street sellers, chimney sweeps, puppeteers and others (see also Bellotti and Parolin 1985). Performances usually take place in the open air, in the streets and squares of town centres or of neighbourhoods, although the group also visits Residential Homes and schools. Typically, performances begin with a parade of traders shouting their characteristic 'cries' to advertise their trade, and enacting brief sketches of 'real life': children playing and teasing the lye seller, women bickering, men flirting with girls and so on. Along the route, the sellers also offer their wares to the audience. A speaker then introduces each 'trade' by its dialect name and by a brief commentary, as the performers come to a halt and settle down to their crafts and activities. Audiences are then invited to mingle with performers, who demonstrate their craft and let people finger their costumes, ask questions and try their hand. Often the parade is accompanied by accordion music, and performers break into old-fashioned styles of dancing and into 'traditional' songs, both local dialect Italian, both of which audiences are encouraged to join.

The commentary, elaborated by the group leader, presents the show as a 'dive into the past' . . . 'whence we will emerge to live in our own time enriched by what we have learnt, aware of the dignity of our forefathers, of their hard work' (December 1987). The theme of the dignity of poverty and hard work was accompanied by that of the 'warmth' of past local society. The traders were presented as emblems of a world in which 'direct human contact' predominated, and traders 'carried out a service for the community' by offering their 'humble wares' to 'smiling housewives'. This was contrasted with 'the cold shimmer of shop windows' dominating 'today's world'. Buying from a milliner was contrasted with 'the coldness of a supermarket, without a smile and a human hand', carrying stuff in woven baskets with using 'horrible plastic bags', and eating sweet potatoes and plain sugar candies with today's 'junk sweets'. Enforced frugality ('modest incomes, modest expenses', 'not everyone could afford cream cones') was held up as evidence of a world where people were content with little ('cheap stuff but appreciated all the same') and used to recycling instead of wasting. The commentary thus conveys an idealised image of the urban past, reminiscent of representations about the social cohesion, piety and morality of past peasant society also found locally, and of a Catholic matrix (see e.g. Bellotti 1983; Bernardi 1986; Guizzardi 1976).[14] However, this narrative is not the only or the main way in which participants and audiences of the ApV remember.

Kinship with the past

The ApV are explicitly conceived and realised as a 'perfect reconstruction' of the past. The group founder explains that some documentation stems from her own recollections and informal research on street trades from the 1950s. Old photos were also used to fashion clothing, and many objects were donated by a local man who has set up a private 'ethnographic museum' of old peasant artifacts. The period reconstructed is the first half of the century. Group members who, unlike the founder, are all local people, also stress the role of their own memories in putting together costumes, 'cries' and acts: 'I remember that as children we used to run after [the lye seller] and tease her – in the performance she was static, silent, so I have introduced the scene of the children . . . each of us introduces ideas and suggestions, otherwise the group would die out' (Anna, about 'her' character). In some cases, clothing or objects used had belonged to the performers' own ancestors: for instance, one of the 'washerwomen' in 1988 wore a black bodice that had been part of her grandmother's wedding dress. Furthermore, her grandmother had been a washerwoman, like her mother and, in her childhood, the performer herself. A striking feature of the ApV is that many group members impersonate trades with which they have a personal link through family history. So, the cream cone seller is the son of the man who last had this job in the 1950s. The straw plaiters, two women and a man in their sixties, worked as straw plaiters in their youth in their family business and now use some of their old tools and handiwork in the show. They became involved in the ApV because a woman in her forties, who wanted to join the show, remembered hearing about them from her father, a doctor whose patients they had been in the 1950s. The former strawmakers, now factory workers, agreed to join and to teach her the craft so she too could be in the group: 'but I am too slow so I am an apprentice . . . they do it without thinking'. Other performers still practice in real life the trade that they perform, like the 'milliner', who is a needleworker; or the 'potter' who is also one in real life. Others still, like the chair mender, were taught the skill by a 'real' craftsman not directly involved in the show.

The performers proudly assert, and describe with relish to their audiences, links with the past that are of either real or putative kinship, that cross time and even, as in the case of the woman hatmaker, class lines. Although ApV participants consider it an occasion for having fun with friends, kinship dominates the performance. Participants also stress the unbroken link with the past in describing the personal impact of performing in the ApV: 'it helped me to remember many things – it's not that I'd forgotten them, but I had stopped thinking about them' (Gina). For some, the ApV also works to restore 'family' memory. So the washerwomen once took their grandmothers and mothers to see the show, and the latter were so moved that 'they cried their eyes out'. Gina, impersonating the rag seller (one of the poorest traders), once went into the shop of her sister (who since her marriage has considered herself socially superior to Gina and does not speak to her), as if to remind her of the very modest social origin that they share.

The ApV is thus experienced by participants as the reawakening of dormant memories that, for some of them, are bodily memories of activities that they no longer practise (cf. Connerton 1989). The show has the same effect on audiences: 'I remember we used to do the washing once a week, how hard it was, we used ash that would leave your hands burning... then the wonderful smell, the beautiful bright white of the clean washing' (two women, between fifty and sixty years old, watching an ApV performance in 1988). A direct link with the past is also mediated by taste, as audiences are invited to try 'old' flavours like cream cones and sweet potatoes. By working at the level of sensory and bodily memory, ApV performances feel very 'authentic' to audiences (cf. Cantwell 1993: 45, 112, 227). They come to perceive an unbroken connection with the past even where there isn't one. So, for instance, audiences praise the 'right' period feel of the faces of performers (who, in fact, look as 'modern' as any of their co-citizens when in normal clothes). So, also, ApV performances, which often take place during local markets or fairs selling 'local' and 'traditional' produce (chestnuts, local cheeses, wine), help to authenticate what are often recent inventions, in the eyes (and tastebuds) of audiences. The sense that this is a show and an interpretation of the past is replaced by that of performing and witnessing something 'real'. This sense is so strong for both audiences and performers that slides of ApV performances are used by the group leader to give 'historically documented' talks about aspects of 'old Bassano'. In 1994, the ApV also visited schools and sent them videos of their performances as part of a town-wide project for children to 'study folk traditions'. At the same time, the performance commentary incited children to 'go to your grandparents, to your elders, and ask them to tell you about the past, that is a mine of precious facts' (September 1994). As this quote suggests, transmission is primarily imagined along kinship channels. So the fact that group members are kin of, or have met and learnt from, the 'old' traders is emphasized and is as much part of what is displayed during the performance as the 'carefully reconstructed' costumes. Participants also routinely mention with pride that 'whole families' are involved in the show. By having present-day family groups act out former families of artisans, kinship is also displayed as the basis for cooperation and the trasmission of skills. This performance thus celebrates work as a form of embodied knowledge transmitted through kinship. It also celebrates the measuring of 'local' time by the lives of individuals and families, and the space of the town as a site for face-to-face material and symbolic exchange.

Bodies in Place

At first sight, the two performances I have considered can be contrasted in both form and content. Carnevale celebrates unrestrained, unpatterned, aimless, 'free' motion of body and mind, expressed in 'imaginative', 'creative' costumes that do not conform to preconstituted norms (e.g. of colour coordination) and that play with 'real' identity. By contrast, the ApV celebrate the patterned, controlled, regulated and purposeful motions and gestures that make up skills. Inventiveness is minimised as performers aim at carefully reproducing past originals, including using old objects, and by assigning the performance of specific trades to people who carried them out in the past, or whose kin did. Emphasis on kinship in the ApV matches its claim to faithfully replicate the past: both envisage 'vertical', obligatory, hierarchical relations between past and present, epitomised by transmission 'down' generations. By contrast, Carnevale's emphasis on creative and bodily 'freedom', 'infecting' people across town, resonates with the symbolic connotations of friendship, a relationship among equals, who come together because they want to.

Overriding these differences are some common themes. Carnevale celebrates leisure as a state of body and mind that flows from 'within' people towards others, and so also fun as an eminently sociable quality of shared time and space. This is encapsulated by the image of noisy, fast-moving, aimless maschere, while the silent, still, 'perfect' maschere 'going up and down the square', and bystanders 'standing still', 'content with watching' and 'ashamed' of 'letting go', seem to evoke the self- and other-conscious demeanour of overdressed Bassanesi during the fashionable stroll in the centre of town every evening and holiday. The eccentric, overstated, cheap costumes of Carnevale may be seen as a parody of, and a counterpoint to fashion and conspicuous consumption, which turn people towards, and even into, objects rather than one another. Unlike fashion, conforming to externally imposed canons of 'taste', Carnevale costumes bring to the surface and loudly proclaim inner creativity and imagination. Unlike fashionable clothes, they are also evidence of personal creativity, insofar as they are handmade, recycling humble materials in innovative ways. A similar theme is found in the ApV, which celebrates work as an act of skilled creation, minimally mediated by technology. Images of handcrafting and of the simple, 'genuine' flavours of unprocessed foods, both of which can be directly sampled by the audience, evoke (or enact) a world in which the body is the means and end of production and consumption, and in which producers and consumers know one another and know how things are made (cf. Cantwell 1993).

Carnevale celebrates 'pure' sociality and face-to-face togetherness, untrammelled by the material symbols of affluence and of social 'distinction' (Bourdieu 1984; cf. Simmel 1950). The ApV celebrates the craft of human hands producing use-value, and learnt through kinship. In this sense, both performances contain an anticonsumerist and antitechnological message. They cast production and consumption as social and sociable acts insofar as they are performed directly by the body, without the mediation, respectively, of conspicuous consumption and of complex technology. The body, construed as a 'natural' entity[15] is called into play in a bid to reduce (selectively) the modern 'complexity' of life (cf. Miller 1995a: 13).

The centrality of the body in both performances is testified by the role of mimicry in them. Both Carnevale and the ApV are presented and experienced by locals as moments in which gestures and motions reverberate from person to person, body to body across space (especially in Carnevale, where emphasis is on synchronic 'participation') and across time (especially in the ApV, stressing diachronic 'transmission'). Local discourse and practice of present-day Carnevale foregrounds the power of bodily expression in communicating with and influencing people ('drawing them in' and so on). Motion is also central in the ApV: celebrated here as embodied knowledge and skill, displaying labour as the direct objectification of able, purposeful action producing use-value. This kind of labour is also presented as the basis for sociality, both verbally and performatively: as the traders weave their way across town, peddling their wares and skills, they turn the street into a site of material and social exchange, and the town into a 'community'. Motions, noises and gestures in each performance appear to materialise social relations: the uncontrolled, inventive motions of Carnevale, friendship; the controlled, patterned motions of the ApV, kinship. By identifying the human body as the matrix of sociality and community, both performances enact some sort of seamless communion, a 'mutual confirmation between myself and others' across space and time (Merleau-Ponty cited in Jackson 1983: 338).

This seamless communion is characterized as essentially 'local', by rooting it in contiguous space and continuous time, highlighted respectively by the image of the body in motion and by that of the body that remembers, in the quite literal sense of recalling the past into its limbs (see Casey 1993; Connerton 1989). The link between sociality and shared time and space is reminiscent of the sociological concept of gemeinschaft (cf. Cohen 1985). In Bassano, it permeates conservation policies in the town centre, of which these performances are a part. Local supporters of pedestrianisation argue that, without cars, the town centre would not only regain its beauty and historical and artistic value, but also 'its original function as a meeting point of human relationing', contributing to recreate 'a town to human scale' (CCS 1992; see Filippucci 1997). In practice, pedestrianisation strives for 'human scale' in the literal sense of removing from a stretch of landscape the mechanical means of long-distance connection. Conservation can also reduce the technological 'complexity' of life in an area: for instance, when tarmac in the piazza was replaced by the 'original' flagstones[16] lighter vehicles for refuse collection had to be introduced, because the stones would not withstand the weight of existing vehicles. Both pedestrianisation and conservation, finally, act upon the sensory dimensions of a 'place': the play of colours and shapes, the feel of the street surface underfoot, the sound and spatiality of streets and squares freed from the rumble and bustle of cars. In this sense, while it draws on nonlocal canons of aesthetic and historical value (codified in state legislation, influenced by national and international scholarly traditions), conservation also strives to realise a sensuous, unmediated bodily experience of space. The bodily experience of space is said to be a 'natural' basis of a sense of place (Tuan 1974; Seamon 1979; Casey 1993). However, the contemporary 'valorisation' of the town centre in Bassano, which includes the performances I have examined, suggests a concerted bid to identify 'locality' with a discrete and continuous spatial and temporal frame, striving to constitute 'place' as immediately experienced physical, social and economic reality.

This way of constituting 'place' may be typical of modern 'global culture' (Wilk 1995). By constituting 'locality' as immediately experienced, localised time and space, the former is disarticulated from broader scales. This apparently contradicts the stated motivation underpinning both these festivals and the centre's restoration: that of having something to show to outsiders. Locals are keenly aware of 'the global gaze', clearly perceiving that it is this gaze that now bestows 'identity' (Wilk 1995: 127).[17] Exposure to extralocal 'audiences' is not new in Bassano; the town has been fully integrated in broader political, economic and cultural systems for centuries, its urban status long construed around access to extra-local resources, powers, ideas and styles.[18] What may be new is the way in which visibility on an extralocal, 'global' scene is predicated upon the self-conscious elaboration of 'locality' as a repository of difference (see Wilk 1995). As the material above suggests, 'local' difference is invested in spaces and practices that are selectively 'simplified' (cf. Miller 1995: 13): that is; brought to a human, localised, spatial and temporal scale. It is as a repository of difference that 'locality' is thus constituted as a spatial and temporal frame that is disconnected from broader ones. This only apparently contradicts total exposure to a global 'gaze': the interplay of absolute disconnection and total connectedness may be central to the perception of 'place' at a time in which (in some parts of the world, including the one studied here) communication is near instant and consumption is 'globalised'. In this context, images and material testimonies of difference may be the only way of creating a sense of distance and placedness both in locals and in visitors (who can take them home to show that they have been somewhere) (see Wilk 1995; Augé 1993; Appadurai 1995; cf. Castells 1996).

In the area of study, a tension between spatial and temporal disconnection and connectedness may now be central to its constitution as a political and economic entity. Since the early 1980s in Northern

Italy, anti-national (regionalist and localistic) sentiment has found expression in political movements advocating fiscal and administrative autonomy and even, at times, independence from Italy (see e.g. Diamanti 1995a, 1995b; Biorcio 1997). While these movements are not electorally dominant in Bassano, unlike some neighbouring villages, anti-national and antistate rhetoric is widely used by local administrators and residents. Part of it is the idea that 'living here', 'seeing with your own eyes', 'smelling' (e.g. the offensive effluvia of a factory) are privileged ways of knowing 'local' reality, as opposed to disembodied ways of knowing attributed to nonlocal agencies, like 'looking at a computer' or 'reading a map' (see Filippucci et al. 1997; cf. Anderson 1998). At the same time, locals regard efficient, capillary communications with the rest of the world as essential to ensure the area's continued 'competitiveness' and prosperity, mainly based on export (see Filippucci 1997).[19] So locals now appear simultaneously concerned to define locality as a bounded, self-contained spatial and temporal reality, and to ensure that it is fully connected with realities beyond it. Specifically, the Bassanesi may elaborate 'local difference' by reference to self-contained space and time in a bid to disconnect 'place' from the encompassing and hierarchically nested spatial and temporal scales that form the nation/state (see Herzfeld 1987). This might be an attempt to reimagine locality as an entity that can connect opportunistically to political, cultural and, especially economic resources and frames beyond it (Europe; the world) (see Filippucci 1997). In this respect, the performances considered above, that stage locality as an absolute, embodied experience for the sake of audiences that, in the aspirations of organisers and performers, include the world (go to it, as the ApV do, or bring it here, as with Carnevale) are truly ways of 'acting local' insofar as, in contemporary Bassano, people's sense of place is expressed by juxtaposing 'local' and 'global' as emblems of total disconnection and difference and total connectedness and sameness.

Conclusion

Performances, like rituals, chart time and space in patterned ways to constitute meaningful experiences (cf. e.g. Turner 1967; Bloch 1974). In the two performances I have considered, the body is used to produce a centred experience of being 'in' and part of a place (see Entrikin 1991: 1; Appadurai 1995; Tuan 1974). It is used in its capacity of means for charting time and space, in ways presented as 'old' and lost by modernity. This is suggested by the self-consciously nostalgic tone, implying that locals can no longer take for granted continuity, or the knowledge of whom and what they owe their existence and identity to

(Nora 1989: 16). At the same time, the body, in its ability to mimic, is cast as the means to render the past less 'other' (Connerton 1989; cf. Jackson 1983: 336). In the same capacity, it is presented as the means to reconstitute spatial contiguity. Both are presented as the basis of localness. Time and space directly apprehended by the senses are made to constitute 'locality' as an independent reality with its own 'truth'.

In these performances, the body is thus imagined as a bounded, self-referential entity, conduit of motion and of sensation, expressive and effective without 'artificial' accretions like fashion and technology: as a 'natural' entity. This way of imagining the body also surfaces locally in discourse and practices concerning health and environmental pollution. Thus, it may be said to address issues in local lives that derive from living by and through industrial production and mass consumption. So in Carnevale, focus on the body as 'natural' tackles critically the centrality of personalized consumption in expressing and maintaining subtle, finely graded social distinctions (see Bourdieu 1984; cf. Featherstone 1991). In the ApV, focus on the body as a 'natural' means of production may address (and illusorily mend) the sense of 'rupture' stemming from the 'consciousness that one is living through objects and images not of one's own creation' (Miller 1995a: 1). In this respect, both performances, even as they are presented and perceived as ways of 'acting local', also display the fact that living 'here' now inevitably entails the constant awareness of also being 'a point in a centreless world' (Entrikin 1991: 3). The body as it is constituted in 'consumer culture' (Featherstone 1991), a monadic entity that must nevertheless endlessly 'mirror' the world outside it in order to give itself meaning and to reproduce itself (see Frank 1991: 61), may be the most appropriate means to express this eminently contemporary experience of place, perched between 'local' and 'global' perspectives and scales (see Appadurai 1995: 208; Rodman 1992; Entrikin 1991).

Notes

1. Fieldwork was carried out in 1987–9, and in 1994–5.
2. Primarily newspapers, collected in the Civic Archive of Bassano.
3. In 1929, part of the regime's policy to promote nonpoliticised forms of recreation for working-class people (see De Grazia 1981; cf. Filippucci 1992).
4. In 1978.
5. In the context of a 'festival of Europe', promoted by the local Christian Democratic administrations in the early 1980s.
6. The best known was that of Viareggio in Tuscany, because of its elaborate papier-maché' floats.
7. I attended in maschera both the 1988 and the 1989 Carnevale, once as a member of a large masque group. I also extensively interviewed the organisers.
8. Although the organisers require maschere to be in 'good taste', that is, not obscene.
9. Less commonly, women as men: 'that's not funny', because women now 'wear

trousers every day'. Reversal may be more effective when it 'lowers' (see Bakhtin 1968). Women did, however, dress up as figures who are normally male, like the Pope, priests, soldiers.

10. In practice, the Carnevale of Bassano cannot compete with that of nearby Venice, and mostly attracts local audiences.

11. Elaborate, fanciful and richly attired maschere inspired by the Venetian eighteenth century but often with abstract themes (e.g. 'the moon') appeared in Venice at the 1978 Carnevale and have since become part of the tourist image of Venice.

12. This was one of the main 'games' of Carnevale, which, in the past, included wearing face masks that covered features and 'even changed one's voice'.

13. In Venice, one day of Carnevale was traditionally devoted to treating and entertaining your kin 'like friends' (see Bernardi 1986: 320).

14. Bassano is in an area that, both culturally and politically, has long been Catholic (see e.g. Lanaro 1984).

15. It is beyond the scope of this paper to explore local ideas about the human body and 'nature', explored in a forthcoming book.

16. Documented in a mid-nineteenth century photograph.

17. So, for instance, when, during my time in Bassano, images of the historic centre were shown on national TV, all those I saw the next day mentioned it as if they'd seen for the first time what they see every day, which had now acquired some added significance.

18. Even though such access was unequally distributed until the mid-twentieth century; greater for higher socioeconomic groups (see e.g. StdB 1980; Berti 1993; cf. Silverman 1977).

'Cose Paesane'

Tourist Performances and Contested Localities in the Italian Alps

Keith Ridler

Introduction

Some ten years ago, in the Val Rendena in the Western Dolomites in Northern Italy, I was invited to film a *Ferragósto* celebration. The term *Ferragósto* refers both to Assumption Day itself and also, by extension, to the August holidays period. It is observed in various forms as a religious and/or secular holiday throughout Mediterranean Europe. The festivity takes place at a time when mass-tourism, both domestic and international, is at its peak. In rural communities, it also coincides with the most intensive period of agricultural work.

In the Val Rendena, before mass-tourism arrived, the day of *Ferragósto* provided a welcome break from heavy work connected with haymaking and harvesting, which could otherwise be continuous from early July through to the end of September. As in the rest of the country, it was celebrated mainly with special masses and a procession. From the early 1960s onwards, as tourism became an important economic force, the event often grew to include locals and outsiders sharing a meal and dancing in the village *piazza* in the evening. On the occasion I filmed, however, the *festa* (celebration) took what was locally a new form. People from several neighbouring villages gathered to enact, in traditional costume, historical skills and past occupations from the days before tourism for an audience composed mainly of tourists. From a celebration for locals, *Ferragósto*, by collective decision, had here become a spectacle for visitors.

This, of course, is a pattern which is increasingly familiar globally and which, in Europe, has led to a notable increase in the number of public ritual performances in recent years as well as to a widely variable series of transformations in their contemporary form and significance

(Boissevain 1992: 1–2). At one level it simply confirms the emergence of what some Italian observers have called a *cultura turistica*, formed specifically in the meeting grounds between visitors and locals in heavily touristed contexts (Bruschi et al. 1987). These days, the 'commoditisation of culture' for tourists this kind of performance implies is so commonplace as to be almost unremarkable, not only to its tourist audiences but also, often, to its local participants (Greenwood 1977: 130–131).

It is no longer as clear as it was when Greenwood first coined the phrase 'commoditisation of culture' that what is going on inside a *cultura turistica* is a simple extension of the logic of capitalist development, whereby cultural meanings, like other commodities, are expropriated by organised tourism interests, be they local or international. As two recent collections of ethnographic work amply document, the cultural impacts and developmental effects of tourism have proved more complex, more ambi- or multi-valent, and perhaps more malleable *from a local perspective* than many anthropologists have, in the past, been prepared to consider (Boissevain 1996; Selwyn 1996). The performance of tourism, and tourism performances, as Löfgren has suggested, are deeply implicated in mapping, strategising around, and contesting local, regional and even national identities (Löfgren 1989, 1994).

In the Italian Alps, at least, it is becoming clear that locals use public enactments like the *Ferragósto* celebration as a way of articulating who they are, marking images of cultural difference for political as well as economic ends, not only with regard to a tourist audience, but in relation to locally contested senses of place and selfhood. In the current phase of tourism development, broadly a move away from mass recreational tourism towards an intensification of ecological and cultural tourism, this also represents a form of local resistance to the positioning of local identities from within hegemonic regional and national cultures. Thus, as with most publicly mimetic activities, such historical enactments can be both 'make-believe' and at the same time, serious political business at a number of performative levels.

The multiple inflection of such events, and the degree of political agency they can display, suggest the need to interpret performances within a *cultura turistica* in terms which go beyond constructions in which locals figure as relatively powerless subjects positioned by a 'tourist gaze', or simply as vulnerable workers for an industry which they cannot control (Urry 1990). In this paper, I explore some experiential and political dimensions of such enactments in touristic contexts. For many locals, the significance of their participation extends beyond the parameters of the *cultura turistica* to embody projected and often contested views of local futures in terms of selective and politicised readings of the past. Thus, in historical frontier regions such as the Trentino, the social poetics of participation in Patron Saint's festivals, military commemorations, and informal gatherings are a potent means of communicating about individual sense of place and selfhood, locality and identity, and how these might be constructed in relation to the regions and nations of the New Europe.

From Enactment to Ethnomimesis

I have begun with the image of an historically enacted public event, but I do not want to suggest that the enactment of historical identities and their significance as a dimension of the life-world in Salamone, the now heavily touristed village I have studied, ends with such *feste*.[1] More broadly, enactment can be said to provide a pervasive idiom and framework, a flexible mode of social poetics, which informs performance in many contexts, differing in scale from public rituals to those relatively private and informal interactions that are, in effect, strategic retreats from the world of the tourist. In these various contexts, historical enactment has at least two common features. Firstly, it is always an embodied performance, which works experientially and stylistically because it is marked off from everyday patterns of expression, and, secondly, it refers itself as a performance to an image of the past. Moreover, to enact, in this sense, is both to *act upon* something – the self, the audience, the setting – but it is also to be *acted upon*, by the historical weight of others' previous modes of experience.

This dialectic is clearly mediated by, and draws deeply on, the mimetic faculty, 'the gift of producing resemblances', in Walter Benjamin's generalising phrase (Benjamin 1979: 160). There is a convincing psychological argument that, beginning with imitation and mirroring in very early childhood, mimesis as the enactment of an Other is a human universal. By means of such mimesis, the physical investment of self in activity, which may be as simple as one's presence, as extensive as the creation of a comprehensive role or identity, is made to signify, as Taussig (1993) has suggested, historical and existential equivalencies and, therefore, continuities. Expressively such enactment may sometimes be 'freer', sometimes less so. While to walk in a religious procession may offer little scope for individual choice, to play the part of an ambulant knifegrinder or a school teacher in a reconstructed school at a *Ferragósto* celebration, calls for a comparatively complex poetics. At either extreme, however, to enact is to 'throw oneself into' an experience outside the mundane, to bring together a self and an other (the audience) in a new light, to create a space for the statement of who one is in a way that is psychologically and socially transformative.

In terms of modes of expression, this impulse is so extensive that

Robert Cantwell, who coined the term 'ethnomimesis' to loosely describe collective and historicised forms, somewhat idiosyncratically equates it generically with 'culture' (Cantwell 1993: 6). More usefully, at the core of Cantwell's notion, is the more restricted sense of eth-nomimesis as the embodied collective representations of an imagined self to an imagined other. Ethnomimetic enactments project a sense of self and grouphood within what he terms the 'noetic "vacuums" or culturally vacant spaces of complex societies', using the body to com-municate statements of identity across 'social hinterlands', mediating conceptions one group holds of another, 'often in response to the other's stereotyped expectations' (ibid.: 6–7).

Predominantly, Cantwell tends to associate imitation, imperson-ation, and the 'figuring-forth' of imaginative equivalence (all charac-teristics of mimesis in general) with festivity, 'enchantment', and a pre-conscious, pre-structural expression of order. In his argument, eth-nomimetic events are strongly associated with ritualised aspects of folk-life as opposed to the somehow less structured forms of élite cul-ture, against which they tend – though not exclusively – to position themselves counterhegemonically (ibid.: 8). From a participants per-spective, however, ethnomimesis as a mode of historical experience played out in a *cultura turistica*, may arguably extend to sometimes include nonrepetitive, spontaneous acts of expression constrained only by the requirement that they fall within the performative idiom of an explicitly historical cultural frame. The range of representation shaped by the dimension of ethnomimetic enactment thus includes not only public ceremonials and celebrations, but is also an experien-tial aspect of the activities of functional and recreational associations, as well as of the poetics of more intimate interactions with tourists and other locals. Thus, in a heavily tourist oriented milieu like that of Salamone, what is ethnomimetically enacted – to cite some examples more or less at random – includes public *feste*, but also a style of infor-mal interaction with tourists and other locals, the performance of music at private parties, and the stylised preparation and consumption of traditional food and drink. The variety of contexts illustrates that ethnomimetic enactments of historical identities in places such as Salamone are a versatile medium within which individual statements of selfhood are made within idiomatic common forms, and an image of social order, community, personhood and the self represented both reflexively and to a tourist audience.

The formal openness of ethnomimetic enactments, however, is not only a question of poetics. Embodied performances of identity are also constructed across different and sometimes contradictory fields of reference in terms of locality and history. As both inward and outward facing expressions of what Herzfeld has called 'cultural intimacy' (1996: 3–6), enacting historical identities is also a complex play on stereotypical constructions and deconstructions of status difference. Statements of historical equivalence imply boundaries, as between locals and tourists, but in many heavily touristed places are also internally contested. Enactments may represent 'common forms' of identity, but this is rarely synonymous with common meanings. In Salamone, historically in a borderland between cultures, claiming particular historical equivalencies by enacting them locates individuals, and often groups, within a particular geopolitical reading of the past, and therefore, commits them to a particular imagined future. To illustrate these connections between performative practices, historicity and locality, I turn now to a description of two local associations in the business of ethnomimesis.

Tradition, Differentiation and Locality: Two Contrasting Associations

> K: Can you explain to me, Carlo, the business of the rediscovery of traditions here in Salamone, the various things that you are doing. . .? For you what is the meaning of this movement?
>
> C: I think that in this society where everyone is seeking to resemble something – people, facts, behaviour – that are represented to you by . . . the television, the newspapers, there is a desire to differentiate yourself. And to differentiate yourself, you have to do something particular that could be, exactly, this search for these old traditions, these old behaviours, perhaps tied to the territory, or to some tool, that not everyone can have, or which, if they have them, is not the same as that which is here...I think it's this, fundamentally this, this desire to differentiate yourself.
>
> K: Differentiate yourself from whom?
>
> C: From the system now, where the difference between here and somewhere a few kilometres away, or a thousand kilometres away . . . is irrelevant.
>
> *(Conversation with Carlo Delpaese, Sindaco (Mayor) of Salamone, July 1995)*

In Salamone, as perhaps in all tourist locales, the interplay between political and poetic dimensions of identity is often couched in a differentiating discourse that pivots on a set of contrastive and sometimes metaphoric categories: us versus them, tradition versus modernity, local versus national culture, cultural versus folkloric activities, authentic versus staged for the tourist, closed versus open circles of local participation. Underlying this discourse lies a wider concern about the globalising effects of mass media and consumerism on local cultural distinctiveness. Pragmatically, this mapping of difference forms an important dimension of the way people experience their involvement in *ongoing* associations and activities which, unlike *Ferragósto* or the even more important patron saints' *feste*, provide a continuous thread in the social life of the village. Along with the physical restoration of the oldest and most central area of the village and the transformation of public *feste*, in recent years the search for distinctiveness has led to the foundation and growth of a number of groups which aim to re-establish and concretise cultural activities popular in the past, and which had disappeared from the village scene. Unlike other existing associations, which do not principally concern themselves with recuperating a sense of the past, these newer groups are focused specifically on the rediscovery and documentation of local history and customs. As with the public *feste* in which some of these groups participate, their regular meetings also provide experiential spaces where sometimes contested statements about identity and its boundaries are performed. However, while such groups may share a focus on ethnomimetic enactments, their fields of symbolic reference may relate to the village as locality in differing ways. Because of this, the statements their members embody and display about the nature and extension of both the contemporary sense of self and its primary historical referents are hotly debated. In the public sphere, they figure in relation to each other as 'sites of struggle' in the search to define such identity vis á vis other associations within the village, as well as other communities in the valley and beyond.

In this light, the contrast between the current political and social orientations of the two associations I discuss next is illuminating. Both have been refounded and have flourished in the last five years; in the eighteenth and nineteenth centuries, both were active in either Salamone or the Trentino before disappearing for more or less lengthy periods. They thus refer to direct models of association rooted in the period of when the area was part of the Habsburg Empire and a unified Tirol. This epoch remains for many Salamonesi (and many Trentini), an idealised 'Golden Age' in which rural life is held to have been well ordered, relatively free of external intervention, and above all, stable. As a nostalgic trope, the years before the Great War are thus sharply counterpoised against a present seen as a moment of extreme political and social fragmentation, though one paradoxically reflected in *cultural* homogenisation, partly as a result of touristic influence.

Both the *Banda Musicale Comunale* and the *Schützenkompanie* (or simply *Schützen* as they are referred to in the village) derive some of their energy from this sentimental referral to an idealised past, but their ranges of reference are not equivalent. For the *Banda* roots itself directly, as we shall see, in village history, drawing on an explicit local charter, whereas the *Schützen* have their origins in Tirolese regionalism as it was played out in the late eighteenth and early nineteenth centuries. In their contemporary form, the *Schützen* are one expression of a broad political movement for the re-establishment of a modern and autonomous Tirolean region reinstating the pre-1919 boundaries of the unified Tirol. This broadened geographical and cultural scope throws into relief the powerfully expressed positions which surround that association and the appropriateness of the *Schützen's* local connection, both in Salamone and in the Trentino generally.

(i) The Banda Musicale Comunale di Salamone

Unquestionably Salamonese, in style and following (at least as far as villagers are concerned) is the *Banda Musicale Comunale*. Originally founded in 1853, it was the second comunal band in the Trentino to register its charter. The archival records held in the *Comune* show that instruments were ordered from Prague and Innsbruck, and that the band was, even by modern standards, an extremely organised and regimented association, with fines being levied for absenteeism from rehearsals and against players who fell asleep at school the following day. It is also possible to reconstitute the composition of the band at this period (nineteen musicians, plus *maestro*) and part of their repertoire. Some twenty-five folios of music were sent in its early days, scored for this type of band, by a Maestro Giorgetti of Pola in Istria, now part of Bosnia, where many Salamonesi had emigrated, and there are scores by local composers from nearby Condino and the village itself. Sacred music, marches, *ballabili* (dance-music) and lyrical passages from opera all figured in the repertoire, suggesting that the band played for popular entertainment as well as religious *feste*. Interest in the band and in music generally must have been high in the second half of the nineteenth century; the village also boasted a church choir and briefly, from 1873 onwards, a *Società Filarmonica* comprising both a *coro virile* (male voice choir) and a classical string quintet. The latter, and its instruments, were absorbed into the Banda in 1877.[2] This first village band flourished for some seventy years after its foundation, foundering sometime during 1914. Although the church choir was able to continue, the band then disappeared until 1991, when it was relaunched at the initiative of the newly elected *Sindaco*.

In fact, the refoundation of the band was a major and risky community project, both financially (in its first year it was underwritten personally to the tune of some twenty million lira by the *Sindaco* and a nonplaying member who is currently president), and in terms of the external image of the community. Its initial meeting in late 1990 attracted about fifty villagers (almost one in ten) of whom forty-three joined; only a handful possessed instruments and even fewer were able to play them or to read music. They ranged in age from about ten to seventy-six, and constituted a wide cross-section of village families, although several contributed more than one player. Instruments, many of them broken and unplayable, were begged from the bands of surrounding villages. Soon, new instruments were acquired in Trento, music teachers hired and courses in readings and performance held. The organisers arranged trips to hear other bands play, and registered the refounded band, still untried, with the federation of comunal bands in Trento.

Under these circumstances, it is not surprising that public opinion amongst nonparticipants in the village and elsewhere in the valley was extremely sceptical about the chances of success. The neighbouring community of Campago, for example, with whom historically there has been intense rivalry, was attempting to raise funds for a new Comune building at the same time without success, and those convinced of the impossibility of either project posted satirical notices announcing that the Salamone band would play at the new Comune's opening. Nonetheless, the band gave its first public performance fewer than six months after its formal refoundation, playing in the village procession for *Corpus Domini* on 21 June 1992. The band possessed no uniforms, so players were asked to wear blue-jeans and white shirts, and the mayor's wife, the night before, tied a bow from black ribbon for each member. The procession took an unusual form: since the band could not march and play simultaneously, the procession halted for each number (they had mastered two pieces, which were repeated several times) before proceeding on to pray at the chapels. In front of the band, the president processed slowly and solemnly, carrying its banner, elaborately embroidered with the village crest and the two dates of the bands foundation and refoundation, symbolising its historical continuity.

Five years later, the band and its nonplaying supporters numbered three hundred and twenty-eight members (making it by far the largest voluntary association in Salamone). Players possessed individually tailored full dress uniforms, which reproduce those of the first Banda, their purchase subsidised by the Comune, and a full range of new and modern instruments. As well as offering a number of public concerts each year, including several as far away as Austria, the band has played in every village procession since its first. Recently it won first prize in its category at the regional competitions in Trento. In the light of the collective struggle to refound it, and its current successes, the band is naturally a source of enormous local pride.

The exterior, public role of the band demonstrates this self-confidence and the desire for display: it is significant, perhaps, that the Comune has spent more than twice as much, some 40,000,000 lira in 1993, on uniforms for the Banda as on instruments. Uniforms are, as elsewhere in Italy, a marked feature of ceremonial life in Salamone. To stand out in a procession from the uniformed firemen, the *Guardia Civile*, the *Schützenkompanie*, the *Gruppo Folkloristico* (in traditional dress) and the religious confraternities, and to compete with the bands

100 • Keith Ridler

of neighbouring villages, is no easy thing. The fact that the uniforms of the band reproduce those of its first incarnation and identify this group with a particular historical period constitutes the most visible aspect of its ethnomimetic message.

Despite this visible distinctiveness, many of the active members of the band are also participants in other local organisations. Carlo, for example, not only heads the *Giunta Comunale*, but also participates in the volunteer fire-brigade and the Banda, and other players are also involved in the local administration (several are on the ruling *lista*), the *Pro Loco*, or other associations, such as the church choir, the *Gruppo Folkloristico* and so on. In a number of cases, players in the Banda are thus also co-members of two or three other associations concerned with the political life of the village and with the 'revitalisation of tradition'. The Banda, simply as a function of its size, cuts across networks, offering the possibility of contacts between members of different political factions and social interest groups. This inclusive aspect contrasts with examples from elsewhere in Alpine Europe. Weinberg (1976), writing about village bands in the Swiss Valais in the early 1970s, argued that there, bands provided a vehicle for family clans' explicit support of local political parties. Even in that much more pervasively factional context, however, the bands displaced and dampened the institutional political divisiveness of local clans. What is important, in the case of the Salamone band, is that village inclusiveness fosters an association with the identity of the whole village, undivided. The band, as a symbolic expression of who Salamonesi are, could be said to fall between the level of internal cultural politics and that of a wider valley identity. Indeed, after the religious processions, its performances are arguably the most powerful collective expression of this internally inclusive sense of 'being Salamonese'.

(ii) The Schützenkompanie

The sense of inclusiveness that the band literally embodies, and which also refers to the village as a whole, is in marked contrast to the Schützen, who, while they have their local headquarters in Salamone and appear increasingly in village ceremonials, have a wider scope of recruitment and of reference.

Refounded in Salamone in 1994, the historical role of the Schützen, from their medieval roots through their emergence as a powerful regionalist military force at the turn of the eighteenth century under Andreas Hofer,[3] was as 'protectors of the land' or 'defenders of the soil' – a local militia functioning at times as a reserve army. With the forced Italianisation of the South Tirol in the 1930s and 1940s, the Italian Schützenkompanie were suppressed. This history, popularly associated with Austrian – as opposed to Italian – nationalism, remains a central historical referent for the Schützen themselves, as well as for the general public, and, as I explore below, explains their ambiguous social positioning and the ambivalence of local reaction in Salamone toward their revival.

Today, the Schützen exist as a widespread and closely linked ceremonial group spread throughout the Trentino, Southern Austria and Bavaria. Internationally, they have a substantial membership and local chapters participate both in strictly local and regional gatherings and also travel for larger ceremonies held throughout the formerly unified Tirol and Bavaria. While military, religious and familial themes dominate such ceremonies, often of a commemorative nature, and target-shooting is part of their activities, the Schützen are not paramilitary, and are viewed in general terms by locals as contributing to the movement for cultural revitalisation.

In the village context, this is also the view the Schützen present of themselves. In a statement published in Salamone early in 1996, reviewing their history and explaining the rationale for the refoundation of the group, the Rendena Company stated:

That of the Schützen is therefore an age-old presence within the life of our valleys, strongly rooted in the convictions of the population and transmitted from generation to generation.

In the rediscovered ideal of a Tirolese European region, the refoundation of the company of defenders should be understood as a reconciliation with our history, putting aside all the strains and opposed positions which today are nonsensical. Even the exercise of target practice, often misunderstood as a militaristic act, is in reality a moment of peaceful historical reference, a leisure pursuit and excuse for sociability.

We participate therefore in the rediscovery of common values with the people of the Tirol and Bavaria, the values of family and community, the awareness of history, traditions and customs which are similarly shared by all the alpine populations: values which are to be defended from the dangers posed by a consumer and individualist culture which today is ever more widespread.[4]

Like the Banda Comunale, public performance, often for a tourist audience, is a central aspect of the Schützen's local presence; on ritual occasions, members wear elaborate Tirolese uniforms, display historical and contemporary banners, and carry historical paraphernalia including antique weapons derived from the original regiments. In a further extension of embodied identity, many male members have grown the lush upturned moustaches often worn by Tirolese men in the nineteenth century. Membership today, however, extends to both men and women (female members are known as *Marketenderinnen* (provisioners), youth under sixteen as *Jungschützen*), and, in its social dimension, being Schützen is, for many, a family activity.

In parts of the Trentino, to the extent that the activities and ideology of the Schützen extend beyond a ceremonial profile and 'folkloristic' intent, they comprise for many people a symbolically and politically problematic cultural statement. The historical dimension of this ambivalence finds its roots in the troubled history of the Tirol and Trentino as historically contested borderlands and as an active front at various times in two World Wars this century. This ambivalence is also echoed in current debates about the role of cultural regions in the 'New Europe'. Almost every distinctive north-Italian language group from the Valdôtain in the west to Friulani in the east has generated political associations which view the decreasing importance of national borders within the EU as a political space in which to establish regional platforms of ethnic identity on the basis of historical models. In nearly all these cases, a central demand is for the reunification of language populations divided, in many cases within the last century, by national frontiers. The Schützen, figured against this background, but straddling German and Italian language populations, seem to some people in Salamone to be the cultural expression of a contemporary ethnic movement with far broader and potentially identity-threatening political and economic agendas.

The ambiguities around this issue are intensified by the play of historical parallels and resonances. Located as they were at the extreme margin of the Habsburg Empire, Rendenesi have nonetheless always been native speakers of a mainly Italian-based dialect and identified themselves as culturally Italian. One implication is that the Schützen are commonly understood by many people as having been an administrative imposition, reflecting outside rather than local interests. While this qualifies the identification of Schützen with a strictly local past, at another level it presents a further categorical difficulty in that they are also felt to represent a distinctive *regional* Alpine history. The problem for nonparticipating Salamonesi thus revolves around a conflicted question of the political mapping of locality. If Schützen are local, how local are they?

This ambiguity is well illustrated by local responses to two ceremonial events in 1995 in which Schützen of the local company (currently about two dozen families) participated. The first was the commemoration, on 21 May 1995, of the eightieth anniversary of the founding of a large military cemetery in the neighbouring Val di Chiesa, a half-hour drive to the south of Salamone. The local Austrian command post, supply depot and hospital were sited very close to the front during the war years. The monumental cemetery, recently elaborately restored, is the last resting place of several hundred Austrian troops (some of whom were ethnically Italian) who had fallen in local campaigns on the Presanella-Adamello massif.

Although local Schützen had described this event to me as primarily a gathering of some of their companies (including several from as far away as Austria), on the day of the commemoration it was clear that while they may have provided the most spectacular element of the display, they were neither numerically dominant nor the most central aspect. Speeches were made by the Mayor of Bondo and the Austrian organisations responsible for the upkeep of the cemetery and were translated into both German and Italian, while masses were offered by Austrian and Italian churchmen. The Bondo village band performed, both at the ceremony and, later that evening, at a concert, which also included alpine choirs from around the Trentino.

The inclusion of the Schützen, who dominated the ceremony visually with a spectacular massed salute fired from reproductions of historical cannons, thrust into the foreground at least one subtext among several related to this event. In broad terms, what was at stake was the desire to recast the received Italian history of the *Guerra Bianca* (the alpine campaigns) as one of the last regional struggles for Italian unification as, conversely, a struggle to preserve an independent Tirolese identity under Austrian rule. This 'irredentist' message, as I have already suggested, operates metaphorically in the present to highlight some contemporary aspirations toward the legitimisation of a broadly Tirolese identity. Thus, the principal leitmotif of the speeches was, as the *Sindaco* of Bondo put it, 'the necessity of overcoming old prejudices, in order to construct the New Europe' and the 'forging of new bonds'. Other speakers preferred time-honoured kinship metaphors, speaking of present day Tirolese and Trentini as having been 'one family' and more distantly 'one culture' for a thousand years. These references to reunification received warm applause from the Schützen and other supporters. Other events surrounding the commemoration were less inclusive, however: a display of historical postcards on military themes held in the *Municipio* was restricted to items from Austrian sources.

When I discussed this event with people in Salamone, there was little negative comment. Members of the Schützen were pleased with the public perception of the ceremony; acceptance and support for the commemoration as a whole were felt to cast a favourable light on their own participation. Nonmembers felt that the ceremony was a validation of a submerged aspect of the local history of the area, and although not closely identified with Salamone itself, nonetheless useful in differentiating local history from the Italian experience beyond the alpine region.

The reaction, however, was more ambivalent some two months later, when the local chapter of the Schützen, whose membership is not restricted to Salamone, although the headquarters are located there, approached the village priest to participate in the village procession for San Giuliano, one of the two patron saints. San Giuliano's *festa*, like the Ferragósto celebration, falls within the tourist season, and is itself marked off from that of San Biagio, the other *santo*

patrone, which is celebrated by villagers during the winter for themselves alone. In what was felt to be his characteristic spirit of inclusiveness, he readily agreed. In the eyes of a number of villagers,
however, even for this explicitly inclusive festival when many tourists
would also participate, the decision was mistaken. Several people
commented to me that while they had no strong feeling about the
Schützen establishing themselves in the village, they did not feel it
was right that they should march in the procession, which was a matter of *village* 'tradition'. This brief casual conversation with Pier-Paolo,
a former *salumiere* (salami maker), nicely reveals an underlying attitude:

> K: So, what do you think of the Schützen being in the procession?
>
> PP: This is something that doesn't concern [*che non riguarda*] our people,
> for me at least. It's a German tradition. If it was done here it was because
> they were obliged to do it by the Austrians. It's got nothing to do with
> us. Everything [in the contemporary Tirol] is different. The way of eat-
> ing, of dressing, of behaving. As far as I'm concerned, their way has
> nothing to do with our traditions. *Non e una cosa paesana.* [It's not a
> thing of our village].
>
> K: But this isn't the case as far as food goes.
>
> PP: But they don't eat *spaghetti*!
>
> K: Yes, but you do eat *canederli* and *speck* [traditional Tirolese foods sold
> to tourists as traditional Rendena products].
>
> PP: Yes, but these were things we learnt from them. *Speck*, you know,
> until twenty years ago we didn't have that here. *I* was the one who intro-
> duced *speck*. I went up to Bolzano to learn how to make it. This was
> strictly a commercial thing. Tourists came up from Milano and we had to
> give them something you couldn't find there, and so, *speck*, we pre-
> sented it as if it was ours. But it had nothing to do with *our* traditions,
> and, as far as I'm concerned neither do the Schützen. Now, they're like
> *speck*, something we've imported.
>
> *(Conversation with Pier-Paolo Santini, July 1995.)*

The metaphorical equivalence of *speck* and Schützen as cultural
metonyms representing, in Pier Paolo's account, 'imported' if not
'invented' traditions, highlights an unresolved vacillation between a
desire to ally local history and 'tradition' with that of the broader
alpine culture and a fear that, in the very process of differentiating
itself from the Italian milieu, Salamone will simply submerge itself in
another *regional* (Tirolese) image. At its most explicit, this ambivalence
is political, and hardly surprising in an area where national ascriptions
have changed frequently within recent history.

Actually, a similar ambivalence appears to exist within the Trentino
Schützen themselves. In 1995, on the occasion of the fiftieth anniversary of the Armistice in Europe, the then General Commander of the

Schützendell'Alto Adige (Alto Adige = the South Tirol), declared that 'the 8 May 1945 did not cancel the injustice committed at the end of the World War [WW1] with the division of the Tirol', and explicitly proposed the return of the Italian areas of the erstwhile Tirol to Austria. His statement alienated some high-ranking members of the Trentino branches of the organisation. Michele Pizzini, cofounder and Deputy Commander of the Piné company (one of the most active Trentino companies) resigned, categorically denying that most members shared this view and criticising the ranking hierarchy of the Trentino Schützen as undemocratic, repressive and overly dependent on policies generated by the more numerous and longer established groups in Alto Adige. On this occasion, Pizzini called for the Federation of Schützen (the umbrella organisation) to declare itself on the issue – as it had so far failed to do (*l'Adige*, 15 May 1995: 12).

Both within and without, then, deep and unresolved ambivalences surround the issue of delineating the dominance of the 'political' versus 'cultural' and/or 'folkloristic' role of the Schützen, and their implications for mapping local identities. On the local stage the unstable (political/cultural) semantics at play leave this group ambiguously positioned in the discourse at work in a cultural space triangulated between tourist performances, 'tradition', and disputed mappings of locality. Ambivalent reactions to their inclusion in local events such as the procession for San Giuliano, and differing interpretations of their role in wider commemorations (such as the gathering at Bondo), can thus, in part, be understood as struggles over the definition of the boundaries of the social field on which essentialist local (as opposed to regional) identities will be charted.

Ethnomimesis, History, and 'Systems of Difference'

The positioning of the groups discussed here suggests that the significance of performances of locality, when viewed from a local perspective, may often transcend the performative field provided by the *cultura turistica* itself. Existentially, in choosing to participate in specific forms of ethnomimetic enactment, individual villagers in Salamone display contested positions whilst making statements of identity in terms which are at once 'given' by the past and yet transformed by the present political and poetic contexts. For individuals, the commitment to associate oneself with either the *Banda Musicale Comunale*, the *Schützen*, or any other of the ongoing groups in Salamone is, thus, far from arbitrary. In one dimension, such a choice embodies a reading of the historical past, quite literally, by clothing the self and displaying an identity. In another, dimension, it states a projective view of the future, staking an individual's identity on a vision of the future topography of the political and cultural landscape. While these constructions of historicity and locality are often performed for tourists, local readings may construct this touristic space as little more than a stage on which a more complex and touristically 'invisible' dialogue is taking place.

From a more experiential perspective, such forms of ethnomimetic enactment can be understood as a kind of performative 'hinge' between these two dimensions, past and present, a moment of praxis, shared and visible, in which Salamonesi work upon their own and other's perceptions of historical experience and thus the nature and parameters of their shared lifeworlds. However, they are also, and at the same time, a hinge between the collective weight of a given history, the 'practico-inert' as Sartre called it, and individual intentionality. Embodying the past in the present is to be worked on by it, but also to work on it, by choosing the meanings with which it will be clothed.

Thus, wearing a uniform, giving a public concert, marching in a procession before an audience of tourists, are all, at one and the same time, ways of publicly differentiating individual and collective senses of identity within a local field and from the homogenising mass culture which the tourists themselves represent. In this light, just as salient as the touristic dimension of the performance, is the need to differentiate oneself from others who are also differentiating themselves, whether this be in the context of the village itself, or more broadly within the field of revitalising local traditions generally. As Cesare Poppi has observed of the highly politicised Ladin revitalisation movement in the nearby Val di Fassa in recent years:

> The grounds for the legitimacy of a minority's claim to positive discrimination and, eventually political autonomy must be firmly established at a given boundary ... [This process] becomes all the more crucial in the age of the expansion of the world system and in view of the persistence of the nation-state. History, language, culture, 'tradition' – whatever the chosen signifier, a unit has to have a boundary to qualify as a distinctive political/jural subject. Whether objectively grounded in historical developments or vindicated by a wholly contemporary claim, a 'turn of events' of some sort is required to signal a change. Under such circumstances, the dilemma for contemporary ethnic minorities constituting themselves as political subjects is how to 'be different' when everybody else, in the age of uniform individualism, seems to be engaged in the same game – how, in other words, a difference between 'us' and 'them' can emerge when the conditions for developing a system of differential characteristics are fast fading away (Poppi 1992: 131).

In Salamone, the contrast between groups that share a common impulse to engage in 'building difference' ethnomimetically through tourist performances and their spatial and political references, encompasses several levels in differing and sometimes opposed systems of 'differential characteristics'. Whether enactments signify allegiance to a local, regional or 'pan-alpine' sense of history, locality and self is thus a framing political consideration defining variously 'open' or 'closed' circles of participation and social reference. Such locally constituted circles of meaning perforce define notions of who are *'la nostra gente'* (our people), to cite Pier Paolo, and what is construed as authentically *una cosa paesana*. As we attempt to interpret tourist performances and their articulation with sense of place, the complexity of how such circles of meaning are mapped and articulated in relation to each other invites us to reassess the weight which we might ascribe to the 'tourist gaze': the actors may literally be addressing themselves as much as the audience.

Notes

1. The current population of Salamone is around 535 individuals: at the peak of the tourist season, there may be as many as 2600 tourists present in the village.
2. Some of this material results from my own trawling through the files held in the archives of the Comune – which were being reorganised during my last period of fieldwork, and from interviews with members of the band. Further material also comes from an account published by M. Mosca, in *Il Garzonè* n.4 (Luglio 1992: 35).
3. Andreas Hofer (1767–1810), the paramount symbol of Tirolean independence, is importantly linked with the Schützen at the turn of the nineteenth century, when peasant militias, for a brief time, achieved political control of much of the Trentino. He is thought in Salamone to have lived for a period at Bleggio, not far from the village. His sojourn there provides some historical justification for the refoundation of the Schützen locally. Hofer's 'peasant militia' distinguished themselves against Bavarian, Italian and French troops during the Napoleonic occupation of Tyrol, briefly succeeding – in 1808 and 1809 – in reinstating the South Tyrol alliance (including present-day Trentino) with the Austrian emperor Francis I.
4. 'La Compagnia Schützen Rendena', *Il Garzonè*, n.10; Gennaio, 1996: 43.

Go Athens

A Journey to the Centre of the City

Penny Travlou

You do not expect your guidebook to be an encyclopaedia. You do not want interminable lists of things. You are not interested in the address of the Lithuanian Legation or the destination of every tram. Certainly you want to be free to choose your activities but you do definitely want to be guided in your choice. You want to be as independent as possible of the nuisance of advisers, from the state offices to the scrounger in the streets. (Kenneth and Davis 1934: 5)

The guidebooks are made to follow them, mainly to read them and rarely to analyse them. (Elissalde 1986: 27)

The journey is a symbol of narrative. (Curtis and Pajaczowska 1994: 199)

For many theorists, contemporary tourists are modern pilgrims who carry guidebooks as devotional texts and follow their advice as to what they should and should not see (Horne 1984; Urry 1990). For some others, however, the guidebook is not a Bible to follow but an ideology of travel that is not actually that of mere tourists. It is a meaningless necessity – some sort of a placebo – imposed on them as part of tourist culture (Elissalde 1986; Cazes 1989; Urbain 1991). The tourists buy the guidebook to do exactly what other tourists do and feel secure that they have with them all the valuable information they need to enjoy a relaxing holiday. Bible or not, placebo or not, the guidebook is influential. For example, if it describes – let's say – Calcutta as 'an international urban horror story' then it might be expected that this is how tourists, too, describe it to each other (Hutnyk 1996: 90). The guidebook is, so to speak, the mediator in the interaction of the tourists with the destination place. The tourist, the sight and the guidebook – as part of the group of markers – are bound in an empirical relationship, constructing the tourism experience (MacCannell 1976). As a marker, the guidebook has the functional role of the informant since it provides important information. In this context, the travel book – as with all the other markers – is responsible for the construction of the image about the place that the tourists form in their minds. Consequently, the tourist does not try to approach the objects but their images; in other words, the object is reduced to a sign, or even to a signal (Urbain 1991). As for the guidebook, it is transformed into a signifier regulating the discourse of the communicated meaning.

Following the above argument, this chapter attempts to look at the ideogrammatic character of Athens – its symbolic representations – as narrated and mapped within guidebooks. A semiotic analysis of the existing travel discourse to Athens is followed by a particular emphasis on the major myths of the city, those which shape its symbolic space: the glorification of the past, the orientalisation of the present and the reification of her population. Various influential foreign tourist guidebooks – old and recent publications – are analysed, including both those that are addressed to mass tourists and those designed for younger, low budget, independent travellers. This retrospective analysis is based on the assumption that the travel narrative describing Athens has changed little since the first guidebook written about that city (Murray 1845). The fact that the same stereotypical images are found in all researched guidebooks makes the travel discourse on Athens a particularly interesting case among travelogues to other tourist places. For instance, a similar analysis on guidebooks referring to India has confirmed that the content of different guidebooks and the representations they portray 'are likely to vary' (Bhattacharrya 1997: 372) whereas in the case of Athens there is an archetypal imagery followed by guidebooks, regardless of publication date.

The guidebooks analysed in this work were selected as comprising a representative cross-section of the available spectrum. The latter is divided into three main periods, characterising the travel discourse on Athens. The first period is dated back to 1845, a few years after the foundation of the modern Greek state, with the publication of *The Handbook for Travellers in the East* (Murray 1845) and its second edition, *A Handbook for Travellers in Greece* (Murray 1854). The narrative style of Murray's books was inspired by the travel literature of that period and is therefore more like a traveller's memoir than a guidebook. However, by the end of the nineteenth century, the genre of writing had changed dramatically and only a few kept up the memoir tradition, whereas the majority of the new publications started to look like recent guidebooks. The second period of the travelogue to Athens is situated in the 1950s and 1960s. During these decades, there is an explosion in the number of tourists visiting the Greek capital as an outcome of the phenomenon of mass tourism. In addition, there is the feeling that Athens was becoming a cosmopolitan city as well as a cultural centre. This idea was encouraged by people like the American writer Henry Miller (1942) who staged one of his novels there, *The Colossus of Maroussi*. The guidebooks published during that period are greatly influenced by literary accounts, even those addressed to mass tourists. From the conducted research, it was found that the majority of the guidebooks published that period were American and were not dedicated exclusively to Greece but to Europe. Athens, therefore, was described with a few details as one of the destination places within Europe. Finally, the third period of the travel discourse to Athens is dated from the end of the 1970s until today and is mainly addressed to the young, independent traveller. During this period, about 700 travel books – Greek and foreign editions – were published (Karpodini 1995). For the first time in the travel literature Athens is treated as a bargain and mapped according to its cheapness. Therefore, the information provided by these guidebooks is limited to some useful information and brief descriptions on history. However, in the mid-1980s, with the appearance of publications such as the *Lonely Planet* and the *Rough Guide*, the style of writing changed again. These particular guidebooks are enriched with more information about the culture and history of the city as well as with the necessary advice for an independent traveller. Nevertheless, they do not escape the tradition of the previous travelogues and thus do not avoid describing Athens with the same stereotypical images.

In general, the guidebooks draw a textual map which describes the few recognisable landmarks and reinforces the pre-existing mythology of the Athenian landscape. The writing of the travel narratives is a form of intertextuality, where the text is dependent on previous texts. An investigation of the origins of the urban myths and the circumstances under which they were formed is of vital importance for the analysis of the guidebooks. What is argued in this chapter is that the people who created the symbolic images of Athens are the nineteenth century travellers to Greece. Their narratives are compared with the discourse of the guidebooks.

A Semiotic Analysis of the Guidebooks to Athens

If nineteenth century travellers are described as mythoplasts, constructing the symbolic images of Athens, tourists may be called 'semioticians', as they read the landscape for signifiers of certain pre-established notions of signs derived from various discourses of travel and tourism (McCannell, 1979). In the case of the guidebooks as part of the travel discourse, the signs are represented and portrayed by the text, the map and the photographs; the reader is only asked to search for the signifiers and understand the meaning conveyed.

Through this semiotic process, the myths are finally denoted and consumed.

The semiotic analysis of the guidebooks to Athens that is given below tries to read the symbolic landscape in a way similar to that of the tourists. However, the analysis is conducted in conjunction with an *'across'* time and *'in'* space approach. This refers to different readings of travelogues where the symbolic images of Athens are represented, first, through a time-narrative and, second, through a space-narrative.

Two time-narratives: the juxtaposition of past and present in the Athenian landscape

Throughout the existing travel discourse to Athens, one thing is clear: there are two different time narratives within the same space; one refers to classical Athens and the other to the modern city. These narratives show a preference and therefore resurrection of the former and a sort of indignation towards the qualities of the latter. As already discussed in a previous section, much of this orientation results from the influence of the travel narratives of the nineteenth century travellers who treated Athens with both 'Grecophilia' (the love of ancient Greece) and 'mis-Hellenism' (the dislike of modern Greece).

Modern Athens

Athens is a Hybrid. The birthplace of Western civilisation, with reminders everywhere of the great classic age, it is today the least Western of all European cities. In one moment, you'll tread where Demosthenes orated and Socrates taught but in another, you'll pass pungent-smelling coffee houses where men alone – scores of them sit chattering about the daily news – just as they do in Cairo or Teheran. (Frommer, 1968: 463)

In one sense, Greece is an aggressively western country that groups its noisy capital with London, Paris, and Rome. . . . Yet to step into Greece is to walk east – into stalls lined with Byzantine icons, past Orthodox priests trailing long dark robes, and through air spiced with the strains of bouzouki. (*Let's Go Europe* 1991: 398)

Throughout the travel discourse to Athens, the latter is portrayed as a 'hybrid' of different images and cultures, even of different geographical boundaries. On the one hand, the city is perceived as a Western capital and compared with other European cities. As presented in the two quotations above, this image of the city mainly characterises the ancient relics found in the urban space. On the other hand, Athens seems also to be a replica of Middle Eastern cities, presenting certain elements of an Oriental imagery. Whenever there is no obvious correlation and similarities to the other metropolitan cities of Western Europe, the narratives on Athens are focused around this stereotypical image. Even if the geographical position of Greece is within the boundaries of Europe, even if Athens is considered as the birthplace of Western civilisation, modern Greece is, for the guidebooks, in an awkward position. The Byzantine and Ottoman periods have resulted in the idiosyncratic development of modern Greece, in many aspects different than that of other Western countries (Gourgouris 1996). Undoubtedly, it is Western culture that perceives difference as 'Otherness' which is nothing but the interpretation of the 'Oriental'. According to Said (1979), the Orient is an integral part of European material civilisation and culture representing the different, the other, the alternative. This happens, especially, in the case where the described place is conceived as inferior and less-civilised, using a narrower sense of the term than the Western.

For instance, in the guidebook *'The Splendour of Greece'*, the author accentuates the Oriental image of Athens and warns the tourist to expect a Middle East city:

> Very often the traveller in Athens finds himself asking inconvenient questions. Walking under that fantastically deep blue sky, he sometimes has to remind himself that he is still in Europe. Athens is oriental. It wears the colours of the Orient. . . It might be Isfahan or Tabriz. Is this, the traveller asks himself, the cradle of western civilisation? . . . Everywhere you go in Athens you meet the Orient. (Payne 1961: 130)

Payne goes even further in his argument by claiming, in an authoritative manner, that Greece as a nation never belonged to the West and that she was closer 'in spirit to Persia than to Rome' (ibid.: 130). This is actually a statement found in many of the guidebooks researched, and especially in those of the 1960s (e.g. Life 1963; Fielding 1965).

It is also evident from the above quotations that the Oriental image of Athens is contrasted with the Occidental. The former is presented either as 'picturesque' or as 'devastatingly ugly' and as providing low quality service, whereas the latter is mainly related to the stereotypical representation of the so-called 'Glorious Past' of the city (see Table 1).

Referring, in particular, to the descriptions of the city as 'a monstrous caricature' where life is presented to be unbearable and hard, the narrative has an authoritative character. It is the way the writers portray their suggestions and advice to the reader that makes the whole discourse authoritative. Because of the ugliness and air pollution of the city, they advise the tourist not to stay more than few days since there is not much to see, apart, of course, from the historic ruins and museums (*Let's Go Europe* 1991; *Versatile Guide* 1996). This authoritative discourse is more evident in the section which describes the quality of service provided by the local tourist industry (see Table 2).

Table 1. Description of Modern Athens

Guidebooks	The Travel Discourse on Modern Athens
Murray 1845: 70	The modern town of Athens was never remarkable for beauty or regularity of construction.
Life 1963: 13	The relics of the past have more sense of life about them than the latest things
Frommer 1968: 463	There is nothing chic about Athens.... However, you will be able to focus clearly on the real aim of your trip: the first-hand experiencing of the great classic Greece civilisation, which shaped our own.
Let's Go Europe 1991: 49	Athens today, crowded with smog, concrete and tourists, little resembles the artistic and intellectual capital of old that gave birth to Western civilisation
American Express 1994: 11	Modern Athens is a young city: the somewhat smug capital of a small Balkan republic, in which the yellowed skeleton of old monuments stand out, like shipwrecks from a deaf and forgotten past, in an expanse of modern apartment blocks.
The Versatile Guide 1996: 117	At first sight, Athens is the sort of place you wouldn't wish on your worst enemy.
Lonely Planet- Web Page 1997	few fall in love with the city. Most visitors never see beyond the nefos (smog) and the high-rise apartment blocks which were built hurriedly.

According to these descriptions, the services are not as good as might be expected. What they suggest, therefore, is that the tourist should be patient and not expect much from the tourist services and facilities in Athens. Most of the time, no argument is provided to justify either the cognitive or the evaluative conclusion: the interpretation appears self-evident and beyond question.

Bhattacharyya (1997) claims that by using this narrative strategy the guidebooks deprive the tourist-reader of any personal evaluation and, correspondingly, encourage them to take for granted all the given advice. She continues her argument by claiming that, most of the time, tourists reject certain hotels and restaurants as they are not included in the guidebook's list. This is particularly evident in the case of the guidebooks to Athens. They give all the valuable and necessary information for a traveller to have an easy, safe, comfortable and cheap journey there by listing the best and cheapest hotels and

Table 2. The Description of the Quality of Services

Guidebooks	Terms Used to Describe the Quality of Services
Fielding's 1965: 1656	About the hotels: trashy low-level beds, so-called 'modern' chairs and tables. Skimpy rugs (if any!), bare walls, excruciatingly jarring taste throughout – typical 'get-back-our-money-fast' decor even in many cases so-called 'Deluxe' houses in the heart of metropolitan Athens.
Fielding's 1965: 1669	Don't look for dining elegance in Greece, because in the routine establishment you're liable to find paper tablecloths, paper napkins, colourless furnishings, and panting waiters who'll toss successive courses at you like ping-pong balls.
American Express 1994: 98	Apart from souvenir shirts and whimsical beachwear; there is little reason to buy clothes in Greece. Neither price nor quality is particularly attractive, and fashions echo the West – at a considerable distance

restaurants – in the writers' opinion – as well as where to shop, and all the useful addresses such as embassies, tourist offices, airlines etc. They even give advice to the tourist about what *not* to buy, eat and drink.

There are few guidebooks that refer to the modern Greek culture, except for some brief reference to the traditional 'bouzouki' scores and dances which give Athens a stereotypical flavour (*Life* 1963; *Rough Guide* 1996; *Lonely Planet* 1997; Rawlins 1997). Even in the case of some reference to the cultural life in the city, their approach is touristically oriented; they reduce the event to a mere sightseeing experience. For instance, in the *Lonely Planet* (1997), the reference to the traditional but underground music of the thirties called Rembetica is summarised in three words: 'worthwhile listening to'. Concerning the most recent guidebooks, few of them refer to modern Greek music, and fewer to pop and rock music which, in most cases, is characterised as 'Western music' (*American Express* 1994: 92).

It is worth mentioning that all the guidebooks analysed in this chapter have a separate section called 'Modern Athens' wherein the tourist might find all necessary information from currency and weather to the best restaurants and jewellery shops in town. The guidebooks dated from the 1950s to the present also include in this section a brief reference to night-life and entertainment. Apart from the latest edition of the *Lonely Planet* (1998), which gives a detailed account of the different entertainment amenities available in the city, the rest of the guidebooks – old and new – refer only briefly to them. First, they concentrate on the Plaka area where most of the taverns are situated; and second they propose live music and theatre shows particularly produced for the tourist clientele. Two of the most frequently proposed tourist shows are the Sound and Light on the Acropolis Hill and the Dora Stratou Company of Greek folk dances (*Fielding's* 1965, *Frommer's* 1968, *Let's Go Europe* 1991, *American Express* 1994). In the *Frommer's* guidebook, for instance, the former show is described as 'a wonder [which] shouldn't be missed' since, as is written further below, 'it's done in sound and light, and . . . the ruins of ancient Athens are the performers' (ibid.: 471). This might be linked with the following myth of the glorification and reinvention of Athens past, where the present life and culture are subtracted from the travel discourse and consequently from the cognitive map of the tourists. In the case of the travel books that describe entertainment and night-life in more detail, they either suggest particular taverns with Greek music in the tourist district or name some night clubs for single male tourists (*Fielding's* 1965, *American Express* 1994), arguing that there are no such things as Western-style clubs and bars. In particular, the *American Express* characterises Athens as 'probably the only major European city, apart from Tirana, where you could sweep the FM range and not catch a single twang of Western rock music' (ibid.: 92). This is somehow an extreme example of an Orientalising image of Athens contrasted with what a Western culture should be. By using that kind of phraseology, the travelogues to Athens strengthen Said's argument about the replacement of the other culture – in this case the Greek – with those self-generated and projected images of otherness that Western culture needs to see in order to orient and understand itself (Said 1979).

The Past of Athens or the Glorification of her Past

The . . . past dominates the present in Athens. (Faubion 1993: 15)

If modern Athens is related to an Oriental iconography, then her historical monuments and sites may be interpreted as an indisputable part of the Occidental 'symbolic imagery' (Daniels and Cosgrove 1988). To be more specific, travelling to Athens is tantamount to encountering the origins of Western civilisation directly, the 'graces of superior civilisation' (Rojek 1993: 112 see Table 3). This is based on the argument that Greece is conceived by Westerners as the birthplace of their civilisation as a result of a globalised viewpoint where all glorious moments, epochs and events are perceived as their own history.

Travellers search the Athenian landscape for landmarks which give credibility to the travel; all signs of a glorious past which is also their own. Using Said's words (1979), travellers experience a kind of déjà vu, where they find themselves trapped into a place that already existed in their mind. One's travel is more a game of recognising than of gazing. Moreover:

> Space is conceived as being already existent, as being divided up into empti loci into which the images by which memories would be recalled, are placed. (Smith 1987: 26)

The tourists, then, before even gazing at the Athenian landscape, carry it inside them in the form of stereotypical images and myths. Usually, they recognise what they already know (Mentzos 1989).

Accordingly, the guidebook plays the role of the pathfinder through time, helping travellers to navigate through the tissue of their recollections; to draw the imaginary map of all the recognisable signs which form the symbolic landscape of the visiting place as they have already conceived it. This is not a spatial (geographical) map, but a temporal one. Apart from walking through the spatial tissue of the city, they try to find their way in her temporal framework. The guidebook, by reducing the city into a few recognisable historical sites, gives the tourist the ability of time-orientation.

The Acropolis in particular seems to embrace most of the tourist interest and therefore most of the travel narrative about Athens. It represents democracy and gives to Athens the credibility of representing the 'birthplace of Western civilisation'. In a sense, the Acropolis is the equivalent of the Eiffel Tower for Paris. For Barthes (1979: 8): 'To visit the Tower is to get oneself up onto the balcony in order to perceive, comprehend, and savour a certain essence of Paris.' The same happens to Athens and her Acropolis: it is her major sign-symbol, which the tourist consumes through a pilgrimage process. *The Versatile Guide* proposes to its reader: 'If you see nothing else in Athens, see this' (ibid.1996: 184). As Downs and Stea (1977) argue, landmarks such as the Acropolis are memorable graphic symbols that capture the identity of the place; they are points of reference, spatial and temporal.

Concerning the language used to describe the Acropolis, most of the monument's descriptions use many adjectives and superlatives as they try to show the uniqueness of the place (see Table 4). They represent it as the major attraction of Athens and one that makes a tourist's visit to the city valuable.

Throughout the narrative of the guidebooks, the Acropolis seems to be superimposed upon the rest of the Athenian landscape. This lavish praise somehow annihilates the city and makes her look unattractive or even invisible to the eyes of the tourist. Furthermore, in many cases – as portrayed in the following quotations – they contrast the monument's unique beauty to the present condition of the city, which undoubtedly has a negative effect on the opinion of the tourist towards the latter.

Table 3. The Glorification of Athens' Past

Guidebooks	The glorification of the past of Athens
Murray 1854: 2	In [Athens] the traveller is, as it were, left alone with antiquity.
Life 1963: 69	A trip . . . to Athens means going home to the spawning grounds of western culture – a 25-century return.
American Express 1994: 148	It is the lure of history that brings many travellers to the Greek capital. It was in Athens, the city of Pericles, Socrates, Plato, Aristotle and Pythagoras, that ancient Greek civilisation reached its maturity.
Rawlins 1997: 9	The city has not changed much over the millennia which separate it from its founding fathers.
Lonely Planet-Web Page 1997	The city of Athens ranks with Rome and Jerusalem for its glorious past.

Eaten by pollution, the Acropolis stands with tragic dignity over a forest of concrete bristling with television antennae. (*Let's Go Europe* 1991: 397)

The Parthenon is magnificent, but stands alone, with almost no other monument to compare to it in size or beauty. (*American Express* 1994: 12)

These descriptions are quite recent, as the urban landscape and morphology of the city have changed during the last three decades.

Referring to the semiological hypostasis of Acropolis, the symbolism of this monument slips from a syntagmatic to a paradigmatic axis, and vice versa. To be more specific, the Acropolis, by representing democracy, stands as a metaphor, whereas Athens' geography is shrunk to the symbolism of this monument and, as a metonymy, is replaced by it.

Mapping the City: The Fragmentation of the Urban Landscape

The above analysis shows how travel discourse to Athens is divided into two-time narratives: one about her past and one for her present, with her inhabitants creeping between them. This time division leads to a fragmentary representation of the urban space. The city appears to be split into several spatial units. On the one hand, there is the historical centre representing the past. On the other, there is the modern part of the city, 'Modern Athens' as it is frequently called within the travelogues, portraying the present space. Moreover, it is this spatial dualism that visualises the Athenian landscape as being in a dialectic of 'outside/inside' spaces, where the inside space represents the enclosed tourist area and the outside the rest of the city. This fragmentation and disruption of spatial continuity is best portrayed in the maps found within the guidebooks. It is not an exaggeration to say that the maps in all researched guidebooks picture only the very historic tourist area, excluding the rest of the city centre (see Figure 1). As a result, the city is confined to a few useful places for the tourist and recognisable historical sites. A very good example of the above statement is found in *The Versatile Guide* (1996) where the author advises the visitor to Athens to take one of two suggested short walks:

> You don't have to take the walks from beginning to end; indeed you don't have to follow them [the two suggested routes] at all. The information in the walks can just as well be absorbed at a cafe table! (ibid.: 176)

It seems as though the city consists only of major monuments, as well as of a few central avenues with all hotels, restaurants, shops and

Table 4. Descriptions of the Acropolis

Guidebooks	Terms used to describe the Acropolis
Murray 1845: 70	The Acropolis is the first object which attracts the attention of the traveller.
Murray 1854: 70	On turning into the Acropolis, the Parthenon rises in all its majesty before you. The finest edifice on the finest site in the world.
Life 1963: 39	Yet in the modern city's midst, the Acropolis with its Parthenon still stands as a shining citadel of an ideal.
Fielding's 1965: 1650	Athens with its Acropolis is the birthplace and heart of Greek culture and Western civilisation, a must for all visitors.
Frommer 1968: 463	To ride from the airport to Athens ... and suddenly to see the Acropolis, high overlooking the city, is literally a thrill that comes once in a lifetime.
Let's Go Europe 1991: 397	The oldest, most sacred monument of Western civilisation.
Lonely Planet -Web Page 1997	The Acropolis, crowned by the Parthenon, stands sentinel over Athens, visible from almost everywhere in the city.

monuments situated there, excluding anything else that does not fall within these categories. In particular, the monuments and sites that the guidebooks suggest as being the main tourist sights of Athens are the Acropolis, the Lycavittos hill and the National Archaeological Museum. They are the locations which validate one's travel to Athens.

> The metropolitan skyline grants pride of place not to commercial skyscrapers, but to two recognisable points of reference; the Acropolis and the Mount Lycavittos. (Faubion 1993: 15)

What the map generally suggests to the tourist is to follow a particular path situated along the boundary line and the enclosed area. Certain things are included and others are not in the tourist gaze. This is exactly what Gritti characterises as '*devoir regarder*', arguing that certain objects in the local environment are narratively marked as worthy of the tourist's attention, whereas other parts of the city are subtracted from their map (1967: 53). The result of this spatial subtraction is the creation of 'enclavic' tourist spaces cut off from the wider urban landscape (Edensor 1998). The main point of dividing the space is the minimisation of the tourist's disorientation. It is this particular point that gives credit to the metaphor of the guidebook – and the map – as pathfinder (Bhattacharrya 1997).

In the case of Athens, the tourist is instructed to walk within the boundaries of the historic centre as bordered by the landmarks of

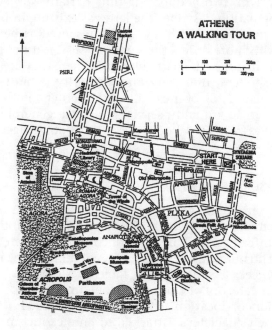

Figure 1. The Centre of Athens (© American Express Guides 1994)

Acropolis and Syntagma Square. An elaborate example of enclavic spaces is found in the *American Express* guidebook to Athens (1994) which, with the help of a map, draws the very centre of Athens (see Figure 1).

The above conclusion brings the subject of selectivity under consideration as it is what actually makes maps inseparable from the tourism experience. Some even argue that maps are by necessity selective, since there is 'no one-to-one correspondence between the spatial environment and its cognitive representation' (Downs and Stea 1977). The same argument may be applied to the tourism experience, as it is by definition impossible for a tourist to walk around the city without following particular directions and paths. Some reference points in the spatial environment help draw the tourist map. This impulse towards cognitive organisation and orientation is often encapsulated in symbols that are easily recognised by people as standing for a particular place. In this way, the guidebooks create a 'monument tourism' dependant on recognisable landmarks, which, by linking to each other, draw paths in the urban landscape (Hutnyk 1996).

In-between Spaces: The Narratives About the Locals

If the urban landscape of Athens is portrayed by the guidebooks as fragmentary, with two juxtaposing time narratives, the discourse on the local population describes the latter as existing in between those spaces. On the one hand, they are represented as being like their ancestors, with more or less the same physical features and qualities. On the other hand, in the particular case where they are connected to the tourist services, hierarchy and authority is built between the tourist playing the role of the civilised Westerner and the Athenian as the provider of low quality services but of a generous personality. Some examples from guidebooks presenting both images are shown in the table below:

a) Discourse of the Other

It is obvious from the above extracts that the local population of Athens is somehow the 'Other'. Through their description, they lose their human features and are objectified. All the given adjectives are abstract and do not really give precise descriptions of the mentality and attitude of Greeks as a nation (see Table 5). Moreover, 'the "Other" is available as a category of choice and investment, innocent of specific determination or location' (Robertson et al. 1994: 202). In these instances, their character is attached to pure exoticism. This process, whereby Athenians come to represent the 'Other', sustains a power relationship: 'The tourists, powerful and civilised, come to view Them, powerless and primitive' (Bruner 1991: 240). It is this hierarchy of power and status that transforms tourism into a form of colonialism and, consequently, contributes to the shaping of the colonial discourse of travel writing (Nash 1977).

However, the portrayal of modern Athenians as reproductions of ancient Greek figures is related to the need of tourists to verify on every occasion the material existence of the 'dream land' they are visiting. The ancient Athens: the cradle of Western Civilisation, still existing because her citizens are recognisable on the faces of the inhabitants of the present city. The closest parallel is with a foreigner travelling in the Athenian metro who visits a classical Jurassic Park inhabited by figures of Greek pottery:

> If Plato is the best introduction to the way Greeks talk, Greek pots are the best introduction to the way they look. . . Take the metro and you will see these same faces everywhere: some even manage to scowl geometrically. (Rawlins 1997: 53)

Thirty-six years before, the same travelogue appears to exist, a realisation that verifies the major argument of this chapter: the representation of the same stereotypical images through old and recent guidebooks.

> Everywhere you go [in Athens] you come upon the classic features. . . One day, while I was walking around Plaka, a horde of schoolboys came roaring out of a street: I had seen the same features only a few minutes before on the Parthenon frieze which is shown round all the walls of the Acropolis Museum. (Payne 1961: 131)

Finally, there is also the case of the guidebooks addressed to the independent traveller, wherein the portrait of the local is either absent or related to the provision of services. For instance, in the *Rough Guide* (1996) and *Let's Go Europe* (1991) there is no special section referring to the inhabitants. The only references, however, to the local population emerge when they want to describe some peculiarities of their behaviour in relation to eating or drinking attitudes as well as to their hospitality.

> For ordinary drinking you go to a *Kafenion* – simple places filled with old men arguing and playing tavli (backgammon), a national obsession. (*Rough Guide* 1996: 179)

> Even more important to know is Greek body language, which can lead to endless misunderstandings. To say no, Greeks silently close their eyes or click their tongues while lifting their heads and/or eyebrows. To indicate a positive, they tilt and bow the head in one motion. A hand waving up and down that seems to mean 'stay there' means 'come'. (*Let's Go Europe* 1991: 400)

The use of 'anomaly' in narratives describing indigenous populations, is a characteristic of travel literature in general (Wheeler 1986; Dann 1999). Within different types of travelogues (e.g. travel memoirs, diaries and books), the writer-traveller searches for all those characteristics – physical and cultural – in local inhabitants that would differentiate him/her from them and amuse readers. 'Without anomaly there is no travel book, no story to tell, and the more wondrous the anomalies the better the account' (Wheeler 1986: 58). Fussell says that the travel writers – particularly British – have 'the unique ability to spot anomalies' as a result of their confidence to 'know what is "normal"' (1980: 170).

b) The Discourse of the Anomalous

To understand the relationship between Athens and the discourse of the anomalous, I shall refer to the existing travel literature on the city which is full of such narratives. Athens is not a literary city of the magnitude of Calcutta (Hutnyk 1996). Since the nineteenth century travellers to Greece, few writers have written stories about Athens. The most famous book probably remains *The Colossus of Maroussi* (1947) in which the writer, Henry Miller, narrates his stay in the city and acquaintance with the Greek intelligentsia of the forties. Several pages

Figure 2. The Stereotypical Image of the Greeks (© Rawlins C. L. 1997)

Table 5. Descriptions of Athenians

Guidebooks	Terms used to describe Athenians
Murray 1845: 69	The Athenians have been noted among their countrymen, like their ancestors, for their superior quickness, vivacity, and disposition to intrigue.
Murray 1854: 50	Those who are best acquainted with the Greeks, cannot fail to remark the numerous and striking features of resemblance that connect them with their ancestors.
Life 1963: 13	Can the nature of the Greeks be summarised? Realism, quickness, and courage.
Fielding 1965: 1649	People? Lovely; very clean; very honest, overwhelmingly kind to Americans
Fielding's 1965: 1667	When the Greeks try to cook like Frenchmen the results are usually disappointing, if not disastrous. When they cook like Greeks, they turn out interesting fare.

of his book comprise descriptions of Athenians who are reified, if not as anomalous, then as different and unique:

> Everybody goes the wrong way, everything is confused, chaotic, disorderly . . . [The Greek] likes to do things with his hands, with his whole body, with his soul. (ibid. 1947: 11, 12)

> A Greek has no walls around him: he gives and takes without stint. (ibid.: 34)

His inspiration is *Zorba the Greek*, a book describing a character who supposedly represents the Greek male figure (Kazantzakis 1952). Zorbas' personality is at the same time passionate and intelligent, such as the main character in Henry Miller's book. Many books and guidebooks written after *The Colossus of Maroussi* represent Greeks in similar ways. For instance, Don Delillo, in his book *The Names* (1983), uses a similar character, Andreas Eliades, as a representation of Greekness. Eliades has the cultural and physical qualities of ancient Greeks as imagined by the West. He is presented as an original thinker, using rhetoric with considerable capacity to communicate his throughts, but in such an unrealistic way that he loses his human character.

Nevertheless, Don Dellilo is not a travel writer as much as a 'place writer'. He uses Athens as a locale, 'as the environment in which to explore inner experiences within a strong sense of geographical identity' (Dann 1999: 164). In his novel, both city and local inhabitants play a background role, giving an exotic character to the actual plot. This writing style dates back to the nineteeth-century romantic travellers and is comparable to what de Nerval named as 'les decorarions du theatre' (Mentzos 1989).

However, the book which best portrays the discourse of anomaly is *Dinner with Persephone* (1996) by Patricia Storace. Storace's one-year stay in Athens is transformed in to a verification of the exceptional: Greeks being different from Western people in a grotesque manner. Whatever does not fit into Western lifestyle, she interprets as anomalous behaviour; a drawback. Her characters are women who obey their husbands' will, men who sexually harass her, people who are obsessed with Orthodox religion, politics and their national identity and who more than anything else behave differently to their ancestors and Westerners. Sometimes her description of the inhabitants goes to extremes in constructing a discourse of negation, which is actually 'one of the characteristic tropes of European colonial imagery' (Spurr 1993; Gregory 1995: 36). Storace's obsession with contrasting present inhabitants with their ancestors is an act of negation. She presents them as being physically alike to ancient Greeks whilst their culture is under criticism. In other words, she depopulates the landscape of present people and then repopulates it with figures of the past. Her interest is focused exclusively on the past of Athens passing the present landscape by with indifference. In fact, Patricia Storace is a modern Florence Nightingale.[1] They both feel disappointed about the present landscape: the former for Greece, the latter for Egypt, using the residents as 'scratches on the face of the country' (Pratt 1992: 58; Gregory 1995: 37).

Alternative Travelogues or the Same Old Story?

Using metaphors such as the above to decipher the Athenian landscape, the guidebooks seem to embody narratives of colonial discourse. Stathis Gourgouris, in his book *Dream Nation*, which I will quote at length, insists on the representation of Greece as 'a nation forever situated in the interstices of *East* and *West* and ideologically constructed by colonialist Europe without having been, strictly speaking, colonized' (1996: 6). For him, modern Greece is mainly a by-product of the European colonialist spirit as an effort first to encapsulate and capitalise on the ancient Greek past and second to secure their own past. In Western discourse, Greece as a modern state was never articulated independently of its antiquity, its existence was necessary for the West to remember its own past. In a way, the relationship between the symbolic landscape of Greece and the history of the West is nothing less than the interrelation of the 'historicity of "us" and the ideality of "them" – the ideality of "them" ensuring the historicity of "us" ' (ibid.: 123; Humboldt 1963). Apparently, the hypostasis of Greece as a nation has been elevated to the state of an 'idealised other' where its people, by serving as mirror images of what Europeans would like to be, represent the epitome of that ideal. As Homi Bhabha observes, the colonial discourse is mainly characterised by mimicry, which is actually the 'desire for a reformed recognisable Other' (1986: 199).

One might expect that the Greeks themselves would portray their nation and culture through different symbolic images and narratives, questioning the validity of Western colonial discourse. In reality, how-ever, the national imaginary of the former and the 'idealised other' of the latter coincide. On the one hand, the sublimation of antiquity served to boost the Greek identity by employing 'ready-made' national symbols (Skopetea 1988). The ancient ruins, for example, were trans-formed into a symbolic (and national) capital. On the other hand, Greeks 'were subjected to so much discursive bombardment about the nature of their being as to learn to respond in accordance with the expectations of their questioners' (Gourgouris 1996: 150).

If the guidebooks are examples of colonial discourse, the brochures distributed by Greek tourist agencies are narratives of mimicry, but reversing Bhabha's definition. In this case, it is not the West which tries to resemble the 'ideal other', but Greeks who identify themselves as such. Instead of producing a new imagery, they reproduce and/or recycle the 'ready-made' one, employing the same stereotypical images. They shape their cultural identity according to what they believe tourists want to see. 'This participation in stereotyping [is] a tacit agreement to domination' (Norkunas 1993: 7).

To support the above argument, I present here an analysis of eight recent publications of leaflets and brochures distributed in central hotels and tourist information offices in Athens. Three of them were published by the GNTO,[2] one by the Municipality of Athens, one by the Prefecture of Athens, and the rest by private tourist agencies. Half of these have the Parthenon on the front page. In fact, the use of sym-bols/landmarks is a familiar part of the rhetoric of tourist promotion; they simplify the procedure of connotation by offering ready-made symbols to the visitor. It is obvious that their intention is to sell the image of a 'glorious past' to the tourist. In the leaflet distributed by the Perfecture of Athens, the first few lines are as follows:

> Athens! Welcome to the place where legend embraces history. Under this Attic land, layers of civilization lead to past centuries, that reach as far as the origin of mankind itself (Perfecture of Athens 1998: 1).

The first few pages of the GNTO brochures are dedicated to the appraisal of Athens as the 'birth place of Western civilisation'.

This is where democracy was born . . . Athens is the symbol of freedom, art and democracy in the conscience of the civilized world. In Athens memory never fades. Wherever you stand, wherever you turn, the city's long and rich history will be alive in front of you (GNTO 1993: 4).

Greece is the cradle of Western civilization, the origin of drama and history and philosophy, the birthplace of democracy. It is hard to imagine what civilized life would be like today without the influence of ancient Greece (GNTO 1995: 1).

Some of the brochures even contain a 'letter of introduction', written by either the editor or an important political figure (e.g. the General Secretary of GNTO, Minister of Culture etc.). For instance, in *Athens Today* – a private publication sponsored by GNTO – the Mayor of Athens, Mr Avramopoulos, plays the role of the host, welcoming the visitor in Athens not as 'a foreigner, but as a guest and "Athenian"' because, as he says, 'Athenians' are not only the inhabitants of the city, 'but all those around the world who have placed the noble, superior values born in the eternal city of Athens in their hearts and mind' (*Athens Today* 1997: 8). Then, he adds the following: 'I welcome you to the city of Athens, the city of culture, the city of light, the historical capital of Europe, your city' (ibid.: 8).

The phrase 'your city' constitutes both an offer and a reminder. An offer of the city to the visitor, an act of generosity; a reminder of the familiarity, of the belonging that the visitor should feel on returning to a place central to the construction of Western culture.

The content of brochures is mainly dedicated to information related to the historic centre of Athens, giving names and addresses of museums, sites and monuments that are worth visiting. In addition, they advise the visitor where to go shopping, eating and night-clubbing. They include such information either in separate sections or through advertisments. In the former case, some brochures use the same content as guidebooks. In *Fun Time* (Konidaris 1998), a magazine distributed free in hotel lobbies, there are separate sections referring to various images of the city, using similar titles and topics to those found in guidebooks. Instead of presenting alternative narratives on the Athenian landscape, they actually function as shorter versions of *Lonely Planet* travel books, summarising the most important information that a tourist might need during their stay in the city.

The analysis of different types of travel literature – guidebooks, travel books and brochures – suggests that narratives about Athens are characterised by intertextuality. In particular, the memoirs of nineteenth century travellers influence the first guidebooks, which in their turn influence recent publications, and finally all previous travelogues influence the brochures of Greek tourist organisations. As a result, all travel narratives to Athens have a common element, that of bestowing Athens with a mythological imagery. As Kabbani argues: 'it is as if the imagination of the traveller, in order to function, has to be sustained by a long tradition of Western scholarship, by other Western texts' (1986: 10). The same stereotypical images and conventional clichés are renewed over and over, so that 'the continuities of travel literature may be traced across long periods of time' (Hutnyk 1996: 40). Probably the main reason for this unifying documentation of the city is to facilitate the traveller discovering and identifying these preconceived images. Alternative representations, outside the stereotypes, are very difficult to maintain, as their existence would cause frustration and disorientation in travellers.

Thus, the guidebooks, by continuing the tradition of travellers' memoirs, portray a fragmented city whose present history is missing and whose urban landscape is shrunk to just a few routes, directing tourists up and down to the historical sites. This particular selectivity of monuments reduces the geography of the city to the mere description of a monumental but depopulated world where the present is absent (Cazes 1989). These textual maps treat the actual landscape as empty spaces to be filled with 'useful' information about facilities and monuments found in the very centre of the city (Smith 1987). At their worst, they represent the urban space as a 'non-place' where 'transit points and temporary abodes are proliferating under luxurious or inhuman conditions (i.e., hotels, museums, airports)' (Augé 1995: 78).

More than anything else, travel literature, and particularly guidebooks, represent 'imaginative geographies' of Athens which, as Said might argue, dramatize distance and difference in such a way that 'our' space is divided and demarcated from 'their' space (after Gregory 1995: 29). They delineate two contrasting worlds, that of the tourist and the local inhabitant, the West and the Orient, Europe and Greece, present and past.

Notes

1. As a young woman Florence Nightingale, later famous for her activities as a nurse in the Crimean War, toured Italy, Egypt and Greece with family friends.
2. GNTO are the initials of the Greek National Tourist Organisation.

Adventure Tourists and Locals in a Global City

Resisting Tourist Performances in London's 'East End'

John Eade

This chapter considers three related questions: What role do guide-books and guides play in the exploration of local space by tourists as they move from tourist centres into the periphery? In what ways do local people resist the performances provided for the tourists by their guides and local businesses? What are the specific conditions shaping the interaction of tourists and locals in a global city? Before examining these questions in detail I shall explain my approach towards the general issues contained within them.

Globalisation: The Interweaving of Global and Local

Contemporary debates concerning globalisation have placed so much emphasis upon the power wielded by transnational corporations and the threat to national policies posed by the free flow of capital around the world that it has become difficult to advance alternative approaches. However, social scientists have presented us with more subtle accounts, which shift the focus away from economic forces to social and political changes and uncover the dynamic interplay between global and local processes (see Appadurai 1991, 1995; Robertson 1992; Lash and Urry 1994; Albrow 1996). Their work undermines claims that we are simply seeing the development of global cultural homogenisation and the flattening of local differences (see Hall 1992a, 1992b; Robertson 1992; Featherstone 1993). Ethnic revivalism, new ethnicities, increasing cultural hybridity and the emergence of new imagined, virtual or diasporic communities are all features of recent globalisation. The 'West' is linked to 'developing countries' such as India through 'new patriotisms' which 'involve rather puzzling new forms of linkage between diasporic nationalisms, delocalized political communities and revitalized political commitments at both ends of the diasporic process' (Appadurai 1995: 220).

These new ways of perceiving the world are contributing to the increasing social and cultural pluralism that is, particularly, a feature of London. It is misguided to dismiss class as a declining, if already moribund, mode of interpreting social divisions. At the same time, other solidarities and boundaries have clearly attracted widespread popular attention during the last thirty years. Single issue movements have highlighted the significance of gender, sexuality, race, ethnicity and the environment, for example, and their tangential relationship to the grand narratives based upon class. Local community campaigns may draw on struggles in far distant countries as local issues become 'disembedded' and stretched across the globe (see Giddens 1990). It would be a mistake to imply that only the relatively well-off in London's changing social structure are engaged in the reworking of perceptions created by the interplay of global and local processes. There is evidence that descendants of comparatively poor (materially) labour migrants in London, for example, are highly adept at negotiating landscapes and constructing imagined worlds which cross local and national boundaries (see Samad 1992; Appadurai 1995; Back 1995; Eade 1997). The more extravagant and naive claims on behalf of the 'global village' need to be challenged by reminders that the distribution of global flows across the world is very uneven (Massey 1994). The global/local dynamic may well be to deepen social and economic inequalities within particular nation-states or create new forms of division. However, in a city such as London there is already empirical support for elements of the theoretical debate concerning globalisation and global/local dynamics (see Sassen 1991, Rhodes and Nabi 1992, Eade 1997). Here we see most vividly the ways in which global flows of people, capital, information, ideas and images are intimately bound up with local social and economic developments.

Heterotopias and the Tourist Gaze

The development of the tourism industry in London was part of the wider process of service sector expansion and the global/local processes which I have outlined above. Yet, while discussion of contemporary tourism has largely focused on central London, the process of global/local interactions can be more easily investigated outside that area. It is in these peripheral localities that a clearer contrast can be made between the official and professional attempts to interpret urban space for tourists, on the one hand, and the alternative knowledges of residents on the other. Here we can more easily examine people's imagined worlds in relation to the changing social and economic character of their localities: the scapes of people's imaginations and the physical urban landscapes which surround them.

John Urry (1990, 1993) has emphasised how the tourists engage in a process of leisurely gazing at extraordinary landscapes or townscapes. Building on Foucault's analysis of the medical gaze (1976), Urry claims that the tourist gaze is 'as socially organised and systematised as is the gaze of the medic' (ibid: 1). 'Professional experts', therefore, play a crucial role in 'helping to construct and develop our gaze as tourists' (ibid.). He proceeds to claim that the auratic modernism based on the nation-state is now being challenged by a postmodern, anti-elitist, nostalgic proliferation of alternative, vernacular histories (ibid.: 130).[1] These histories encourage tourist intrusion into local backstages (see MacCannell 1984; Greenwood 1989; Boissevain 1996) – an intrusion which may be greeted by various forms of local resistance (see Boissevain 1996: 14–20). Most research on tourist/local interaction has been undertaken well away from densely populated urban settlements. The most relevant analysis, for my purposes, is Heidi Dahles' work on tourist narratives in Amsterdam (see Boissevain 1996: 227–46). She is well aware of the ways in which the tourist gaze is variously constructed for different types of visitor as Amsterdam's public authorities seek to encourage tourism in the competition for global flows of capital, people and information.

However, her subtle analysis of two kinds of tourist narrative needs to be balanced by a more revealing account of how local people react to the commoditisation of their 'backstage'. Furthermore, Amsterdam's competition with other European cities for these global flows through tourism requires a more thorough engagement with the wider debates concerning globalisation and global/local dynamics outlined above. My chapter, therefore, tries to move the debate on by locating a particular form of tourism within the context of London as a global city.

London: A Global City

In her book *The Global City* (1991), Saskia Sassen brings London, New York and Tokyo together as global cities on the grounds that they share certain economic features. They are:

> Sites for (1) the production of specialized services needed by complex organisations for running a spatially dispersed network of factories, offices and service outlets; and (2) the production of financial innovations and the making of markets, both central to the internationalization and expansion of the financial industry (ibid: 5).

The emphasis which Sassen places upon financial institutions and the service sector needs to be placed in the context of the long-established role played by commerce and services across London (see Feldman and Stedman Jones 1989). Since the 1970s, the predominance of services over production has strengthened even further. Between 1984 and 1994 the contribution of the financial and business services sector to London's Gross Domestic Product (GDP) rose from 29 percent to 39 percent while the contribution of manufacturing correspondingly declined from 18 percent to 11.5 percent. Financial and business services had also expanded across Britain during that period. Even so, in 1994 London's disproportionate reliance on those services was indicated by the 39 percent of GDP contributed by finance and business in the metropolis compared with the national average of 26 percent.

These changes, which were shaped by the City of London's role within global capitalism, deeply influenced the changing shape of social divisions across the metropolis. The City had long enjoyed a dominant position within the world's financial and business markets. Changes in the way capital flows were handled during the 1970s and 1980s provided new opportunities which City firms eagerly seized. Despite Britain's declining share of world trade, the City of London remained a major centre for global corporations and for commercial businesses and 'cutting edge' industrial enterprises serving these corporations. These developments have led to a reordering of class distinctions. The new rich within the business and financial sector, information technology and the media have developed lifestyles which jar with those of the traditional middle class (see Lash and Urry on the emergence of a new service or information class and the work of Castells 1989, 1997 on the informational city). What united both kinds of 'professional workers' was a keen awareness of the material advantages accruing from educational achievement, the ability to cope with the new modes of information production, collection and analysis and the capacity to operate within the rapid flow of capital, information, ideas and images across local and national boundaries. Local social solidarities, therefore, engaged with global flows and were not simply flattened by a global juggernaut. People's perceptions of local class, gender, ethnic and racial distinctions were reworked in ways which require new sociological categories (see Albrow 1996, 1997; Albrow, Eade, Durrschmidt and Washbourne 1997). Although traditional manual jobs continued to decline between the 1970s and 1990s, new working-class jobs were created by those servicing the new wealthy through small businesses and individual operations across the service, information technology and new industrial sectors. Those who did not benefit materially from the interlocking of global and local processes were the homeless, single-parent families, unskilled manual workers and others who did not possess the qualifications to gain access to the new information class. So, while average earnings in London were a third higher than the national average during the 1990s, unemployment was also disproportionately high.

Long-standing differences between areas across London resulted in large numbers of unemployed, single-parent families and ethnic minorities occupying the most deprived, inner-city boroughs. In 1991, ten of the fifteen most deprived boroughs in England were located in the metropolis. At the same time, some of these inner-city boroughs contained an amount of very expensive accommodation, especially in 'Docklands'. London's position as a global city was shaped by tourism as well as by the financial and business services discussed above. London vied with Paris as the most popular city tourist venue in Europe (see Law 1996: 18). Media debates about London's future emphasised the importance of infrastructural improvements so that the city would continue to be seen as an attractive place in which to both work and play. London also held a pre-eminent position within British tourism: a dominance which was established by the mid-1970s. According to Eversley, by 1976 75 percent of the tourists were spending 'at least one night in the capital' while in 1984 it was estimated 'that 64% of all visitors to the UK came to London' (Law 1996: 157). Many of these tourists stayed in central London which contained a high proportion of the famous tourist sites and hotel accommodation. (We must also note that not all overseas and domestic tourists stayed in central London – 15 percent of overseas tourists and 46 percent of domestic visitors stayed with friends and relatives whom we might reasonably assume lived in the suburbs).

Guiding tourists across Spitalfields in London's East End

Gentrification and the tourism industry

Spitalfields is a ward in the East London borough of Tower Hamlets. The locality lies outside the tourist heart of London. Although the tourist 'honeypot' of the Tower of London is not far away to the southwest, only the adventurer/explorer visits Spitalfields, attracted by the historic Petticoat Lane market and the restaurants and cafés established by the locally dominant Bangladeshis. Tourists and other visitors who are also interested in social and architectural history are drawn here by the traces of previous migrants (French Huguenots, Jews and Irish) and the echoes of a darker past (the 'Jack the Ripper' murders).

These traces exist within a bustling neighbourhood where working-class Bangladeshis have occupied some of the most dilapidated council housing in the country and endure high rates of unemployment and overcrowding. Close to these council estates lie the ward's conservation areas, where white middle-class immigrants have invested in property whose value rose to over £500,000 in some cases during the housing boom of the late 1980s. These sharp social and cultural divisions have played a part in the ward's lively political campaigns (see Eade 1989; Forman 1989). However, Bangladeshi residents are linked to a wider world where class solidarities are overlaid by ties to Islam, Bangladesh and their district of origin, Sylhet, as well as generational, educational and gender differences (see Gardner and Shukur 1994; Gardner 1995; Eade 1996). The process of gentrifying and prettifying this area of Spitalfields has resulted in working-class residents, who are mostly Bangladeshis now, becoming ever more concentrated in their council redoubts to the east of the ward. As the Tower Hamlets' borough plan warned these residents during the 1980s, the western part of Spitalfields will eventually be absorbed within the 'City Fringe' which runs along the borough's border with the City of London. In the process, the ethnic character of West Spitalfields is weakening and the adventurer tourists will have to explore the 'eastern tracts' beyond Brick Lane if they are to find 'authentic natives'.[2]

Poverty, ethnicity and danger

A vivid insight into the ways in which this locality is represented to tourists can be gained from one of the many guidebooks available on London. The *Automobile Association's (AA) Explorer London Guide*, for example, dedicates a special section to Spitalfields later in the book. Christopher Catling, the author, covers the familiar themes – Jack the Ripper, the immigrant history and ethnic mixture, Hawksmoor's celebrated Anglican church and Brick Lane, 'the heart of a large community of Bangladeshis, Pakistanis and Indians' (1996: 187).[3] The locality is introduced by a section in bold type which concentrates on Spitalfields' immigration history, poverty and continuing ethnic character:

> A visit to Spitalfields provides the opportunity to sample the surprising contrasts of London's East End. This working class neighbourhood has long been a home to the poorest of refugees. Its character was first formed by Huguenot weavers, whose houses still have skylit attics where handloom weavers worked all the hours of daylight to produce fine silk clothing. After the Huguenots came Jewish refugees from Russia and Poland, specialising in furs and leather, only to be followed more recently by Bengali immmigrants, who now toil in the same 18th-century buildings over sewing machines and steam irons, producing garments for sale in London's clothes shops and street markets. (1996: 186)

Here we see the social divisions of class and ethnicity outlined in a form that establishes continuity between past and present. Visitors to the locality are encouraged to gaze at the Georgian buildings which signify this continuity. What the passage fails to reveal, however, is the wider context of class division, conservation and property speculation. Many of the Bangladeshi garment factories have been moved out of the Huguenot houses across the conservation areas of Spitalfields and the streets are gradually being gentrified or turned into more up-market offices and shops which service the City of London.

The attempt to attract cultural tourists and other visitors through a more 'trendy', chic image is described in Catling's discussion of the large, former Fruit and Vegetable Market in West Spitalfields:

> The area is now earmarked as the 'Covent Garden of the east', although there is still much work to be done on the building and development. It currently houses a craft market (open daily except Saturdays), a food market and a Sunday market. (ibid.: 186–7)

While the market may attract outsiders, it offers few employment opportunities for local Bangladeshi residents. Moreover, the new mock-Georgian housing developments around the market are not designed for relatively poor Bangladeshi and white locals, but for people working in new service class jobs across the City of London and in gentrified areas such as West Spitafields. Gentrification and prettification poses a problem for those who wish to continue representing the locality in terms of 'Dickensian' London and the Jack the Ripper shock-horror narrative. The murders of six local women took place in 1888 across Central and West Spitalfields, but in the conservation areas the signs of urban decay and poverty have been swept away. Those undertaking the Ripper night walking tours have to exercise their imagination more and more as the streets and lanes are refurbished. Local estate agents have played a crucial role in the 'upgrading' of Spitalfields, and yet they also have an interest in maintaining the international notoriety of the area. As one estate agent explained:

> You've got to keep a bit of the original Jack the Ripper territory because, obviously, that's a great big pulling point for the tourists around here. It was around Spitalfields that a lot of the supposed murders took place . . . so you've got to keep that otherwise you'll lose what was . . . the East End of London and what people remember of it. If you talk to the Americans all they think of is: 'Have you got the fog?' and 'Where's Jack the Ripper?' and 'Isn't this quaint?' and they're the sort of people that want to see these Georgian buildings. (Quoted from Eade 1997: 135.)

In the *Explorer London* discussion of Jack the Ripper, Catling chooses to establish a link between the 1888 murders and changing public tastes. He refers to 'a growing taste among the public at large for crime and detective stories, such as The Adventures of Sherlock Holmes which Sir Arthur Conan Doyle began to pen in 1891' (1996: 186). To the observant reader the reference to Sherlock Holmes establishes another connection – with the museum created by the Sherlock Holmes International Society on Baker Street near Madame Tussaud's. The Insight guidebook to London shows another way in which the Jack the Ripper story can be interpreted. The events of 1888 are presented as part of a history of violence where Bangladeshis as well as white women are the victims:

> The area ... has a gruesome past. It has been the scene of race riots against the Bengalis by the extreme right-wing National Front. In an earlier era ... Jack the Ripper terrorised the streets, murdering five prostitutes, identified by his gruesome trademark – a double slash of the throat. (1995: 177).

At night, the locality can be dangerous for visitors as well as locals, since 'Brick Lane and neighbouring streets have yet to defeat the problems of racism and it can still be foolhardy to walk there alone at night' (ibid.). These warnings did not deter the more adventurous tourists who were looking for an 'authentic', local experience. Indeed, the hint of danger may have encouraged the kinds of people who visited Soho, London's 'red light' district, and its equivalent in other cities (see, for example, Dahles in Boissevain 1996). Brick Lane had become widely known as a centre for good value, exotic shopping and eating. Explorer London, for example, describes Brick Lane as:

> Lined with shops selling exotic groceries, brightly printed fabrics and saris and the simple restaurants here serve some of the cheapest and most authentic curries to be found in London. (1996: 187)

The developments across Spitalfields have revealed the sharp contrasts between rich and poor which have long been a feature of this locality. However, the social composition of rich and poor has changed as the new wealthy in business and financial services, professions servicing the 'global city' and those in the media move into the conservation areas while Bangladeshi factory operatives, shop workers, waiters and chefs occupy the nearby council estates. At the same time the gulf between white and Bangladeshi residents must not be overstated since a few of the Bangladeshi second generation have moved, or are moving, into middle-class jobs.

Performing for tourists and local resistance

Having outlined the social and economic developments within this particular locality of the global city, let us consider briefly the contested character of tourist performances in Spitalfields. The first involves the use of the old Truman Brewery on Brick Lane for popular entertainment while the second focusses on one of the evening walking tours for overseas tourists.

Beer had been produced at Truman's Brewery since the early eighteenth century, but during the late 1980s Grand Metropolitan, a conglomerate which had bought up the family firm, decided to close the brewery. Part of the large site consisted of the original eighteenth century buildings which were protected from radical architectural surgery. While the fate of the more recently constructed areas of the site was debated, Grand Metropolitan attempted to exploit the commercial potential of the eighteenth century buildings through the establishment of a music hall. It was hoped that large parties of revellers would be attracted by entertainment and food which conjured up nostalgic images of a late Victorian and Edwardian 'East End'. Publicity leaflets invited people to enjoy:

> An evening of rare rapport and sophisticated sauciness . . . Escape from reality into a world of abandoned frivolity, scrumptious suppers and bargain beverages. Each week will bring named artists at prices only we can afford, complementing the musical director, our master of ceremonies, a bewitching bevvy of beauties – and the legendary Dockland Doris. Dine before the show. A scrumptious three-course dinner served each evening. Latkas a speciality. (Eade 1997).

Local Bangladeshi community activists sharply criticised this attempt to extract commercial advantage from Brick Lane's historic buildings. Their criticisms were delivered from two contrasting ideological positions. The secular activists who led local youth groups pointed to the failure of such ventures to provide jobs for the Bangladeshi second generation. As with so many tourist initiatives around the world, the revenue generated did not 'trickle down' to local residents in any obvious way. The second objection to the performances laid on for outsiders was based on moral rather than economic grounds. Religious leaders at the nearby Brick Lane mosque were offended by the kind of entertainment provided. They were especially affronted by Dockland Doris – a drag act. In a locality where Muslim leaders were attempting to inculcate notions of Islamic correctness among the second and the rapidly growing third generation of Bangladeshi settlers, the bawdy humour of these evening performances appeared to be inappropriate and decadent. Docklands Doris's drag act also touched on a highly contentious but rarely debated issue among Bangladeshi activists – the appropriation of local space by gay men. The early involvement of well known gay men in the gentrification of Spitalfields disrupted stereotypes of heterosexual, familial East End communities (see Brown 1998: 84–86). There was also an extensive history of working class gay space in the dock areas to the south of Spitalfields. Yet, although some young Bangladeshi men appear to have contributed to the East End's gay tradition (ibid.: 80–82), any overt public display of explicitly gay behaviour by young Bangladeshis was unlikely given the attitudes espoused by their elders. The Brick Lane music hall may have encouraged the image of Spitalfields as a gay or transexual space and provide an East End alternative to Soho's growing reputation as the West End's 'queer space' (ibid: 90). However, for conservative Bangladeshis such an image only increased their antipathy towards the entertainment provided in the disused brewery. Muslim leaders could take little comfort from the eventual collapse of the music hall since the historic buildings have recently been used as a disco bar. Local hostility towards entertainment for non-Muslims had scant impact on public performances inside buildings, but it could affect the ways in which people appropriated the external world of local streets.

A recent incident involving one of the walking tours provides an illustration of competing appropriations of the same space. Tourists were taken round the streets of Spitalfields and Whitechapel by various guides who dwelt on their 'Dickensian' past and placed particular emphasis upon the Jack the Ripper narrative. A more scholarly, less sensationalist approach was taken by Bill Fishman, a renowned Jewish professor of local history who had been 'born and bred' in nearby Stepney (see, for example, Fishman 1988). Although he had retired from academic life and lived in Wembley, he regularly returned to the East End to take groups of American Jews on his walking tour. These tours attracted the attention of passers-by who would sometimes comment on the professor's account. As the numbers of young Bangladeshi males frequenting the streets grew so did the potential for conflicting interpretations of the same space. Almost inevitably a confrontation recently took place outside the Whitechapel Underground Station – a meeting point for the walking tour and a busy shopping area used by local Bangladeshis. Bill Fishman's description of the area to an audience of Jewish American students was interrupted by some young Bangladeshi men who (reportedly) pushed through the group shouting offensive slogans. Given the strong anti-American feeling among local Bangladeshis during the Gulf War (see Centre for Bangladesh Studies 1994) it is surprising that such an incident had not occurred earlier. Indeed, this particular incident has to be seen in the wider context of the increasing Islamisation of public space in the area (see Eade 1996), the more aggressive appropriation of local space by competing Bangladeshi gangs and the deep suspicion of white people shaped by a long history of racist attacks (see Keith 1995; Harris 1996/7). Although Bill Fishman wanted to reveal 'his East End' to visitors through a highly informed guided tour, his performance was increasingly conditioned and constrained by varying Bangladeshi appropriations of the same space. The painful confrontation outside Whitechapel Station emphasised the conditions created by the interweaving of global and local processes. His attempt to relive a local Jewish past for Jewish American tourists offended Bangladeshis who considered this part of the East End to be theirs in ways which excluded the 'enemies of Islam'. Conflicts between the US and its allies on the one hand, and Muslim countries such as Iraq, Iran and Sudan on the other, affected the ways in which Bangladeshis interpreted locality in London's East End. The struggles affecting the 'imagined community' of Muslims around the world engaged the passions of Bangladeshis frequenting the streets of Whitechapel and Spitalfields. In defending 'their' locality against its appropriation for certain tourist performances they were, in a very small way, challenging the power of what they considered to be the Muslim community's enemies across the globe.

Conclusion

The tourists who come to gaze at these areas of London are adventurers. They want to move away from the traditional 'honeypots' of mass tourism in central London and are attracted by the 'unique' characteristics of the areas. These characteristics are constructed by guidebooks, for example, in terms of cultural heritage, titillating danger and the exotic. They enter localities where residents are differentiated from one another by a complex interweaving of class, ethnic and racial boundaries. Tourists gain some insight into this local diversity through such introductions as guidebooks which assume the existence of a 'middle ground' for their analysis of local changes. This 'balanced' approach shuns the more radical interpretations produced by local political and community activists – and sociologists! Although issues are not trivialised, there is a conscious attempt to lay a superficial gloss over developments. This strategy is related to the desire to uncover the essential character of a particular locality. What this desire again ignores is the way in which essentialisation obscures process. The attempt to fix, to establish uniqueness, is challenged by the dynamic and the fragmentary, but this struggle is not allowed to interrupt the representation of locality to the outsider. Tourists are not the only ones to look at certain representations of urban space. Local residents also gaze at selected aspects of their locality, but some at least acknowledge that what they are envisioning is shaped through an engagement with flows which cross local, regional and national borders. Bangladeshi residents are particularly aware of this engagement and the need to negotiate between different and often conflicting worlds.

These worlds are constructed through the imagination, but they are not only imaginary constructs as they connect with social and cultural institutions. They express the sense of being caught up with the flows of people, capital, information, images and ideas which cross national boundaries and, as in the case of the Muslim or Islamic community, construct an imaginary global fellowship. These global flows interweave with local appropriations of space, as the analysis of tourist performances in Spitalfields and Whitechapel revealed. Here local/global understandings of space sometimes confront the images of a safe place for tourist entertainment constructed by the guidebooks and guides. A safe local world of 'Dickensian' nostalgia might be provided inside local properties, but out on the streets the adventurous tourists are more vulnerable to local resentments. Here the divisions of ethnicity, race, gender and sexuality can be expressed with intense passion as different interpretations and uses of the same space collide. Performing for tourists can involve locals who have the opportunity to express forcefully their own understandings in ways that may deter future tourists from adventuring so far from the honeypots of the West End. Perhaps the Jewish American visitors will be replaced by Muslim tourists attracted to an 'authentically Islamic' area of the global city. Another possibility is that the two groups could even pass each other as they are led through the same space by their respective local guides.

Notes

1. See also Raphael Samuel's analysis of unoffical knowledge and vernacular histories in his formidably detailed *Theatres of Memory*.

2. It is surprising that Pakistanis and Indians are mentioned since the overwhelming majority of South Asian residents are from Bangladesh. However, Catling may be thinking of the commercial enterprises in the area which are owned by non-resident Pakistanis and Indians.

3. I am being ironic. Later in the paper I will look more closely at the ways in which visitors to Spitalfields can be likened to other tourists in search of authenticity.

4. Docklands displays some of the aspects of the defensive city so powerfully decribed by Mike Davis (1990) in the context of Los Angeles.

DISTANCIATED PLACES

Welcome to Flintstones-Land

Contesting Place and Identity in Goreme, Central Turkey

Hazel Tucker

In Goreme village at the heart of the Cappadocia region in Central Turkey, a group of five local men were planning to open a new office called 'Bedrock Travel Agency'. When asked why they would give this name to the new business, one of the men answered 'Why not, Goreme *is* Bedrock, isn't it!'.[1] Many other tourism businesses in the village also follow this theme; there is the Flintstones Cave Bar, Flintstones Motel-*Pansiyon*,[2] Rock Valley *Pansiyon*, and so on. The businesses and their professionally crafted sign boards displaying these names incite a particular view of Goreme among tourists. As one English man expressed it: 'With all the Flintstones stuff, like Bedrock this and fairy-tour that, it takes out the spirit of it being a real place. It's more artificial – it's a Cappadocia theme park'.

Of course, Goreme is not a theme park, a fantasy-land created commercially for tourists' entertainment and recreation. It is really quite real, even in the sense conveyed by MacCannell (1976, 1992), Urry (1990), and Munt (1994), when they discuss the 'real' type of tourist who seeks to travel to natural as opposed to contrived places in order to experience what they perceive as the authentic. The volcanic landscape of Cappadocia with its giant rock cones which local people call 'fairy-chimneys', has been eroding and reforming for millions of years. The soft rock has been dug out for habitation for centuries, and 'even today', to use a tourism advertisement's words, 'many of these caves and grottoes serve as homes and store houses for peasant families. Whole villages of cave dwellers still exist'.[3] Goreme, in this view, is represented as a 'real' place and is importantly perceived as such by many of the tourists who go there.[4] The question arises then as to what happens when tourists who came to Goreme following touristic images of a real cave village find themselves in a place they perceive to be more like an artificial Cappadocia theme park.

Another question that we may ask concerns the villagers who are carrying out these Flintstones performances. A growing interest within the anthropological literature concerns the ways in which local people react to, negotiate and resist the 'tourist gaze' (see for example many of the articles in Boissevain [ed.], 1996).[5] This gaze, to use Urry's (1990) term, inevitably includes touristic representations in travel imagery and promotional literature as well as the actual looking of the tourists themselves. An example is found in Abram's (1996) discussion of the people of Cantal's wish to shake off the 'shame of peasantry' imposed on them by the rest of France; they do so by representing themselves as traditional in an old-fashioned and wholesome sense rather than a backward and ignorant one. The question which arises here in relation to Goreme is why it is that those villagers mentioned above, who perform a Flintstones theme of the village for tourists, are apparently conceding to a representation of themselves as comic, and possibly ignorant, cave-dwellers. In this chapter I show how it is that rather than conceding to this image of themselves, the villagers may in fact be resisting it through their Flintstones performances.

Tourist and tourism-related discourses generally convey an idea that there are two broadly opposing types of tourism and tourist places: the vulgar, fun-loving type taking place in contrived sites; and the real, authenticity-seeking type occurring in real and natural settings (Urry 1990; Cohen 1995; Munt 1994; see also Selwyn 1994, 1996). It is further assumed that today there is a general 'shift from the natural and authentic to the artificial and contrived' tourist attractions and places, and together with this, 'related changes in tastes and preferences of tourists' (Cohen 1995: 12). Dichotomies, or at best continuums, are constructed between such concepts as travellers and tourists, romantic and crass, authentic and contrived, real and fake.

In reality (if I may use that word), where ideas of place, otherness and ourselves are influenced through tourism in highly complex ways, such dichotomies and continuums might not hold. By looking closely at the tourist site of Goreme and considering the questions suggested above regarding the performance of a Flintstones-land, I will demonstrate how it is that the continuum between authenticity and the contrived might collapse, so that its two extremes are merged in identities and place. I will do so by looking at the processes whereby the lives and identities of the local people involved in tourism have become reconstructed and somehow re-'contrived', and also by placing these processes in the context of what might be described as a 'postmodern' ethos working within contemporary tourism.[6] In other words, this chapter is an attempt to understand what is taking place when a local Fred Flintstone tells me that Goreme *is* Bedrock! First though, in order to relate this particular performance to its context, I will begin by taking a look at some of the wider processes of place and identity construction which occur through tourism in the region.[7]

The Politics of Representation and Tourism in Goreme

The area in and around Goreme village consists of soft volcanic rock, which has gradually eroded to form natural cones and columns. For centuries these 'fairy chimneys' have been carved and hollowed to form dwellings, stables and places of worship which pattern the 'troglodyte' village of today. Tourism, which has grown rapidly in the region since the mid-1980s, has led to an aesthetic valuing of these rock cones and dwellings, serving to promote their preservation along with the 'real lives' of the 'troglodytes' who inhabit them. This theme of preservation forms a seam which runs right through tourism discourse concerning the Goreme region. Examples of this include the setting up of a 'Save Goreme Committee' by a non-Turk who has managed a *pansiyon* in the village for many years, and a section in the recently updated version of the *Lonely Planet* guidebook entitled 'A Future for Goreme'. Such sections are not a usual feature in the *Lonely Planet* series, but the writer, in this case an English woman, had spoken to the instigator of the 'Save Goreme Committee' and felt keen to promote awareness among the visiting backpackers of the cause of Goreme's preservation.

The aesthetic valuing of the rock structures and cave-dwellings is manifested perhaps more concretely in the workings of the Goreme National Park and a regional Preservations Committee under the national Ministry of Culture, both set up in the 1980s with the broad aim of preserving and restoring the historical and cultural heritage of the area. Although the 'living' village, the inhabitants of which today are Muslim Turks, is within the boundary of the preservation area, the main foci of the region's 'heritage' are the hundreds of caved Byzantine churches in the area housing well-preserved thousand-year-old Christian frescoes. Many of these churches are encompassed within the Goreme Open Air Museum, which is situated two kilometres outside of the village. This museum is probably the most well-known and popular tourist site in the Cappadocia region, annually attracting over one million international visitors in the late 1990s,[8] and playing a prominent role in the representations of the Cappadocia region in tourism promotional literature; Cappadocia is represented for tourism as a largely Byzantine and Christian site.

However, as suggested above, another tourist attraction of the region is the contemporary living culture of the villages in the region, it is represented to tourists not only as a 'traditional' rural culture, but also as the life of a people who still live in caves. Goreme is one such village which, along with the 'fairy chimneys' and caved Byzantine remains, is considered within tourism discourses to be an asset which should be protected and preserved.[9] This view can be seen in the words of a leaflet prepared in the mid-1980s by the National Park directorate:

> The Goreme Historical National Park, shall be protected and developed, so that the present and future generation can benefit from the scientific and aesthetic nature, as well as the natural and cultural values.
>
> The picturesque village life, the activities of the villagers, the small volcanic farming areas and the farming methods and the crops. . . All these peculiarities, the tufa rocks and fairy chimneys as they are in traditional relations, are adding to a moving and vivid view. . . The preservation of this traditional view is the main theme of the administration, protection, presentation, and the development of this historical National Park. At the application of the National Park, the main policy has been adopted that the population living within the boundaries of the park should be one of the main important elements, as well as giving support to the resources.

Strict regulations have been imposed by the preservation committee prohibiting the construction of large-scale buildings in the Goreme valley, and restricting the alteration of any of the cave and rock structures in the area; the villagers must remain 'in traditional relations' with their rock houses. Though both preservation and planning are ultimately under the control of the regional committee, which has divided the village and the surrounding area into various zones with different purposes and different levels of building permission available, a limited amount of ground planning is undertaken locally by the Goreme Municipality office. In general, this local office seems to be largely unaware of a desire expressed within tourism discourse for the village to retain its cave-village character in the quaint and traditional sense, and has gradually cleaned up, modernised and 'beautified' the village centre for the tourist visitors.[10] Consequently, frequent clashes arise between the local and the regional/national level authorities with regards to the shape and future of Goreme as a 'tourist place'.[11]

Another factor which further complicates the politics of preservation and restoration surrounding Goreme village concerns the appropriation by the government of parts of the village as 'disaster zones' under the Disaster Relief Directorate. These processes occurred during the 1960s and 1970s previous to the application of Ministry of Culture interest, when many cave and 'fairy-chimney' houses, deemed too dangerous for habitation owing to severe erosion and in some cases collapse, were evacuated and their residents rehoused in government-built houses at the lower, flatter end of the village. At that time a general move towards more 'modern' and 'prestigious' housing was instigated, and that lower part of the village remains as the main 'building zone', although construction there must also be granted permission by the relevant authorities. When tourism really got under way during the late 1980s, however, many of these rehoused villagers began to reclaim and restore their old homes for the purpose of making *pansiyon* businesses. Although all evacuated houses officially belong to the state treasury, this kind of activity has largely been tolerated because it has meant that such old properties are restored and maintained. This tolerance, along with the recent removal by the Department of Infrastructure of the 'disaster zones', is indicative of an increasingly powerful interest in the preservation of the old village.

The move of the villagers to restore and make tourist accommodation from their previously abandoned cave homes is indicative itself of an increasing awareness among the villagers of the aesthetic and economic value of their cave houses and 'cave-life'. It is generally cheaper and easier to build and move into the new area at the lower end of the village because of the lengthy and difficult process of obtaining permission from the Preservations Committee to make any alteration to houses in the old sector of the village. However, the old sector is gradually being given a new lease of life with more and more properties being bought and sold for residential as well as business/tourism purposes. A trend is occurring whereby those villagers who have by now made some financial capital from tourism, and also foreigners or long-term tourists who seek a romantic retreat in Goreme,[12] are restoring and moving into the old cave houses.

Not all of the residents of this area maintain the same aesthetic evaluation of the old cave houses, however, and many villagers complain that these parts of the village are neglected in terms of 'modernisation', such as road surfacing. Along with villagers' general complaints, this point was illustrated to me during my fieldwork when I painted scenes of the old houses in the 'back' streets of the village. When I sometimes left out certain aspects of the scene, such as loudspeakers and pylons, which I viewed as unattractive blips on the otherwise romantic landscape, women friends and children who surrounded me would always point out the omitted parts, wanting me to fill them in. Such features of the landscape which indicated 'modernity' were shown here to hold quite a different aesthetic value for the villagers compared with myself.

Furthermore, villagers often feel restricted with regard to what they can and cannot do to their own houses (similar processes occurring in rural Greece are recorded by Williams and Papamichael 1995). When I commented on the darkness of a young woman's cave kitchen, for example, she said, 'Yes, but we are forbidden to make new windows or shelves or anything in the rock. Before it wasn't forbidden, but when tourists came here it became forbidden'. Another villager told me: 'In some ways we are lucky because tourism has brought work and money, but there are also many forbidden things, and expensive things. We can't do anything – we need permission for everything. Even on little alterations to our houses we must use the right stone and so on, and we can't build new caves for the animals'. Indeed, many villagers have been brought in front of the law as a consequence of alterations undertaken on their rock houses, many of which were carried out to convert the houses into tourist *pansiyons*. Together with the actual appropriation of the rock structures by the government, this building and alteration legislation manifests itself among villagers as a sense of a lack of choice and control over the homes that they live and work in, and a recognition that the loss began, as the young woman quoted above said, 'when tourists came'. These complexities in the preservation rhetoric surrounding Goreme convey the tensions created by the conflicting sets of values regarding Goreme local identity and place.

However, one of the nationally imposed laws which seems to have worked more in the favour of local villagers, albeit indirectly, is that which restricts the construction of large buildings in the Goreme area. A notable consequence of this legislation is that outside business interests in the form of large hotels are kept, on the whole, *outside* the National Park boundary. Tourism business in the village has therefore tended to develop on a smaller, locally owned scale. Since the mid-1980s, many of the villagers have become entrepreneurs and the owners or part-owners of *pansiyons*, restaurants, tour agencies or carpet shops, and today almost all of the villagers in Goreme reap direct financial benefit from tourism.[13] Moreover, the village men who run these small businesses can consequently enjoy a significant amount of control over their relations with their largely 'backpacker' customers. The politics and legality of representation can be said to have worked at least partly on the side of the local villagers, a significant point, as we shall see, in view of the apparent paradoxes inherent in the Flintstones performances; it is because of this direct involvement in and control of the tourism business and relations with tourists that these performances are in fact less paradoxical than they appear at first glance.

Relations with Tourists and Negotiating Identities

The processes of tourism development in the village have led to the social and physical division of the village into two spheres (Tucker 1997). As mentioned above, the village has been zoned for ground planning and preservation purposes, and it is the central area of the village which is the designated *'turizm'* zone, and on which the municipality office concentrates in terms of the development of tourism facilities and tourism appearance (for example, surfacing the roads, planting trees, installing street lamps and so on). The back residential streets, which radiate out from and wind upwards away from the centre, remain less 'modernised', and this is also the area where villagers who do not work directly in tourism, such as women and the elderly, continue with their agricultural work and the general running of the household. Consequently, except for the enclaves of tourism to be found in the cave-house *pansiyons* which are now dotted throughout these old streets, this back area has come to represent something akin to a living museum for tourists, where local people may be gazed upon, encountered and photographed as they live out their daily lives among the caves.

Many tourists go to Goreme with expectations of experiencing something of the 'real' pre-modern lives of the contemporary cave-people of Goreme, in order, as a Canadian tourist expressed it, to 'experience the simpler, pure life that we've lost'.[14] Such tourism is said to be about seeking authenticity in other times and other places in order to somehow restructure the fragmentation of contemporary life (see, for example, MacCannell 1976; Sack 1992), and such tourists are chasing the myth of the 'authentically social' – to use Selwyn's (1996: 21) words, a myth which characterises the 'other' in the following way:

> The character of this other derives from belonging to an imagined world which is variously premodern, precommoditized or part of a benign whole recaptured in the mind of a tourist. This is a world which is eminently and authentically social. Thus what makes a tourist destination attractive is that it is thought to have a special 'spirit of place', which derives from the sociability of its residents. Or, to put it another way, in successful tourist destinations the natives are friendly.

These ideas could not be more closely echoed than they are in the words of a middle-aged lawyer from the US, who has been visiting Goreme repeatedly over a number of years. He said:

> I feel really at home here, there's something magical about this place. Part of it is the incredible way that this community deals with the indoor and the outdoor. There's such a natural relation with the environment . . . and I don't just mean because it's in a cave, but there's a kind of easy communion between the indoor and the outdoor in the way that the people live, and the way the architecture is done and so on. And I found the people to be incredibly friendly the first time I came here.

Although the extent of this quest for the 'authentically social' is likely to vary greatly among tourists, such idealisations concerning the Goreme people and place are repeatedly expressed by many of the tourists in the village. Such expressions convey the idea, which is also expounded in much of the tourist literature concerning this region, that the villagers are living a premodern life which is uncorrupted by the many vices that modernity has inflicted on 'us' in the contemporary Western world. Tourists often wander through the back parts of the village, in particular, looking for experiences of and interactions with these others, hoping perhaps that some of the 'authentically social' will rub off on them. Whilst wandering around in the back streets, tourists may be invited to sit and chat with villagers, or to help in activities such as gathering fruit or nuts off the trees. They may even be invited in to 'come and look inside a real cave house'. Whilst such encounters are unlikely to move beyond the imaginations that each party has of each other, they are taken as 'real' encounters and contribute to the richness of the tourists' travel experience, even if only because they constitute good stories for fellow travellers and friends at home. Meanwhile the villagers adopt a self-image which is mirrored back to them from the tourists, developing an understanding that they are 'interesting for tourists' precisely because they live in caves.

Down in the central and tourist areas of Goreme, the kinds of interactions that tourists and villagers have are quite different from those described above. Here, tourists do not so actively seek the 'real' cave-people, since they generally view tourism practice as counteracting, and even destroying, the 'authentically social'. In the tourist arena, therefore, the tourists are 'serviced' and 'entertained' in a way that provides for their more practical needs in the forms of food and accommodation, transportation and information, and in a way that suits their general quest for fun and companionship with other like-minded 'travellers'. Nonetheless, this arena should ideally be consistent with the touristic representations of the particular locality, and so it is that many of the tourist *pansiyons* are set in restored village cave-homes, providing the chance for tourists to sleep in their 'very own cave'.

As these *pansiyons* and the other tourist services are mostly owned and run by the Goreme villagers themselves, these villagers have learnt over the past ten or fifteen years, during the main growth period of Goreme's tourism, that tourists *like* sleeping in the caves. An accommodation office which *pansiyon* owners have collectively set up in the village bus station is full of images advertising the cave-rooms in which tourists can choose to sleep. Indeed, both the villager entrepreneurs and the villagers in general, who are more than able to observe the 'performances' of tourists staying in their village, can see the enjoyment had by the tourists, not only in the fact that they are *in* a cave village, but also in imagining that they too, for a while at least, are cave-people themselves. To some extent then, interactions between tourists and villagers take place within a context of play.

The idea of the playful tourist has been developed in particular by Dann (1989) in his assertions that tourists can be childlike. This idea links with the concept of *liminality* in tourist experience (see MacCannell 1976, Graburn 1983,1989), the process in ritual where the usual order of things is removed and rules reversed.[15] Furthermore, the process of *liminality* draws closer the supposedly contrasting tourist experiences and practices which are on the one hand playful and fun, and on the other more serious and pilgrimage-like (see Graburn 1983). These concepts, however, have so far only really been discussed in the tourism context in as much as they relate to the experiences and practices of tourists. The temporary nature of the tourist's stay means that the tourist experience of a place and its people has a certain 'virtuality' about it, never achieving a sense of reaching the 'core' of the place.[16] Tourists are therefore forever on the edge, in a sort of liminal zone, and so that is where tourism workers must come to meet them.

What has been neglected, then, in discussions of *liminality* in tourism, is the sense in which local people who 'host' the tourists might also experience some sort of suspension of 'normal' life, free to some extent from the usual rules, and able to join in with the 'play' of tourism. Whilst the *pansiyons*, restaurants and tour agencies are places of work for the Goreme men,[17] they are also contexts in which the men are relatively free from the village way of life and village rules. This idea was expressed in an interview with a village entrepreneur when asked how he felt when in his pansiyon:

> It's like a free zone – I can't walk in shorts on the street but I can here. So I must be careful to change when I go back into Goreme. I can't walk with a girlfriend through Goreme holding hands . . . so I'm happier here – I feel more free.

This sense of being apart from the village life whilst in the tourist 'enclaves' is perhaps confounded by the point that, during the summer tourist season at least, the men are working more or less twenty-four hours everyday. Many of the men who work in the tourist arena pointed this out as a significant feature in their experiences of being employed in tourism. During the summer, they may rarely go home – even if their home is only some metres away from their business, and they become neglectful of village events such as weddings and funerals. So, although the tourist 'hubs' such as *pansiyons* are within the village, they become places where the men who work in them may feel that they are outside of village life for a while, and consequently that they are free, in their interactions with tourists, to play and experiment with their own identities. They are therefore able to join in together with the tourists in the fun and fantasy of the tourist experience, and in Goreme this includes the playful performance of being troglodytes in a cave-land fantasy.

One local entrepreneur told me the following about how this play resulted in his use of a Fred Flintstones characterisation:

A few years ago in this pansiyon, there were four Aussie girls sleeping in the cave in the fairy-chimney – I was born in there – and I had to give them an early morning call and, just for a joke, I shouted, 'Wilma wake up!', and they said 'We're coming Fred!' . . . and so they gave me that nickname, of Fred. And they sent other tourists here later, telling them to go to Fred's place . . . It began like that – and they liked it – and they sent me socks of Fred Flintstones, alarm clock of Fred . . . and then I decided to call the bar Flintstones Bar. It's a really good name, because it's in the rocks, a real cave, like the Flintstones, it's the Flintstones bar – the Flintstones movie – it's so famous in the world . . . but it's fun – of course – people come here and I invite them to come for a drink in the cave bar – and they say this is fantastic – who did this? And I say I did that.

Goreme has consequently become a fantasy land of caves and troglodytes, a sort of Disneyesque Flintstones World where tourists can stay in a cave room in somewhere like 'Flintstones', 'Peri (Fairy)' or 'Rock Valley' Pansiyon. There are tours of the area entitled 'Mystic Tour', 'Fairy Tour', and 'Dream Tour', which can be chosen from cartoonified regional maps and booked in the offices of the 'Stone Park Travel Agency', 'Magic Valley Tours', or soon to be 'Bedrock Travel Agency'. At night, there is the 'Flintstones Cave Bar' or 'The Escape Cave Bar and Disco', 'set in gigantic medieval donkey stables' where you can watch a 'traditional Turkish belly dance act', 'dance to the latest in dance music', 'join in traditional Turkish folk dance', and enter a 'beer drinking competition'. 'Every night is an experience in real Turkish culture and great fun', in a get together with some of the local troglodytes, who might tell you about how they were born and brought up in a cave, how the fairy-chimneys come alive at night, and how you should call them Fred.

One particular Fred these days introduces himself to newly arrived tourists as a local cave-man. He points to a cave and tells tourists that he was really born in a cave right here. He also calls his dog 'Dino', and he collects Flintstones paraphernalia to decorate the office of his *pansiyon*. Fred was indeed born in a cave-room of the house which has now been converted into the *pansiyon*. However, he might be viewed today as a caveman in something of a *post*modern sense rather than the premodern sense that seems at first to be conjured up in some aspects of tourism discourse and the tourist literature concerning Goreme. For Fred is a lot more cosmopolitan than tourists might at first imagine, since he has lived a large portion of his life in Holland, where his parents had migrated, and from there drove trucks up and down the length of Europe from Scandinavia to the Middle East. After several years of this work, Fred returned to his home village and converted his family property, complete with fairy-chimney, caves and stone-built rooms, into a *pansiyon*. This business developed along with many similar tourism businesses in the village during the late 1980s, and expanded to include a large cave bar which is named 'Flintstones Bar'.

In the cave bar, Fred always has a lot of stories to tell to visiting tourists. He tells of the way some tourists who have stayed there in the past behaved rudely and arrogantly towards him, thinking that he would not understand because he would not be able to speak German or Dutch. 'People think I'm stupid because I was born in a cave!', he says, 'they don't believe I know anything about Europe, about where they come from, but I do, I know very well'. In one incident, Fred was proud that he had been able to tell one such tourist exactly how to drive to his address in Denmark and, refusing the beer that he had won in the bet, told the tourist, 'Look, don't put us down, you must never put people down. You must never think of yourself as above others'. Fred's stories usually have this same theme; that of how he emerged as righteous and not 'premodern' at all, by successfully contesting attempts, be they by customs officers, immigration police, or European tourists, to put him down for being a Turk, and what is more, a Turk born in a cave.

The important point here is that the use of Flintstones imagery in his performances for tourists also has a place in Fred's assertions of a 'contemporary' and 'with it' identity. In the first place, the link with the famous American comedy cartoon is in itself an indication that Goreme village is not so premodern as to not be linked up with the global network of terrestrial and even satellite TV. Further to this, though, it is the actual way that the imagery is manifested in the per-formances by the villagers, and the way it is negotiated together *with* the tourists, that becomes significant here. The Flintstones imagery is generated largely through an idiom of irony which arises in the inter-actions between the tourists and the villagers who 'host' them. It is this sense of irony which enables the men, through their perform-ances, to both play to and at the same time resist the 'premodern' caveman representations of themselves in tourist discourse.

Men like Fred are aware of the role that the 'cave' identity plays in Goreme's tourism business, and for this reason they accept and con-tinuously perform this identity to the tourists. By doing so, they are playing directly to touristic representations of themselves and also bringing themselves into the foreground of the tourist experience. However, the villagers are well aware of the derogatory connotations which might accompany the identity of being 'Cavemen from Cappadocia' and, not being prepared to accept an identity which merges with a sense of unmoving tradition and backwardness, they choose to present themselves and Goreme as a sort of comic fiction. It is through a sense of fun and irony in their interactions with tourists that the men are able to renegotiate and divert some of the representations placed upon them by tourism discourse and the complex multiplicity of authorities and tourism bodies who assert a need to preserve that 'cavey' identity. Indeed, in some parts of the village the 'real' cave-life does remain 'preserved', and there tourists may wander and have their more serious experiences with the 'authentically social'. In the tourist realm, too, the villagers are retaining their 'cavey' identity. Here though, they are doing so together with the tourists (the same tourists who may at times be more serious) in an ironic twist through which they are able to bring the ascribed premodern identity into the realm of the (post)modern.

Experiencing the Hypo-reality of Goreme

For the tourists, the Flintstones characterisation in Goreme is experienced in a variety of ways. The four Australian girls mentioned by Fred in the quote above clearly enjoyed staying in a cave-room and playing the 'Flintstones game', whilst some others may feel that the Flintstones characterisation is so obviously contrived for tourism that it, to their annoyance, blurs their experience of being in a 'natural' cave place. However, whilst the discourse of preservation of 'tradition' is very much at work in Goreme, the performances of the villagers themselves, in their interactions with tourists, become increasingly multifaceted regarding their presentation of a 'traditional' identity. What is more, the desires and experiences of the tourists simultaneously come to match this multifaceted presentation by becoming more ambivalent concerning the 'traditional' in the village. Goreme village, both in its dividing into two different spheres and in the performances of the Flintstones characterisation played out, appeals to the ludic tendencies which tourists have alongside their desires to experience the village as a real 'cavey' place. As the village and the villagers change to become increasingly touristified, so tourists seem to be prepared to accept that touristification, as long as they are having fun and as long as they get a sense that the performances are embedded at least partly in the 'real'. An example of this process can be seen from this short anecdote told to me in conversation about the Flintstones theme with a local entrepreneur:

> I was talking to some tourists who I met on the street in the centre, and I said, 'Let's go to the Flintstones Bar', and they said, 'Oh no, it's too modern'. I said, 'Have you been there yet?' – They thought the name was too modern, too artificial, but they hadn't been there. But when they went to the place, they had a different idea, because . . . it is in a cave! (he laughed), and very natural!

This point highlights a problem existing with discussions about tourism that convey the idea that there are two opposing ideal types of touristic places and touristic experiences that can be characterised by such concepts as natural and contrived, real and fake. Such discussions generally assert the view that places, together with touristic experiences of those places, can only be one thing or the other. However, it seems from close analysis of touristic processes in Goreme that, not only are the two combined, thereby appealing to various touristic tendencies at the same time, but that the experiences of 'real' and 'fake' may even be collapsed into one. Indeed, it has been widely noted in recent academic discussions on tourism that the contemporary touristic experience is characterised by a suspension of 'the saliency of the boundaries between . . . fact and fiction, reality, reconstruction and fantasy' (Cohen 1995: 20).

This point, however, is most often discussed in reference to the proliferation of contrived or simulated tourist sites such as theme parks, and the touristic perception, highlighted by Eco (1987), of the fake as more real than the real. Goreme, on the other hand, is a natural place and has a 'traditional culture', and is importantly perceived as such by the tourists. Yet, because of the 'fantastic' landscape together with the Flintstones characterisations played out in the touristic centre, the village can be imagined and experienced, alongside the real and traditional, as somehow artificial. The landscape of Cappadocia is naturally formed and yet is perceived by tourists as being so weird that it is often described as 'Disneyesque'. It is like a 'huge adventure playground', tourists say, a sort of 'moon world', 'like a different planet', 'it's unique, visually stunning, weird, the most abstract place I've ever been to'. As one tourist said as she stood looking at the rock shapes pitted with steps and doorways carved through centuries of real lives, 'I'm having a hard time believing this is real. I guess I've been influenced too much by Disney World where they make things like this out of poured concrete'. The suspension here of the boundaries between the modes of experience marked by reality and fantasy are striking.

A further example concerns a young American tourist I spoke to in Goreme. He viewed his travel as an escape from the rat-race back home and his 'unethical' job as a maker of videos and computer games, but found himself feeling keen to return to the US so that he could set about making a computer game of Cappadocia. The game would feature moonscape valleys and underground networks of caves and tunnels, and the player would enact an early group of Christians fighting off the attacking Hittite or Persian armies. This man's ideas are indicative of a developing global culture of tourism which accepts anything or any place being produced and reproduced, moved and recontextualised in any place whatsoever. Usually regarded as postmodern, this process marks the proliferation and increased consumption of experiences generally characterised by 'stylistic eclecticism, sign-play, . . . depthless-ness, pastiche, simulation, hyperreality, immediacy, a melange of fiction and strange values . . . [and] the loss of a sense of the reality of history and tradition' (Featherstone 1995: 76). From an analysis of touristic experience in Goreme, it seems as though such experiences might be at their most intense in the tourism context.

In an age of simulation and a world where one moves freely and easily between the real and contrived, there is instilled an absolute belief that the real thing is capable of being reproduced. Therefore, 'the "completely real" becomes identified with the "completely fake"' (Eco 1987: 7), and the ability to distinguish between the two is lost. Theme parks, then, are not only created worlds of fantasy, but places of hyperreality where 'absolute unreality is offered as real presence' (ibid.). Here, latex crocodiles in the Amazon jungle are more lively than the real thing, for example, and two-dimensional pictures can come to life. The point for Eco is that the simulation seems more real than the (really) real.

My point concerning Goreme, however, is that if simulations are experienced within the postmodern ethos to be more real than the real, then what we have left is the real appearing to be more fake than the fake. Some tourism then, may become travel in hypo-reality (or hyper-fakality), and that, I suggest, is what is happening in Goreme when tourists have trouble deciding whether it is a 'real' place that they are in or a Disney World created out of poured concrete. Furthermore, this also seems to be the spirit in which the English tourist quoted in the opening paragraph of this chapter shared the following, and here I quote a fuller version of his words:

> It's pretty cheesy, you can't take it seriously. I said when I came here a few years ago that it was like a film-set, but now it's more like a theme-park – but it's really nice at the same time – but it's really unreal – with the fairy-chimneys like they were made out of polystyrene – they're mad formations that you wouldn't think could be formed – and with all the Flintstones stuff, like Bedrock this, and fairy-tour that, it takes out the spirit of it being a real place – it's more artificial – it's a Cappadocia theme-park.

This experiencing of a sort of *hypo*-reality in Goreme does not necessarily interfere with tourists' enjoyment of the place. Though tourists may have come to the village initially with a desire to experi-ence the 'traditional' in a more 'natural' sense, and whilst a few tourists do experience tension in the juxtaposition of new and old, real and contrived, most seem to be able to suspend the importance of such serious matters quite easily as long as they are having fun. This fun is often coupled with a sense of irony on the part of the tourists, an irony which concerns their useless attempts at 'off-the-beaten-track' travel, and their obviously fruitless search for 'authentic experiences' in a place that is obviously not authentic at all.

This is where, in Goreme, we may see the collapsing of the supposed dichotomies between real tourism and contrived tourism, and between the 'real' type and the 'fun' type of tourist. The place itself can be experienced in both the extremes of real and fake, authentic and contrived at the very same time. The tourists are willing and able to indulge plentifully in authentic experiences with 'other' peoples, and at the same time to play with Disneyesque experiences of fantasy and fun. There is no longer an either/or situation, but one where the poles of the postmodern continuums are inextricably mixed. To only talk about simulations and how they are more real than the real is to miss an important point in the actual processes of tourism taking place, for simulations *are* only simulations. For real places on the other hand, to be experienced as fictional and fake, is to bring the experience of real and fake into one.

Conclusion

Whilst Goreme village is represented in tourism discourses as a 'traditional' village of cave-dwelling peasants which might be gazed upon and preserved under a shroud of 'authenticity', in the tourist arena within the village, tourism services display names and imagery which engage tourists in a sense of fun and irony by presenting Goreme as a Flintstones fantasy-land. It is precisely through this sense of irony that the Flintstones characterisation played out in touristic performances simultaneously feeds and diverts certain touristic representations of the Goreme people and place. So, although the Flintstones characterisation works to convey the 'other' identity which is expected from tourists, it also, I have suggested here, goes some way in defying the complex multiplicity of authorities that have a hand in managing tourism in the area. The local men are reinventing, and even recontriving, their 'cavey' identity, and in doing so, are resisting something of the 'traditional' and 'backward' identities placed upon them, and thereby some of the limitations and frustrations they face under the weight of the hegemonic discourses concerning the value and preservation of *their* place and life.

Moreover, this characterisation reforms a sense of equality in the men's actual interactions with the tourists they meet, as it openly acknowledges an awareness of representations of themselves and Goreme, and brings them together in a sort of communitas of irony *with* tourists. Simultaneously, this play on the Goreme cave-life works within a postmodern ethos to meet the tourist's desire to be in a place which is both real and yet fantastic at the same time, and to encounter people who are both 'authentically other' yet also fun and fictional. It seems that even the serious authenticity-seeking tourists can also enjoy some fun, and this fun is plentiful in the fantasy of being troglodytes in a Flintstones-land which the tourists can play out together with their 'hosts' in the liminal zone of Goreme's touristic sphere.

As a last point, this analysis of tourism in Goreme has been, in many ways, a viewing of the interface between global and local processes in the contemporary world. It might be pertinent to consider here, though, the point that the tourist's liminal experience of fun in this Disneyesque fairy-chimney land is only temporary; the tourist can enjoy moving in and out of, as well as playing with, the realms of the real and fictional, because in the end the tourist always goes home. For the local villagers on the other hand, this fantasy land *is* home, and so if Goreme is becoming Bedrock, then where is their reality?

Notes

1. 'Bedrock' is the name of the rock-cut town in which the 'The Flintstones' live. These American comedy cartoon characters anachronistically live out a 1950s American life-style in rock houses and in 'cave-man' style. The central characters are Fred Flintstone, who is a nice but rather gormless guy, and his wife Wilma. They have a pet dinosaur named Dino.

2. 'Pansiyon' is the local term for a small-scale tourist accommodation unit. Most of the pansiyons are converted from villagers' homes, and many of them are 'cave-homes' since, in the main period of tourism development in the village during the late 1980s, villagers began to understand that tourists enjoyed the experience of 'staying in a cave'.

3. This is quoted from a tourism promotion video entitled 'Adventures in Turkey', produced by *Explore Worldwide Ltd,* 1989.

4. The tourists' search for an authentic cave village in Goreme is discussed in Tucker, 1997.

5. Here I follow Odermatt (1996) in his use of Urry's (1990) concept of the tourist gaze to refer to representations and presentations of local peoples, environments and their pasts for tourism.

6. The 'postmodern' touristic ethos refers to the apparent trend characterised by a particularly kaleidoscopic and hedonistic tourist experience, uncompromising consumption, and the 'nivellation' of tourist attractions (see, for example, Baudrillard 1983; Cohen 1995; Feifer 1985; Pretes 1995; Urry 1990).

7. This work is based on ethnographic research carried out in Goreme village between 1995 and 1998.

8. This figure was taken from the statistics gathered from ticket sales by the museum.

9. Here I am referring to discourses generated by the travel and tourism literature concerning Cappadocia, the Ministry of Culture and National Parks directorates, and tourists themselves.

10. As I go on to point out, this lack of awareness by the Goreme Municipality Office is somewhat out of step with many of the villagers who, having more direct contact with tourists through their privately owned businesses, *are* aware of the tourists' desire to experience a quaint 'cave-village'.

11. These clashes, however, should not be viewed as separate from the political dissatisfaction which may generally be felt at the local level when the management of the locale becomes increasingly drawn under regional and national auspices. This point was illustrated in the Mayor's telling me in an interview that: 'The Culture Ministry staff make decisions from their desks without even seeing Goreme. They give building permission to those who have the right "contacts" and those who give bribes. So according to me, the Culture Ministry doesn't help us at all'.

12. A similar process is described by Waldren (1996, 1997) in her discussion of 'outsiders' moving into the village of Deia in Mallorca.

13. Estimates were given to me by villagers, for instance, that approximately 90 percent of the village residents today depend financially on tourism business. For discussions of similar findings regarding the possibilities of local benefit and control in 'back-packer' tourism as they may be compared to the 'mass' tourism industry, see, for example, Hampton (1998) and Wilson (1997).

14. Here we are reminded of the Rousseaun notion of the 'noble savage', as well as the *orientalism* of Said (1978) upon which much contemporary tourism seems to hinge.

15. Following Turner's description of ritual (1973), which in turn is based on Van Gennep's earlier work of 1909 (1960).

16. It is interesting to consider here what happens if and when tourists do begin, by being invited to stay in local homes for example, to get a sense that they are becoming more deeply embedded in the 'core' of the place; tourists in this situation often express a sense of claustrophobia, and a desire to pull back out of the situation and place and to move on to a new place where they are again unknown. The tourist condition therefore is characterised by *wanting* to be on 'the edge' of places and peoples for a while, where it is possible to experience this sense of freedom and play. The visitor's and incomer's experience has been looked at in various works by Kohn (1994 and 1997).

17. I say 'men' here because it is almost entirely the men rather than women of the village who run these businesses. Because of the strict gender segregation in Goreme society (see Marcus 1992 and Stirling 1965, 1993 on gender segregation in Turkey), the women's domain is considered to be centred in and around the household, and it is inappropriate for women indigenous to Goreme to work in tourism, or to be present in the touristic realm (the centre of the village, *pansiyons*, and restaurants and so on).

Performing Place

A Hyperbolic Drugstore in Wall, South Dakota

Eve Meltzer

In the southwest region of the state of South Dakota, in the eastern part of Pennington County, at 43 degrees, 59 minutes and 63 seconds north latitude and 102 degrees, 14 minutes and 55 seconds west longitude, to be exact, waits the town of Wall (Fig. 3). The heart of Wall (and perhaps its belly, or indeed any other anatomical metaphor we could think up) is its drugstore, "Wall Drug," the only pharmacy within a 5000-square-mile area. In what follows I will pursue the case of this little cow-town with a population of about 800 residents, and its drugstore, which opened in 1931. It was then a twenty-four-by-sixty-foot structure. Today, Wall Drug has grown to a fifty-five-thousand-square-foot, 'world-famed' tourist attraction. Such fame – unexpected, hyperbolic, and curiously earned – has been realised through a play of signs, space, places and absences.

Today this pharmacy-turned-tourist sight[1] occupies almost the entirety of one block of Main Street, which is only a few blocks long. While it makes its claim to fame in the phrase 'The Largest Drug Store in the World', Wall Drug looks more like a giant souvenir store. Inside one finds a maze of shining pine hallways covered in memorabilia and connecting the dozens of smaller shops within: a rock shop, a pharmacy museum, a homemade fudge store, a bull and harness shop, an art gallery, a chapel that seats 60 and a boot store that stocks 6000 pairs of cowboy boots, to name only a few. There are innumerable momentoes, beginning with the more classically kitschy: pens with kinetic jackalope that float back and forth across the Great Plains landscape when tilted; transparent spheres filled with liquid, depicting Wall's 80-foot plaster dinosaur in a snow storm, as well as collectable spoons, patches, and thimbles from every state. There is the outlandish and sight-specific: 'Roadkill Helper' (a novel spin-off of the well-known 'Hamburger Helper') and corrugated 'Macho Toilet Tissue'

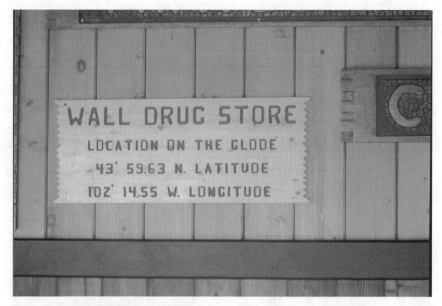

Figure 3 Wall Drug Store sign.

labelled with the trademark phrase, 'As Rugged as the Men that Use it.' For bigger spenders, Wall Drug has a 2.5 million-dollar Western art collection, part of which it sells as prints, postcards and originals for 90 cents to 9,000 dollars.

Still, this drugstore insists, there is more: a bricolage of Western themes, homestead historicity, the chronicles of the long-time proprietor Hustead family; buffalo burgers, homemade ice cream, cheap coffee, and fresh hot doughnuts; horse twitches and saddles; family photographs, historical and genealogical documents; a stuffed horse and a 6-foot rabbit, both of which are there for you to be photographed on or alongside. Hundreds of newspaper and magazine articles featuring the drugstore are displayed next to images of Geronimo and Annie Oakley and just down the hall from a rare collection of 14,000 turn-of-the-century photographs of western South Dakota, Montana, and Wyoming.

I spent one week here; my lasting impression is one of simultaneity and too muchness – too much to read, decipher, gloss over; a week was insufficient. Walking through this store, one has the experience of sudden intoxication. Its immediacy assaults the senses with everything up-front and visible, on display for you. It demands your interpretation. Tourists are, after all, as Jonathan Culler (1981: 127) writes, 'the unsung armies of semiotic[ian]s', interested in everything as a sign, engaged in semiotic projects, reading places, spaces, and landscapes as sign systems.[2]

However, most walk away after an hour, dismissing Wall Drug as a 'tourist trap'; but then the point will have been missed. There are hermeneutical hazards attendant to the study of places like this. Questions of taste or cultural merit often overlook more lasting questions: What does it mean and how does it signify? On our way to Wall these questions will have been our guide. I will argue that auxesis and irony – that is, amplification and double-voicing – are the master tropes of this site. Let us add to that pair the work of *paradox – para doxa, a going against our common senses*; but certainly let us keep the related *oxymoronic – the pointedly foolish* – to one side.

My curiosity with Wall Drug derives from an interest in the work of distantiation (vis-à-vis Marxist, psychoanalytic, and contemporary hermeneutical figurations) and the attendant notions of displacement, deferral and disavowal. During my visit to Wall Drug, it occurred to me that we never really get there. We are always en route and just when we think we have arrived we find ourselves faced with a profusion of semiosis that directs us back outward, somewhere else, looking back from afar upon this place. First we must surmount geographical distance. Such a task Wall Drug lays before us in its unrivaled roadside sign system which advertises both regionally (Fig. 4), in Nebraska, Minnesota, Wisconsin, Iowa, the Dakotas, Wyoming, and Montana, and in far-away, unlikely locations such as Pakistan (Fig. 5), Korea, Saudi Arabia, and Germany, among others.

Without ever having stepped foot inside the drugstore wherein absolute presence and utter materiality dominate, we are made aware that semiosis is the language of this sight. Wall Drug has been made famous by its roadside signs, of which it apparently just can not get enough. Since Dorothy Hustead came up with the idea to advertise free ice-water on a hot, summer day in 1936, hundreds of thousands of signs have been erected roadside, including the best-known ones on Interstate 90 running from Wyoming to Wisconsin (on one 45-mile stretch of highway, I counted 53), and abroad: the North Pole, the Acropolis, on London buses, to name only a few (e.g. 'SHANGHAI TO WALL DRUG STORE, 9,066 MILES').

Just outside of Wall there is one sign, put there to alert the passing, would-be tourist. It reads, 'YOU ARE MISSING WALL DRUG'. A sign so apropos to Wall Drug, it seems to offer itself to be taken at its word. It directs us to look for the locus of that 'missing.' Yet we do not find it merely in the most obvious spot, just beyond or many miles from the attraction, perhaps having driven by without stopping. Surprisingly, the locus of that 'missing' shows itself equally inside Wall Drug, once we have arrived. We are, in other words, always missing Wall Drug and this, precisely, is the nature of the sight. This roadside sign alerts us that the quality of this place is most activated by the quantity of distantiated references to it. As such, I

Figure 4 Wall Drug roadside billboard, US Midwest

want to argue, Wall Drug has acquired its touristic value by dint of being absent.

Until Lady Bird Johnson's highway beautification programme eliminated many roadside signs, there were 28,000 Wall Drug signs in South Dakota alone. In the early days, anyone could post a sign anywhere, and so Ted Hustead did, all across Wisconsin and over the Big Horn Mountains. Today, the Husteads have lost track of the number of signs that advertise Wall Drug apart from the 300 plus posted on private properties, signs for which they must now pay rent.

In the westbound drive from Sioux Falls, South Dakota, one can see just under 100 signs in the 220-some miles to Wall. There are signs that advertise free or cheap stuff (e.g. 'FREE MUSEUM – WALL DRUG', 'FREE ICE WATER – WALL DRUG', 'COFFEE 5 CENTS – WALL DRUG'),those that call attention to those things the Husteads claim as

Figure 5 Wall Drug roadside billboard, Pakistan

the sight's attractions (e.g. 'ORIGINAL WESTERN OIL PAINTINGS –
WALL DRUG', '6 FOOT RABBIT – WALL DRUG', 'TRAVELER'S CHAPEL
– WALL DRUG') signs that lure by troping or with a rhyme (e.g. 'WHO
HAS THE GALL TO BYPASS WALL', 'WALLCOME – WALL DRUG,'
'HAVE YOU DUG WALL DRUG?'), and those that inform us how
many more miles we have left to drive. Both along the road and at the
site there are also signs that are built upon a particular sort of fame
which affords a glorious, if illusory, gratification (e.g. 'WALL DRUG –
AS TOLD BY NATIONAL GEOGRAPHIC', 'FEATURED ON TODAY
SHOW – WALL DRUG'). Here, fame performs subjective relocation,
another mode of absence, which effects the circulation of oneself via
one's name in the realm of others' minds and speech. The outside
recognition of those who come to know, visit, and spread the word
about Wall Drug, serves to extend and aggrandise the store.

In the touristic imagination, the suspense of distance this sign system installs makes Wall Drug a destination in its own right. The store
is a wonder amidst the Badlands just 534, now 447, only 198 miles
ahead. Once we have arrived, distance is reproduced through the
semiotic separation effected by the multitude of photographs, memorabilia, signs and documents on display inside the store. For example,
we might visit the Hustead Pictorial Hallway: a long, narrow, hallway-
like space which holds an exemplary collection of photographs

memorialising the Hustead family, friends, and experiences. The Hallway displays hundreds of photographs, one of which documents the taxi driver who escorted Bill and Marjorie Hustead in Kenya during their travels, another of Senator Bill Bradley and his wife standing in the Hallway; and many others of people whom the average visitor will not recognise (e.g. Karen Poppe, Head of Personnel at Wall Drug, with husband Ken on horseback). We are also invited to visit the publicity wall, an extensive collection of newspaper and magazine articles reviewing Wall Drug. In every case, the point is this: at Wall Drug one will not find the standard touristic attractions that transform a place into somewhere to go to see something worth seeing. Consider the Eiffel Tower in Paris, the Basilica of the Virgin of Guadalupe in Mexico City, or the Grand Canyon in Arizona. In each case, the main attraction is largely *there*: at the Eiffel Tower, we ascend an engineering feat; at the Grand Canyon, we gaze or descend into a natural marvel., and while at the Basilica, we hope to glimpse the *tilma* – admittedly just an index to a sixteenth century miraculous event we can no longer directly access, which indeed is only present through the mark it left on a piece of cloth and on a nation of believers. Significantly, however, the *tilma* is singular and centrally enshrined there, unlike the vast array of memorabilia back at Wall Drug. Here, the main attraction is the drugstore's unrelenting self-celebration and self-promotion wrought by a marvellous obsession with semiotic transport. We go to Wall Drug not to see one thing or another, but to participate in and perpetuate the wonderful work of aggrandisement that such semiosis performs.

Distance, therefore, has engineered the 'faming' of this small town family business, a distance hyperbolised, insofar as this sight locates itself ever-elsewhere. The store exists somewhere only over and against a distant memory, whether personal (of the Hustead family) or regional (of the Great Plains and South Dakota region) and in relation to some far-off place (Vietnam, Paris, London, etc.). Thus, this obsession with semiotic articulation and deferral also performs a location, creating a place that locates itself *anywhere but here*, anywhere but in the town of Wall at our famed, main attraction. Wall Drug can hardly be said to exist at such and such degrees, minutes and seconds north latitude and west longitude. The drugstore as a sight is precisely where we are not, always somewhere else. Our efforts to pursue its insistent precision of place are undone by that place itself, which has gone to such efforts to lay claim to that locality. In fact, we could go so far as to say that the tourist attraction is somehow *where it is not* because upon arriving we will be psychically sent away again, to another time or place. Wall Drug, in effect, upsets our notion of 'being there', of locality as presence *without distance*.

Wall Drug sets for us this challenge: to question location, the quality of geographically 'being there', as irreducibly material. To suggest that locality is excluded from construction, that the matter of place (the earth beneath our feet) is prior to the act of signification, is to say that being in situ is not about physically being on the spot. Rather, I am proposing that the site in situ may be a performance, to a great extent not about being on the spot at all, but rather, at a distance, situated vis-à-vis a somewhere else that ranges from 'just around the corner' to the other side of the globe. Ultimately, the materiality and signification of the location of Wall Drug turn out to be deeply imbricated. The materiality of place can neither be reduced to a system of signs, nor reduced to the irreducibly material grounds of a site.[3] Our trip to Wall Drug will, finally, be an attempt to negotiate the tricky terrain of such a geologically and semiotically knotted place.

The signifying displacements mobilised by the creators of Wall Drug do not, however, diminish the touristic attraction of the drugstore. In fact, displacement augments this place – the immaterial makes matter matter that much more. This notion should be familiar: it is the presence of an absent referent that makes up our well-acquainted notion of signification at work. Indeed, absence can be understood to be a necessary condition for signification. Cinematic theorist Christian Metz (1982: 57) has argued that 'in order to understand [a] film (at all), [one] must perceive the photographed object as absent, its photograph as present, and the presence of this absence as signifying'.[4] Along similar lines, yet still more profoundly, psychoanalyst Jacques Lacan (1977: 65) has gone so far as to insist that the linguistic signifier engenders the thing.[5] He writes, 'the world of words', which for our purposes we might generalise as the world of systematised signifiers, 'creates the world of things' by bestowing upon the chaos of the 'here and now' the presence and permanence of a concept.[6] For Metz and Lacan, matter only means when it has been displaced by a sign.

We must distinguish Wall Drug from the likes of Dean MacCannell's (1976: 115) midwinter zoo,[7] already well-known to semioticians and tourist scholars as a tourist attraction where visitors proceed methodically from empty birdcage to empty birdcage, nonetheless engaged with and eagerly discussing the informational markers attached to each. There, indeed, the sign (informational marker) is taken to be the thing (the would-be sight itself, the birds). Wall Drug takes this cue for meaning-making seriously by proliferating the absences found at MacCannell's zoo. At the drugstore, absence is not the exception, but the rule, for above and beyond the excesses of what is present at Wall Drug – the souvenirs, comestibles and collections – the sense of 'not being there' still retains the greatest presence of all. This cow-town drugstore's main attraction is its vast display of markers that point not to something that should be there and is momentarily absent (à la

MacCannell's birds) but something that was never intended to be present.

In Wall, moreover, absence is mobilised such that we no longer find both sight (that is to say, the attraction – the thing that we have come to see) and site (i.e. location) in one and the same place. Having gone to that place, or places, we must question in what way we have arrived: corporeally or semiotically. Not surprisingly, our predicament has begun with the very question Wall Drug's popular bumper sticker also asks: 'Where the heck is Wall Drug?'

I want to continue now by pressing the following query: why here? Why in South Dakota? Why, finally, at such and such degrees longitude and latitude? Could this sight have bubbled up anywhere? If we cannot reduce the ground of a site to its signifying markers, then what specifically about Wall, as place, makes for Wall Drug, as performance?

The Scopic Experience in Place

My visit to Wall Drug serves to unpack the *sight/site* pair, this relationship between seeing and location. Wall Drug enacts the play of these terms which are the coordinates between which the formation of every tourist attraction must occur: the becoming of a place (site) into something worthy of being seen (sight). In his account of the semiotics of tourist attractions, *The Tourist: A New Theory of the Leisure Class*, Dean MacCannell presents his paradigm of 'sight sacralisation' by which a site or object becomes reified as a sight through successive phases which stage the increasing imposition of distance between tourist and thing toured. Sacralisation begins with *naming* (the official designation of a sight), moves to *framing and elevation* (addition of the formal aspects of display), *enshrinement* (setting the thing within space/walls), *mechanical reproduction* (creation of prints, models, or effigies) and ends with *social reproduction* (the naming of groups, cities, and regions with the same name as that of the attraction; the faming of the sight).[8] Exemplary of those things Wall Drug claims as its 'attractions' are the life-size 'Chuckwagon Quartet', whose animated figures sing and play every 15 minutes, a replica of Mt Rushmore (while the real one waits just over an hour away) and a collection of silver dollars set in the counter top at the dining room cashier. However, we can hardly see the 'sight'-worthiness of those things. Contrary to its own claims, I would argue that what makes Wall Drug a sight is the very wonder that there could be something remarkable, something beyond the ordinary of this place, in this place.

In that spirit, during my stay in town, the Wall Community Center had posted a message to the passers-by on its glass-encased announcement board affixed by its front door. It read: 'HAVE AN EXTRA ORDINARY DAY' (sic) – perhaps by chance, perhaps out of ignorance, or better still, I would like to believe, to call attention to the play mobilised in the meeting of the two words, 'extra' and 'ordinary'. 'Ordinary' signifies the usual custom, the regular plan, that which is unremarkable and utterly continuous. Its prefix – 'extra' – is left not fully conjoined, just set alongside its latter half as if to remind us whence this town and the sight that has famed its proper name, whence this *remarkable beyond* has sprung: out of the ordinary, the thoroughly commonplace. Or maybe the imperative commands us to pass the day more ordinarily than usual, 'extra' ordinarily, a supplemental dose of the quotidian.

That sign made perfect sense there, where the terrain of vast prairie lands and endless skyline is punctuated only with church steeples, grain elevators and telephone wires. An essentially agricultural area, the 'ordinary' of this place historically has meant severe economic problems and proportionately fewer resources than have the East and Midwest. This is the territory where barbed wire means big business, and barbed wire is fully suggestive of the unrefined and relentless hardness of the Plains.

> They say that heaven is a free range land,
> Goodbye, goodbye, O fare you well;
> But it's barbed wire for the devil's hat band;
> And barbed wire blankets down in hell.[9]

South Dakota terrain has been tested by problems of the 'dirty' '30s. Appropriately, it is those destitute days that are memorialised by Wall Drug: in 1931 the original proprietors, Ted and Dorothy Hustead, bought the only drugstore in town, then a town of 326 people, most of whom were farmers who had been wiped out by the Depression or drought. Therefore, 1931 provides the moment in spite of which the store has made its rise to fame that, in recent, peak years, has brought in over $10 million in sales a year. Today, one-third of Wall's population work at Wall Drug and tens of thousands will visit in a single summer day. The marvel of Wall Drug for tourists, economists and locals alike, is the peculiarity of its success notwithstanding its locale.

There is an additional ironic twist to Wall Drug's situation, which shows itself when considered against other sights of its kind in regions – most often California and the American Middle West – that endeavour to attract tourists with the suggestion of an aberrant abundance of natural resources. Karal Ann Marling (1984: 66) and Paul Fussell (1980) have both discussed the ways in which these wayside places sell themselves through the dissemination of tall-tale postcard imagery: 'Bizarre hypertrophied vegetables or Brobdingnagian fruits reposing on large wagons and railway flat-cars; outsized birds and poultry, often so large as to threaten human life and the balance of nature; immense fish and rabbits large enough to be saddled and ridden'.[10] If the function of this sort of imagery (like the Iowa postcard that depicts giant cobs of corn underscored by the caption 'Iowa: Where Corn is King') is to draw tourists with the implication of an anomalous fecundity unique to a particular area by exploiting the modes of disorder and disproportion through which the gigantic operates, by hyperaggrandising that which already stands in the touristic imagination for the essence of these places (what more does the tourist expect from Iowa than corn?), then the commodity through which Wall Drug inaugurated its advertising campaign is particularly paradoxical.

On a hot Sunday afternoon in 1936, Dorothy Hustead dreamt up the idea of advertising and giving free ice-water. Ever since, Wall Drug has become 'The Ice Water Store' and is better known for its free ice-water than for any of the sundry souvenirs it sells. That free ice-water could synecdochically supplant this South Dakota drugstore, that this part-for-whole would be so successfully put into play in Wall Drug's grand and profitable advertising scheme, is quite unlike the iconic, giant corn that almost predictably has come to stand in for Iowa. In 1936, ice was in fact quite scarce. It was neither native to the area nor a natural resource for which the area would instinctively be remembered. Bill Hustead explains:

> Out in the open spaces in those days, very few people had ice. I delivered ice house-to-house all through high school; everybody had ice boxes. To get this ice, we'd take a 150 pound block of ice – we'd get hundreds of them out of the rivers and dams [during winter] – and we'd put them then in sawdust houses: they'd be stacked up two-stories high, and covered with sawdust in between [and] all around them. And then we'd start out in the spring taking them out. By the first of September they'd be down to about 75 pounds. So . . . we would wash them off with a hose and get them all nice and clean, and then saw them up in pieces that fit in a grinder, and we would hand grind them and we would have ice for drinks, and also to make ice cream with. So when you put up a sign for free ice-water, there were dang few people [who] had ice to put in the water! Most [travelers] carried their water in canvas bags that would kind of leak and the evaporation would cool the water down. But to come in with a gallon jug and be able to fill it with ice, that was quite a treat back in those days.[11]

In the early days the hyperarticulation of ice-water amplified the value of a real commodity, gratis though it always has been for the Wall Drug tourist. This articulation is quite unlike the hyperbolically ample, thoroughly native, over-grown Iowa corn. That Wall Drug could sell itself by the very thing its site did not have, distinguishes its economy of fecundity from other tourist attractions of its kind.

So to continue our query: what *is* Wall Drug? What is there to be seen? The attraction is not simply self-promotion and fame, but more precisely, such hyperbolic fame in relation to the place in which it happened with its geological, geographical, historical, and economic valences. We must uncover these valences in order to conceptualise how the drugstore has made itself matter not only so disproportionately to its utter ordinariness, but by means of such 'extra ordinariness'. The 'extra ordariness' of this sight we find in its noteworthiness against the odds, the drugstore's astounding emergence from the backdrop of the hardship of the early days, of the Plains environment and its limitations, of the insistent perpetuity of the visual landscape of the Dakotas. Through its collected concatenation of images and objects, Wall Drug memorialises a family business that 'made it' in the most overreached, overwrought sense of small-town success. Wall Drug is bigger than any drugstore in a town of 800 people ought to be. We are, moreover, presented with a tautology of colossal proportions born from an alchemical exchange that temporarily transforms water into ice, and then, into cash. Wall Drug has effected an exchange that mobilises a non-product, and turns it into a desirable, albeit ephemeral, real product. Water into ice into cash, exchanged, like straw for gold.

In this search to uncover the semiotic richness of the play between our two homonymic signifiers, we should be aware of the fact that by the 1920s, tourism had already become the number-two industry in South Dakota. After the Good Roads movement of the 1910s initiated the facilitation of travel, Yellowstone and the Black Hills began drawing the newly mobile across the prairies. In 1935 alone, 200, 000 people visited the still-unfinished Mt Rushmore, and by 1937 a state tourism publicity agency was established within the Department of Highways.[12] Brochures printed in cool colours depicted South Dakota as an oasis to its prospective tourists: 'The nights are cool and provide the proper temperature for restful and energizing sleep. . . Night covering is required, but no mosquito netting is used. The Black Hills have no mosquitoes'.[13] In 1938, only two years after Ted and Dorothy Hustead made their first efforts towards turning their near-broke pharmacy and soda shop into the emporium it is today, US highway 16 was completed, followed shortly by highway 14 – both roads leading to Wall.[14] Our main attraction therefore must be seen *in situ*: situated amongst several other 'must see' places to which South Dakota's tourist industry also gave rise: Crazy Horse Memorial (sculptor Korczak Ziolkowski's no-federal-funds vision, a 50-year work-in-progress mountain sculpture of the Sioux warrior on his horse), Custer State Park (South Dakota's 'originary' tourist sight, owing to President Coolidge's 1927 summer visit),[15] the 1880s Village (a recreation featuring 'Cisco', the horse Kevin Costner rode in *Dances with Wolves*), Prairie Dog Town (a petting colony of prairie dogs that eat peanuts from your hand) and Mitchell's 'The World's Only' Corn Palace (a civic auditorium built in Moorish style, redecorated yearly with giant murals made of corn, grains, and grasses).[16]

Wall Drug is at home in this place. Situated amongst its fellow land-marks, it rivals them with its rhetoric of American aspiration and a drive to stick-to-it. Wall's drugstore is a testimony to those rhetorics that puff-up the incidental and those theatrics that aggrandise the commonplace. It submits itself to an amplification, fashioning itself under the trope of *auxesis* through the grandiosity of its success and its insistence on making itself known. This cow-town drugstore reckons with the scale of the ordinary, and exhalts and inflates of the excess of the familiar and everyday provided by its own surrounds.

The town of Wall sits on the northern edge of the Badlands National Park, one of South Dakota's most celebrated attractions. We need to consider the Badlands as an exemplar of another sight on site and a place in relation to which Wall situates itself, performing its place, constituting its very locality. Wall was founded in 1907 and shortly thereafter was marked as the 'Gateway' to the Badlands National Park. Wall takes its name from the 200-foot-high geological formation skirting the edge of the Park: an abrupt break from the flat prairie land to the rough formations just miles from the townsite. This break forms an eight-mile barrier which for years had been known by cattlemen as the 'Wall': a towering, multihued precipice of sedi-mentary rock that stretches for 60 miles.[17] The town of Wall, as it turns out, is deeply inflected by this name insofar as it memorialises the geology of its situation. Perhaps the most significant and signifi-cating effect of the shape of the land is summed up by the tragic, oft-recounted tale of the May blizzard of 1905. This unpredicted storm is said to have pushed thousands of cattle and horses over the sharp drop-off of the 'Wall.' They were left to perish, entrapped between heavy snow and barbed wire fencing. The 1938 edition of the Federal Writers' Project, *South Dakota Guide*, describes the 1905 event:

> The storm, starting as rain, gradually turned to snow which fell steadily and thickly. Riding in on a strong north wind, the blizzard howled across the open stretches with unleashed fury. What had been balmy May weather soon changed to the bitterest storm a severe winter could offer. Striking at a time when livestock had just shed winter coats, the blizzard forced the bewildered animals to drift with the wind until they floun-dered helplessly into snow-filled draws to die. Barbwire [*sic*] fences of homesteaders added to the toll, for large numbers of stock drifted against them and piled up.[18]

In this edition of the South Dakota guide, the retelling of this tragic event that 'left in its wake utter ruin for nearly every stockman in the western part of the State', occupies the greater part of the brief description afforded to the town of Wall.[19] This is all we are told of Wall: a singularly devastating event wherein nature performs unexpectedly and perniciously. The guide offers this event to encapsulate what one might want to know, or better, what one might need to know about Wall. This town – the very shape of the land on which it sits – speaks of catastrophic proportions, anomaly and unpredictability.

Twenty years later, a second edition of this South Dakota guide was published. It reads almost exactly as does its original, with the exception of one alteration. The very paragraph recounting the well-known narrative (I heard it at least five times during my stay in Wall) of the 1905 misfortune wrought by an unforeseeable blizzard had been omitted and then replaced. In its stead, Wall Drug had stepped up, earning the following mention:

> The WALL DRUG STORE is one of the most advertised concerns in the State and, for many, one of the biggest disappointments. Highway signs are posted for hundreds of miles in all directions and during World War II signposts in N. Africa, France, Guam, and Australia pointed the way to this enterprising store.[20]

Notwithstanding the curiosity that the earlier edition failed to mention the existence of Wall Drug, by that time already a noteworthy aspect of its town, more significant is what we might call the metaphorical displacement from the edition of the 1930s and the figurative replacement enacted by the 1958 reinscription of the WPA guide. In the first edition, Wall figures as a place teetering on the verge of catastrophe (natural, economic and otherwise), a site emblematic of 'a country of extremes, evinced by the fact that a mild May day, may, in a few hours, be changed into one of biting cold'.[21] In the second edition, Wall Drug is of notable 'concern to the state', but still a great disappointment. In the contiguous movement between the two inscriptions, Wall Drug takes on the weight of the place of the former, the affect of 'on the verge' combined with its own concerns that the WPA assigns to it: specifically, one of failing to live up to its well-advertised name.

There is also the irony that Wall would be the 'Gateway' to its backdrop, these 'bad' lands – a 244,000 acre, grassless maze of rocky spires, eroded domes and washed-out gaps. 'A part of Hell with the fires burned out', General George Custer described it.[22] While this incidental town has made its rise to fame through the travel of tourists, the very same town opens onto the monument that has earned its own monumentalised, proper name owing to the problem of travel through it. 'Mako [land] sica [bad]', the Native Americans called it, and the early French explorers used the expression 'mauvaise terres' when confronted with the impossible task of navigating through the barren land of marvellous formations, ghostly peaks, and lofty pinnacles.[23]

Before highway engineers shaped the passes, travel across the wall of cliffs was limited to one steep wagon trail and a few trails which could be negotiated only on foot or horseback.[24]

It is also remarkable that although Wall has been dubbed the 'Gateway' to the Badlands, the town is not, nor has it ever been, one that must be passed through – as the figure of a 'gateway' would suggest – on the way to the National Monument. Looking at a map of the town and surrounding area, it is clear that each of the roadways that access Wall enable visitors to tour the Badlands without ever entering the town of Wall, without having to make one's way through this so-called 'gate'. In this way, Wall's having been given the name of 'Gateway', a seemingly spatial and site-specific conferral, at the very least simply indicates a town-builder's bending of the word in an effort to position Wall, if not physically, then conceptually in this region, to figuratively attach it both to the monumentality of the Badlands space and to the celebration that its monumentalised name enjoys. This second name endows Wall with a title that claims for the town the very sort of positionality it does not have. Thus, the town is not only marked by the monumentality it gains from this conceptual positionality of contiguity to this nationally recognised sight, but it also fixes and grounds itself always-already as a 'gate', a place on the borders or at the fringe, one which we must merely be passing through on the way to somewhere else.

As such, the town of Wall seems doubly inscribed with the idea of transport: on the one hand, semiotic transport, and on the other, corporeal and material. Wall's physical position vis-à-vis the geological 'wall' on which the town sits could be said to duplicate the notion of semiosis as a mode of being not present or, we might say to push the comparison, en route (in the mode of its system of roadside and internal signs and memorabilia). Here we are confronted with Wall's physical situation – its actual position within its greater landscape – as reiterative of that semiosis. Thus semiosis presents itself in its naturalised form at the interface of cultural and physical landscape.

In effect, Wall Drug reveals the performance of place. Further still, Wall Drug shows us how place per se is performative: constitutive of its own situation. Yes, Wall Drug is a spectacle *in situ*; but that site – the 'where' that we locate at 43 degrees, 59 minutes and 63 seconds north latitude and 102 degrees, 14 minutes and 55 seconds west longitude – signifies through performative enactment. The landscape itself participates in the effecting of that sense of locality. Insofar as Wall performs its precise location, it also renders ironic that precision and the very idea of locality as materially determined. The drugstore shows us how place is a mode of doing, not being. That is not to say that place 'is not' (i.e. not to deny it ontologically), but that its mode of being is enacted by many attributes, from the shape of the land and the climate to all that inscribes significance into the idea of that place. Between place and performance, irreducible materiality and enacted meaning, this hyperbolic drugstore is constituted in relation to the innumerable other places from which we have been asked to imagine it.

Back inside Wall Drug, there is at least one wall which documents many (but still by now there must be countless more) of these places: one photograph shows a South Pole sign, and another, a sign at the Great Wall of China. There is one in Vietnam. Another displays a helicopter-mounted sign that survived the 1968 Tet Offensive. Still one more shows a friend of the Husteads by a sign in Bolivia. Another in Amsterdam: '5,397 MILES TO WALL DRUG'. Another in Korea. '5,541 MILES TO WALL DRUG STORE', reads a sign at Easter Island. So now we know we have arrived at our destination. Now, we are supposed to say, 'we are there'. Standing before these curious photographs and newspaper clippings collected over the years, we come across an article that wants to out-do all the rest. It reads: 'WALL DRUG SIGN MAY GO INTO SPACE', and it is almost easier to conceive of Wall Drug in space than to conceive of ourselves there. Indeed, we know well what it would mean for this drugstore to make it to the moon before us. To date, we know outer space semiotically, by the signs and symbols carried, planted and broadcast from there. The moon, for example, rarely comes to mind unmediated, without the marker of a national flag that says, 'we were here'. This newspaper clipping details a drugstore sign meant to be carried by the US astronaut Charles D. Gemar as one of his personal flight kit items aboard STS38, a mission that launched on November 15, 1990 and returned five days later. Gemar proudly indicates its text: '178 MILES STRAIGHT DOWN TO WALL DRUG'. Finally, a sign that offers up Wall Drug's perfect foil: outer space as a largely uncharted and untravelled nowhere. 'Imagine that!' we say, with our eyes to the sky and our feet in this place.[25]

Notes

* I am grateful to Margaretta Lovell, Kaja Silverman, Dell Upton, and Paul Groth for their support and dialogue in the preparation of this paper. I also want to thank the Hustead Family for their hospitality during my stay, their on-going contribution to my research, and above all, for their imagination. This paper is dedicated to the memory of Ted E. Hustead (1902–1999).

1. Throughout this paper I use the word 'sight' as opposed to 'site' to stand in for 'tourist attraction' following Dean MacCannell's (1976) formulation. For MacCannell, 'site' signifies location and 'sight' signifies that particular locality rendered touristic or worthy of being seen.

2. Jonathan Culler, 'The Semiotics of Tourism', *American Journal of Semiotics* 1, no.1–2 (1981): 127.

3. Here I am drawing in part on Judith Butler's (1993) discussion of the significance of matter in the first chapter of her book, *Bodies that Matter*. Although my topic differs largely from hers, the introductory questions that she poses there concerning materiality as a sign of irreducibility and the indissolubility of materiality and signification have greatly aided my thinking. See Judith Butler, *Bodies that Matter* (New York and London: Routledge, 1993) pp. 27–55.

4. Christian Metz, *The Imaginary Signifier: Psychoanalysis and the Cinema*, trans. Celia Britton, Annwyl Williams, Ben Brewster and Alfred Guzzetti (Bloomington: Indiana University Press, 1982), p. 57.

5. Jacques Lacan, 'The Function and Field of Speech and Language in Psychoanalysis', *Ecrits: A Selection*, trans. Alan Sheridan (New York and London: Norton, 1977). P.65.

6. Lacan p. 65.

7. MacCannell p. 115.

8. MacCannell pp. 44–5.

9. Walter Prescott Webb, *The Great Plains* (New York: Grosset and Dunlap, 1931) p. 295.

10. Paul Fussell, *Abroad, British Literary Traveling Between the Wars* (New York: Oxford University Press, 1980) p. 167 cited in Karal Ann Marling, *The Colossus of Roads: Myth and Symbol along the American Highway* (Minneapolis: University of Minnesota Press, 1984) p. 66.

11. Bill Hustead, interview by author, tape recording, 15 November 1997.

12. Shebby Lee, 'Traveling the Sunshine State: The Growth of Tourism in South Dakota, 1914–1939', *South Dakota History* 19, no.2 (summer 1989): 219, 222–23.

13. Lee pp. 222, 199.

14. Lee p. 219.

15. Lee p. 196.

16. Jerry Shriver, 'Kitschy Coup: When it Comes to Corniness, South Dakota Leads the Field', *USA Today*, 18 August 1995, final edn.: D4+.

17. The American Legion Auxiliary, Carrol McDonald Unit, *Eastern Pennington County Memories* (Wall, SD: The American Legion Auxiliary[c. 1965])p. 9.

18. Federal Writers' Project, Works Progress Administration, *A South Dakota Guide*, American Guide Series (Pierre, SD: State of South Dakota, 1938) p. 290.

19. Federal Writers' Project, Works Progress Administration (1938) p. 290.

20. Federal Writers' Project, Works Progress Administration, *South Dakota: A Guide to the State*, ed. M. Lisle Reese, 2nd ed. (New York: Hastings House, 1958) p. 268.

21. Federal Writers' Project, Works Progress Administration (1938), p. 290.

22. Federal Writers' Project, Works Progress Administration (1958) p. 318.

23. Federal Writers' Project, Works Progress Administration (1958) p. 318.

24. Paula M. Nelson, *After the West was Won: Homesteaders and Town-Builders in Western South Dakota, 1900–1917* (Iowa City: University of Iowa Press, 1986) p. 11.

25. In 1989, US Astronaut Charles D. Gemar met Ted Hustead at the South Dakota School of Mines and Technology. There Gemar was presented with this 12" × 24" Wall Drug sign. Gemar intended to carry the sign, however, owing to NASA's policy of disallowing in-flight commercial endorsements, Gemar's mission ascended to 145 miles orbital altitude, the Wall Drug sign never having been aboard. Charles D. Gemar, interview by author, 17 August 1998.

Farming, Dreaming, and Playing in Iowa

Japanese Mythopoetics and Agrarian Utopia

Charles Fruehling Springwood

In 1993, Hori Haruyoshi, a forty-three year-old Japanese freelance copywriter living in Hiroshima, decided to build his very own baseball field. The field he wanted to build would be a replica of a baseball field in Dyersville, Iowa. Dyersville is where Hollywood's 1989 *Field of Dreams* was made, a film about an Iowa farmer, Kinsella, who is guided by mysterious voices to destroy his cornfield and replace it with a baseball field. He obeys this voice, and as a result, a surreal world of magical events unfolds, and ultimately, Kinsella's deceased father is brought back to life. The real-life owners of the farm where the scenes were shot decided to maintain the ball diamond as a backyard souvenir, of sorts. Then, as the much hackneyed phrase goes, life imitated art when – just as character Terence Mann predicted that if Kinsella kept his field in the face of growing financial pressures 'People Would Come' – visitors from around the United States and later international tourists came to see this field (see Springwood 1996).

Now a secular tourist mecca of sorts for baseball aficionados, movie buffs and enthusiasts of commercialised pastoral landscapes, the site became an object of fascination for Hori, who had grown up playing baseball, Japan's most loved team sport. When the movie was released in Japan in 1990, in conjunction with a visit by the Iowa governor and state business leaders to solicit Japanese investment, Hori saw it along with millions of other Japanese, quickly making it at that time the highest grossing foreign film. Fascinated by the film's mythopoetic bricolage of emotion, pastoralism, baseball, spiritualism and nostalgia, united by an odd narrative of Americana, and indeed, impressed further by the story of an Iowa farmer who dared to keep a Hollywood Field of Dreams in his own backyard, Hori became committed to –

obsessed with – building his own version of this pastoral diamond in land-scarce Japan.

In this paper, I outline an intimate portrait of Hori's project, understanding it to be a cultural performance simultaneously motivated by and productive of a global political economy in which anything and everything is commodified. Hori seeks to locate his *self* meaningfully, within a transnational circulation of the signs, symbols and experiences of this 1989 film. To understand his project is better to understand the global cultural economy and the particular contours of global cultural flow. It reveals the pivotal role that the commodity of advanced capitalism – more than ever now *image* and *simulacrum* – plays in creating novel cultural fields for new consumer classes. Finally, Hori's Field of Dreams offers a snapshot of global capital as dynamic and processual, for capital, as Marx clarified, is a process, necessarily incomplete and always emerging.

This ethnographic research offers a glimpse of what people actually do *with* popular televisual commodities produced by transnational interests such as Universal Studios. I argue that the *circulation* of the Field of Dreams narrative effects the *dispersion* of 'America'. However, the dispersion of sign-commodities is a radically uncontrollable, unpredictable process. Indeed, what starts out as a dispersion of America often becomes the *displacement* of America.[1] Mr. Hori authors his materialised landscape from a privileged position of class, as well, and his project is read as a practice of leisure, a playful form of self *emplacement*. Cultural geographer Stacey Warren noted:

[Cultural technology's] role in creating the landscape is indisputable, but analysis cannot stop there. Half of the hegemonic process is missing; we must still ask how people incorporate these places into the cultural practices of their everyday lives, and how these places form part of the 'moving equilibrium' of an always contested, always changing popular culture. (1993: 183)

Hori's engagement with the Field of Dreams narrative reveals a fetish for the televisual commodity which allows him to engage prior ways of imagining 'America', as he has come to imagine this nation through the eyes of a postwar, middle-class Japanese man. Within the spaces that emerge from the dialectic between the practices of consumption and the activities of production, the consumer reconfigures *through practice* a range of possible meanings of texts and signs. This particular spatial image of America's bucolic heartland has been utilised in idiomatically Japanese ways. In fact, ultimately, Hori's consumption of the Field of Dreams allows him, as well as those who also participate in his dream, to creatively *Other* 'America' and Americans, and thus, his landscape is an empowered representation of 'America'.

Agrarian Mythopoetics and the Authenticity of Peasant Resistance

Hori formed a financial group in 1993, *Tomorokoshi no Kai* ['The Corn Association'], to raise money for the field. Ultimately, with the help of Kazuyoshi Masuda, Hori secured rights to a 1.5 hectare rice-paddy located in the isolated village of Takamiya, about sixty kilometers north of Hiroshima. Just as the movie had parlayed the pastoral aesthetics of corn into a central symbol, as luscious, technicolor green stalks of the plant traced the outfield arc of Kinsella's field, Hori insisted on recuperating this icon of America's heartland. In staging his landscape, he planted specially-ordered corn seed, a crop rarely seen in Japan, in his outfield. He named his team, for whom the field would be hometurf, the Corns, and he designed their green and white jerseys. Each season, the players ceremoniously 'harvest' the corn in the outfield, captured by home video and snapshots, then grill the 'ears' along with chicken over coals in foul territory along the third base line. The performance is suggestive of a suburban 'fourth of July' celebration in the US.

A rice-paddy was transformed into a corn-laced baseball diamond. The displacement of rice – a plant used repeatedly throughout Japanese history to fashion and refashion the Japanese self (Ohnuki-Tierney 1993) – by corn, the ostensible metonym of American pastoralism in the film, was conspicuously ironic. Hori hesitated when I asked him to articulate why and how rice might signify *Yamato damashii*, the Japanese spirit, but he spoke enthusiastically about the articulation of corn (maize) with America; indeed, he referred to Joseph Campbell's writings in discussing the centrality of the plant to the mythos of native American peoples. Initially, as a researcher, I struggled to unpack this curious celebration of corn as a quintessentially American sign, and I attempted to tease from Hori and his teammates a more thorough articulation of some deeper significance to this peculiar symbolism. Locating corn as *essential* to the national persona of America by tracing its history to native American societies seemed to me a provocative move by Hori.[2] Ultimately, however, these players merely identified and enacted an existing metonymic corpus of American heritage signs, one already including corn, fashioned previously through centuries of discursive work in the United States. Because the movie had already encoded it as such, a corn stalk proved to be a crucial, if flattened and overdetermined, sign in order to completely fashion an authentic American baseball field.

The Field of Dreams narrative predominant in the United States turns on the articulation of nation, sport and agrarianism, and thus it compares favourably with a set of Japanese discursive practices to locate the contemporary national identity in terms of traditional, rural villages of a Japan seemingly vanished. Indeed, it is the articulation of particular themes from the *Field of Dreams* and similar nostalgia heritage movements in the US with the historical imaginaries of the Japanese people that suggest the possible reasons for the film's remarkable success in Japan. There, as with so many other industrial nations, a nearly complete transition among the polity from farmer to urbanite was accomplished between the 1850s and the 1970s. As Japan has become one of the most urban nations, its sentimentality for a rural past has flourished. A discourse has emerged, constructing the countryside as the authentic space of the national spirit, and the material consequences of this nostalgia include a 1980s government programme – spearheaded by then prime-minister Nobuko Takeshita – to fund the making and remaking in the hinterland of 'old hometown villages', or *furusato zukuri* (Robertson 1991; Smith 1997: 167–171).

In the middle of the nineteenth century, Japan was nearing the end of a period of over 250 years of feudalism, ruled by the Tokugawa military family and their descendants under a system of highly centralised state control. Although they occupied the honorary second rung of a stratified social system, the peasants experienced great material poverty and burdensome taxation. The state and the samurai class it supported relied upon the peasantry to produce large quantities of rice, a staple valued as a sign of class distinction. Many historians suggest that rice was a key symbol of various Shinto fertility rites, such as the New Year's offering as early as the beginning of the Medieval period (1185–1602), while others (Amino 1980; Tsuboi 1984) argue that non-rice grains continued to be significant even into the Tokugawa period (1603–1886) (see Ohnuki-Tierney 1993). It appears that rice-producing peasants rarely consumed rice on a daily basis, and that urban dwellers began eating rice daily only by the middle of the Tokugawa period (Sasaki 1983: 292).

This is not to suggest that rice was not desired. Indeed, during the Tokugawa period – often characterized as an era of peace and stability – a number of 'rice riots' occurred, in which peasants demonstrated against taxation, and in some instances actually demanded rice for consumption. Although such uprisings seemed to alter little the overwhelming strength of the Tokugawa shoganate, they did reveal the great frustration of the peasantry, and by the middle of the nineteenth century their material consequences were not insignificant. In 1886, a disturbance lasting two weeks in Nishinomiya was led by women demanding cheaper rice. A month later, poor peasants from a district near Edo (Tokyo) attacked four rice dealers, 'triggering 450 raids in several hundred villages' (Ohnuki-Tierney 1993: 38).

By 1868, a new form of government was established, structured by an oligarchy ruling in the name of the emperor (Meiji). Reforms were attempted, as many peasants were made landowners, only to be once again heavily taxed, this time based on land values, and 'rice riots' continued. In truth, the lives of farmers changed little from the Tokugawa period into the middle of the twentieth century, though there were increasingly fewer of them. However, in the process of nation-making that characterised the Meiji state, an agrarian mythos (*nohon shugi*) was resurrected to establish the countryside as the heart of a new social order. The early part of the century was marked by government efforts to seek support from agriculturalists for production of rice and to locate with the rural polity the possibility of a strong link between the people and the army, and also by the emergence of a literature glorifying *inaka*, or the authentic rural Japan, as an escape from expanding urban centres (Gluck 1985).

Japan, like many nations, returns variously and repeatedly to these constructed notions of agrarian utopia, and it has again during the past fifteen years, when the *furusato* has become a common tourist space. Several members of Hori's Corns baseball team mentioned that their fascination with the Field of Dreams film centred on the persona of protagonist, Ray Kinsella, who throughout the story resists the pressures of bankers seeking to foreclose on the farm, even though he is losing money by keeping the baseball field rather than planting corn. Kinsella's actions are hardly the stuff of a quintessential agrarian revolt. Of course, in the end, he keeps the field, magically people from all over come to visit, and – effecting a genuine capitalist utopia – without even thinking about it, they each hand over twenty dollars. But Japanese audiences are drawn to his dilemma.

Nearly every Japanese who spoke to me about the film said that the actions of Ray Kinsella revealed a truly remarkable essence. The word used most often was *makoto*, which indicated a great admiration for the resilience of this character who, despite great pressure to do otherwise, listened to the film's magical voice and followed his own intuitions. According to David Plath (1980: 47), 'If any single idiom can be taken as central to the many Japanese vocabularies of growth it is the notion of reaching out for "sincerity" (*makoto*), of striving to act from motives that are totally pure ... Whatever its form, however, pure action is totally absorbing. It is human "peak" experience in its Japanese guise. In such moments you are no longer hampered by awareness'.

Clearly, the *Field of Dreams* is not representative of a classic Japanese film of any genre, but what emerges is a sense of several features of the narrative that suggest a context for the film's overwhelming reception in Japan. From the economic tensions surrounding ownership of agricultural real estate to the actions of certain characters to its melodramatic veneer, the story contains themes that seem to resonate well with Japanese audiences. In a society preoccupied by its own national debates about the significance of the farmer, the 'traditional' rural village, and new ideas about personal freedom and space, the story of an Iowa farmer's ability to incorporate his love of baseball (the most popular team sport in Japan) and his agrarian existence into a highly manicured, *bonsai*-like, utopic baseball field struck a popular cord.

Space, Time and Freedom in Contemporary Japanese Identity

I read Hori's enactment of the Field of Dreams narrative and his repro-duction of the Dyersville landscape as a practice in/of late capitalism, in which the global social order has been informed by 'the transform-ation of reality into images' (Jameson 1983: 125). However, Hori's par-ticular engagement with this American baseball diamond is nuanced by a Japanese cultural idiom that turns on the relationship of an indi-vidual with certain objects or spaces in her everyday life. I believe that for Hori, the prevailing significance of the field is that it is his very own space, where he can imagine his very own world, and manage his very own baseball games.

In recent years, a remarkable sociolinguistic phenomenon has emerged in Japan which highlights a new, contemporary set of atti-tudes and structures of feeling about individualism and personal, pri-vate freedom. A new idiom of selfhood thrives through personal relationships with material objects that seemingly extend individual freedom. This is illustrated by examining an array of English words that have been adapted to the Japanese lexicon. These borrowed English morphemes are seldom recognisable once adopted into Japanese. For example, *sarariiman*, from 'salary' and 'man', refers to the stereotypical lifetime employee of a Japanese company. The newer understanding of Japanese individuality and personal mobility is con-veyed by a series of *mai* words. Specifically, the phonetic pronuncia-tion of the English 'my' has been transport into contemporary Japanese, glossed in romanisation as *mai*. Examples include *maikaa* (my car), *maikon* (my computer), and *maihomu* (my home). These coinages emphasise the novel meaning that such contemporary objects or spaces have for a new generation of Japanese, and they reflect new options for the individual, such as the opportunity to travel at one's own pace (*mai pesu*), and the luxury of personal, private space (see Passin 1980). David Plath (1990: 231) explains:

> These *mai* words suggest the individuating potential of owner-user mass technology, of machines that empower the mundane self to expand into new domains of action and imagination. By their linguistic form the *mai* words imply that this self-machine linkage is so novel that it cannot be adequately communicated by conventional Japanese terms for person-hood. . . Such material symbols as the automobile and the modern

private home have] become a master metaphor for personal freedom within an industrial order.

Hori, indeed, seems to have procured for himself an attachment to space and the freedom it promises in a fashion clearly informed by the *mai*-generation.

Hori was convinced from the outset that by building this baseball field he would be doing something significant. Hori and his supporters were quite conscious of the emerging narrative about their actions, and they sought to control, indeed author, this story. Before ever meeting Hori in 1997, I viewed a 100 minute video which he sent to me titled 'Ore tachi no hiirudo obu doriimsu' (Our Field of Dreams). It is a fairly high-quality documentary, directed by Hori himself, chronicling the evolution of the field's construction, beginning with the initial ground-breaking. Ultimately, it was made available for purchase for 5000 yen ($40) at the field and in a few regional stores. Hori and his friends are seen struggling to transform what had been, in reality, a nearly flooded, uneven, and inhospitable landscape into a Hollywood diorama.

They are seen driving borrowed construction equipment, using arms and wheelbarrows to remove boulders, digging trenches to lay a large drainage pipe, among many other tasks. In one scene, they offer a brief, Japanese-style prayer before hoisting a large log to form a bridge. The struggle to smooth and drain the once-terraced rice paddy would take about two years. The narrative foregrounds the physical labour required to construct the site, even more clearly than the movie highlighted Kinsella's efforts. The group nature of these efforts is emphasised, and the documentary inscribes Hori's story with the notion of hard work, and work as moral form, very much in the tradition of a Japanese ethos of *samu*, or disciplined work as a pathway to Buddhist salvation. Usually, work on the site usually occurred on weekends and holidays, and members of the Corn Association would stay in the farmhouse adjoining the emerging baseball diamond. In the evenings, viewers see them eating, drinking beer and sake, and even sleeping in futons. All of these scenes of work and play are punctuated by short, on-site interviews with Hori, who discusses how it feels to see his dream taking shape – and there is no doubt that it is *his* dream and that he is the 'visionary', even though the documentary foregrounds collective effort. Groups, especially in Japan, have leaders, and Hori appears to demonstrate for the Corn Association members an understated spiritual will. However, the building of the field was a deeply emotional event for many in the group, as two Corns teammates fight back tears in the video as they stand, along with Hori, on a stage at the opening. Having drawn upon their own funds and having organised several fundraising activities, including concerts and flea markets, to date the group has raised over $40,000 for maintenance of the field.

Hori grew up playing and loving baseball as a child in Tokyo, having moved there from Nagano with his family. He played sandlot baseball, never playing in high school or college. His persona is striking. A conspicuous facial tic punctuates his speech, which is soft, articulate and distinguished by philosophical musings. Both in person and in the video, he commands the, perhaps self-motivated, presence of an artist – seemingly avant-garde. At the end of my research, as I was leaving, he handed me a copy of another 110 page manuscript, titled 'Washira No Hiirudo obu Doriimsu' ('Our Own Field of Dreams'),[3] which he hopes to publish. It, too, chronicles his love affair with baseball, the movie, and the construction of his field.

Writing advertising and public relations copy in Hiroshima, he lives a comfortable middle-class life in Japan, married with one son. Unlike the Hollywood narrative that so inspired him, family is not a significant part of his involvement with this site. While in the US, the movie and the Iowa tourist spectacle have been engaged as celebrations of American 'family values' and nostalgic reunions between sons and their fathers, Hori's many weekends spent building the site represented time away from family. This is the case for all of the men who join Hori to work and play at the site, a group including several business executives, engineers, a travel agent, a teacher, an advertising executive, a car salesman and a shop-keeper. One woman has been part of the group from the beginning. Single, Fuji is a furniture maker who lives and works in a small room attached to the farmer house next to the site. She is the team's pitching ace. With the exception of Fuji's presence, the Corn Association approaches their play in a fashion generally typical of the masculinely gendered social relations of leisure. Specifically, Japanese men commonly pursue leisure activities in groups, away from their families. In urban locales, sons often see little of their fathers (Allison 1994), and neither Hori's son or father figure prominently in his relationship to the field. One way in which the Corns' social relations diverge from common masculine leisure practices in Japan is that they do not reflect Hori's work-a-day relations. Males-at-play typically are males who work together, but since Hori's work is solitary, no such corporate social formations exist.

Before arriving to meet Hori's group, I was expecting a slick, highly-produced site based on prior knowledge of Japan. Perhaps, I thought, Hori's field might surpass the one in Iowa for beauty, precision and symmetry. I envisioned a site embodying a vast array of commercial interests and corporate sponsors, Japanese-style. To the contrary, Hori's field is modest, and the corn he took great pains to grow is short, the grass in his outfield is sparse, and the playing surface remains bumpy. Still, with the homemade bleachers and scoreboard, and the gorgeous rural surroundings, the field has charm. From the bleachers, one can see beyond centrefield, across the highway, a series of colourful building tops poking through trees, several hundred yards up the side of a small mountain. It is an amusement park, a New Zealand theme park (see Yoshimoto 1994: 193). Hori's story was written up in several newspapers in 1995, when the site was completed, and over 1,000 tourists purchased tickets to appear at the grand opening, September 3, marked by a three-game inaugural tournament, including the Corns and the Tokyo Cooperstown Fouls, followed by a rock concert.

Each summer, Hori and friends return to sow corn and prepare the field. The Corns invite several teams to compete with them on the field. Late each June, as noted previously, the corn is harvested, followed by a barbecue. There are no grand efforts to advertise, and in contrast to the Dyersville counterpart – which continues to receive over 20,000 tourists each summer – no more than 1,000 visitors came in 1996 and 1997 combined. This does not disturb Hori, for whom the site seems to function now primarily as a mythopoetic playground, a spacious get-away nestled in the mountainous agrarian landscape sufficiently far from Hiroshima. It is a place of refuge, where he can bring his own baseball team to spend weekends and holidays. To be sure, the public sign-value of his exploits remain a part of his pleasure and desire; but the significance of the site as a private space (albeit one framed as Hollywood simulacra) has emerged as paramount. In Japan, where open land is scarce, and where the cost of real estate is prohibitive, Hori has authored a space seemingly available only to millionaires. Yet, this middle-class intellectual has crafted what many must dream of, a rural, 'American' baseball field one can call one's very own.

Consuming America and Performing *Kokusaika*

During a critical scene near the end of the film, the avuncular character Terence Mann offers the following words in claiming baseball to be the spiritual glue of the American ethos: 'The one constant through all of the years . . . has been baseball. America has rolled by like an army of steamrollers. It's been erased like a blackboard – rebuilt and erased again. But baseball has marked the time. This field – this game – it's part of our past. . . It reminds us of all that was once good, and it could be again'. This prose is representative of a much larger discursive corpus conflating baseball and America, and such discourse has also penetrated Japan, where baseball is hailed, simultaneously, as a metonym for both America *and* Japan (see Springwood 1992).

Japanese society has developed a highly nuanced fascination with America and its commodity-images. In particular, the popularity of visits to and images of rural America has marked recent years, as US tour agents catering to Japan book tours of anything from the Iowa home of *Little House on the Prairie* author, Laura Ingalls Wilder, to the Field of Dreams site in Dyersville. My fieldwork at the Dyersville site was complemented by examination of another baseball nostalgia site in the US, the baseball Hall of Fame in Cooperstown, New York (see Springwood 1996). This site has also been extremely popular among Japanese, and a description of one such engagement allows for a broader understanding of what, precisely, Hori's place-making signified.

On September 29 1990, a dream that had been conceived by Kunihiro Kurata in December 1989 was consummated when an amateur baseball team – the Osaka Old Kids – played a game on Doubleday Field. Then fifty-year old Kurata, employed by an Osaka advertising firm, decided to visit Cooperstown and the Baseball Hall of Fame, since he happened to be in the United States on business. He trekked to this upstate locale in the middle of winter, after the crowds had vanished. Although its once green, manicured outfield was by then snow-covered, Doubleday Field – with its large sign reading 'Birthplace of Baseball' is what impressed Kurata most. The 'historic' mystique of the place called to him, and Kurata decided to return to Cooperstown in the summer to play a game of baseball with his recreational team, the Old Kids. In an interview with a Japanese journalist, Kurata said:

> I only understood after visiting. Apparently, when the baseball sanctuary was first established, there was quite a bit of resistance to locating the Holy Land of baseball in a remote town 400 kilometers from New York City. . . However, once they visited this place, like I did, they were struck by the power and the beauty of the natural surroundings, and realized that as times and the generations change, this spot will always remain the same, thus making it the perfect spot to preserve the past. (Yatsuki 1990: 14)

His discourse is barely distinguishable from public relations copy about Cooperstown's bucolic essence.

Kurata and his colleagues play *kusayakyû*, literally 'grass baseball', a recreational genre, whose participants are said to play with youthful enthusiasm. Specifically, they play *nanshiki*, which is very similar to softball in the US, in which a softer, rubberised ball is used. Several of Kurata's *kusayakyû* teammates joined him in a pilgrimage to Cooperstown, where they hoped to play a special match against the people of the New York village. Finally, with the help of officials from the Hall of Fame, a match was arranged against the Leatherstocking Base Ball Club, a group of locals who perform a version of 1840s baseball at the Farmer's Museum. One of the Osaka Old Kids, Michiro Kizaki, was accompanied by his fiancée so that they could be married on the historic field. A celebratory goodwill summit emerged, with the Old Kids staying at Tunnicliff Inn, on Main Street, where they hosted several drinking parties for their hosts. The Old Kids presented to their hosts a commemorative designer towel, embossed with the Japanese characters meaning 'every ball has a soul'.

The teams faced off for two games, one according to the rules of *nanshiki*, and one played following the 1858 Massachusetts rules. Among the various thank-you notes the Leatherstocking Club received, a letter with the following passage incorporates the pastoral allegory central to baseball nostalgia in both the US and Japan. It is printed as written, and the conspicuous second language errors remain: 'Reminding beautiful Cooperstown that was surrounded by woods and lake, my heart was filled with emotion. I can picture one scene by one scene of the best day – beautiful contrast between street trees and the row of houses, vivid green lawn in Doubleday Field, splendid Hall of Fame and Museum, people's gentle eyes, contact with heart, and your warm reception'. More poetry than prose, this sentiment embodies the affective component of the touristic gaze and consumption of place.

Japanese people who travel to the United States and incorporate 'American' cultural texts and spaces of leisure into their worlds underscore James Clifford's argument, as he seeks to illuminate the 'global world of intercultural import/export in which the ethnographic encounter is already enmeshed' (1991: 100). According to Clifford, 'If we rethink culture and its science, anthropology, in terms of travel, then the organic, naturalizing bias of the term culture – seen as a rooted body that grows, lives, dies, etc. – is questioned. Constructed and disputed historicities, sites of displacement, interference, and interaction, come more sharply into view' (1991: 101). From the Osaka Old Kids travels to Hori's field, we can see one aspect of a much larger process of Japan consuming America. Mitsuhiro Yoshimoto (1994: 195) argues that:

> In postmodern Japan, everything is commodified, including the sense of nationhood. America is, therefore, just another brandname, like Chanel, Armani, and so on. We can, of course, read a sign of colonial mentality in the Japanese craving for 'America' as a brand name; however, we can also cynically say that it is only part of the system of differences which needs to be reproduced perpetually for the survival of the Japanese capitalist economy.

The emergence of this fetish for 'America' articulated with a national movement of the 1980s and 1990s known as *kokusaika*, or internationalism. Japan has become preoccupied in recent years with its position vis-à-vis the global process of internationalisation. What began as a sort of political slogan became the ubiquitous, fashionable rhetoric of politicians, universities, corporations and even home economics clubs: we desire to 'internationalise' Japan (see Goodman 1993: 221–226). Participation in this novel ethos of pursuing the foreign as a way to signify one's cosmopolitan, international attitude is viewed skeptically by some, as representing merely a lifestyle choice, emptied of possibility from the outset. Yoshimoto (1994: 198) writes:

> this new logic of postmodern nationalism – or what Frederic Jameson refers to as neo-ethnicity – is euphemistically called *kokusaika* or internationalization. While domestically it means the presence of more imported goods and image-formation, externally it refers to the phenomenon of more Japanese going abroad . . . What *kokusaika* does not include is precisely one of the most fundamental ways of internationalizing Japan: the genuine acceptance of foreigners and those Japanese who are too 'contaminated' by foreign cultures.

Indeed, the authors of several papers in Mannari and Befu's *The Challenge of Japanese Internationalization* (1983) also read *kokusaika* as a novel form of Japanese nationalism, wherein the engagement with the foreign, especially the American, as a mode of consumer taste, serves to reproduce the Japanese identity as quintessentially different, and *essentially* not international.

The Field of Dreams in Takamiya is one instance of this effort to sustain cultural engagements with Western commodities and the global *flow* of Western cultural capital. We see the subtle convergence of a variety of transnational interests around the production of this Field of Dreams site. For example, Wendol Jarvis is in charge of the Iowa film board and has worked with the Iowa Department of Commerce to enhance Japanese investment in his state, using the popularity of the film as an economic promotional tool, and he was invited to come to Takamiya with the Ghost Players. An Iowa investor, Al Vigil, who recently purchased an interest in the Dyersville site, read about Hori's project in the Washington Post (1995). He and the Ghost Players, a group of Dyersville area farmers – mostly ex-collegiate baseball players – who formed a team in the image of the returned-from-the-dead players in the movie, made plans to visit the Takamiya site and play the Corns. The Ghost Players, several of whom actually appeared in the film as extras, have become somewhat well-known, having appeared at various state and county fairs, in television commercials and even in a Japanese rock video.

Arrangements completed, the Ghost Players, Al Vigil and Wendol Jarvis all arrived in Takamiya on May 11, 1996 to meet and play the Corns. It was the consummate moment of Hori's life, as well as that of many other Corns players. The appearance was publicised, and several hundred spectators arrived to photograph and to shake hands with the Ghost Players, who represented a living embodiment of the televisual realm. These men were, in essence, Hollywood, America and Iowa. The all-white, all midwestern team defeated the awe-struck Corns, 12–5. In a fashion typically Japanese, Hori was preoccupied, anticipating the Ghost Players' disdain for his less than technicolor replica. To his relief, they approved of his efforts, saying that he had done a

'Good job'. To this day, with a pleased grin Hori often recites that compliment, in English. Indeed, he uses the phrase to thank the Corn Association members at the end of his 110 page manuscript. The Field of Dreams, then, is at the centre of a transnational (trans-Pacific) space of cultural exchange which builds on pastoral nostalgia and popular images of the midwestern United States.

I agree with David Mathews (1997: 90) that 'the mere consumption of American commodity-signs cannot be equated with the Americanization of local cultures'. The readings of the Field of Dreams narrative in Takamiya contrast with those found in the US, where the predominant themes are conservatism, masculinity and the nostalgia for a lost bond between fathers and sons. In Japan, involvement with the story turns on a fascination with America, and much more so than in the US, the Field of Dreams is about baseball. The intensity with which the Corns approach their baseball is unmatched in Dyersville, and Hori expressed surprise that Americans read the significance of the film in terms of fathers and sons; his father has never even visited the site.

Lash and Urry described the conditions of globalisation that anticipated and informed a practice such as the Corn Association and its Field of Dreams as 'disorganized capital', with the sea of change in modern society, in which 'large organizations, workplaces, and cities are of diminishing significance for each individual, the processes of forming, fixing, and reproducing "subjects" is increasingly "cultural", formed of available "lifestyles" not at all based on where one lives or whom one knows, that is, on those who are immediately present' (1987: 276). In transnational space, the practices and signs of the cultural sphere flow more rapidly, less constrained by 'stable points of operation', and they serve to reproduce a boundless stock of 'lifestyles' for subject formation (Palumbo-Liu 1997: 15). Importantly, such movement complicates any sense of stable or essential national subjectivity. That is, one might ask, in what sense are the practices of Hori's Corn Association even Japanese? Of course, they are informed by various historically constructed Japanese *habituses*, but to attempt to analyse the full range of the association's recontextualisations and materialisations of a Western text by resorting to some notion of Japanese culture would be counterproductive. Indeed, it is wrong also to argue in the first instance for one or even a small, stable set of 'American' readings of the Field of Dreams narrative.

'Although the essential hyperreality of contemporary culture has meant that America is everywhere but nowhere at one and the same time, the popular signification of America, and hence that of American cultural products and practices, is necessarily contingent upon the unique complexities of national cultural conjunctures' (Andrews 1997: 91). The Hiroshima production with the all-white Ghost Players, and

Hori's field more generally, might be an attempt to construct a Japanese version of America in which the United States is viewed as white, spacious, bucolic; a nostalgic utopia. These readings of America would be, of course, imaginary, but evidence suggests that, in fact, Iowa, pastoral baseball fields and abundant rows of corn are images with which Japanese society constructs stereotypes of America. In a sense, then, when Japanese people visit this field, they may indeed be practicing a form of *Othering* which takes America as its object, much in the same fashion perhaps that White America 'Others' Native America with productions of commercialised Indian Villages. Of course, this is not the only image of America prevailing in Japan; the bucolic America is an America Japan *longs for*, and the Field of Dreams stereotype competes with visions of America as filled with guns, drugs, and violence – an America in this latter instance that represents Japanese society's worst fears about its Western ally.

Haruyoshi Hori represents a new class of consumer, and this class is distinguished by 'the pivotal role that commodities may play in objectifying the life spaces of' individuals (Lee 1993: 175). He and his associates are a manifestation of an emergent process integral to late capitalism, wherein the consumer is obliged not only to consume but to also imagine him or herself in the act of consumption. Intelligent and well-educated, Hori is perceived by those around him as an artist, and this image is also one embodied in his persona. His artistic visions and investments, however, are structured by, in this case, the global televisual commodity, in whose flow he is intimately bound. These commodities have become the means through which identity, culture and difference are communicated. The problem Hori represents for the cultural analyst is how to read the prevailing dialectical tension between the global market of the commodity-sign and the consumer. Lash and Urry (1994: 133) argue that this late economy of signs and space implies a radical break with aesthetic modernism, which revealed an autonomous, reflexive subject characterised by expressive depth. The circulation of images in the current global culture, however, involves not aesthetic subjects, but rather flattened objects. Consider the cultural career of Hori in the context anticipated by Lash and Urry, who claim that, 'Here it is not the agents who decide, reflexively among the symbolic objects, but the objects which choose the agents' (1994: 134). Some will read Hori as a flattened subject, but his passion is not imaginary. Hori and the Corns have become transnational tourists, who, without even leaving their prefecture, experience a simulated mobility through their mediation of the signs and symbols of the Field of Dreams. They have enacted a genuine ethos of *kokusaika*, literally inscribing their lives with the most American of all baseball diamonds. They are the *perfect* consumers (Lee 1993), and as authors of a novel culture of consumption and informed by a transnational flow of capital, they embody new forms of exchange and modes of locating self within the commodity. Clearly, in performing America, they construct a space where the flow of signs and pleasures complicates all prior distinctions between producers and consumers (Fiske 1987).

Acknowledgements

Funding for this research was made available through the Artistic and Scholarly Development Grant, provided by the Mellon Center at Illinois Wesleyan University. The author wishes to thank Al Vigil, C. Richard King, Cheryl Springwood, Chris Thompson, and Teri Sato.

Notes

1. I am indebted to C. Richard King for insight regarding this notion of the 'displacement' of 'America'.

2. There exists a rich tradition of linking a contemporary American identity to an agrarian, maize-centred and Native American past. Indeed, the annual celebration of Thanksgiving ritually invokes a mythical reading of the social relations between European colonists and Native Americans, enacted over a shared meal that included, at its centre, corn.

3. Washira is translated here as 'our own'; it is a colloquial phrase common in the Hiroshima area. It implies an emotional, vernacular and even masculine attachment to the space or object in question.

BRING IT ALL BACK HOME

The Power of Metaphors in Tourism Theory[1]

David Chaney

In their introduction to a recently published collection of papers on social theories of travel and tourism (Rojek and Urry 1997), the editors provocatively attempt to capture tourist studies within the broader project of cultural studies. The tourist industry, in the number of people it employs, in the scale of economic transactions involved, and in the range of social, cultural and environmental impacts, has become a dominant feature of the modern environment and is therefore a topic relevant to all the social sciences. Rojek and Urry, however, seek to initiate a 'cultural turn'[2] in tourist studies and believe their book sustains the following claims:

> that tourism is a cultural practice; that tourism and culture hugely overlap; that tourism as a cultural practice and set of objects is highly significant or emblematic within contemporary 'Western' societies organised around mass mobility; that tourism has largely to be examined through the topics, theories and concepts of cultural analysis, especially the current foci upon issues of time and space. (1997: 5)

My purpose in this paper is not to dispute these claims. Although I accept that the industry of tourism, its organisation, structures and consequences, can and indeed must be discussed within a number of disciplinary perspectives, I believe that the distinctiveness of tourism as a form of leisure requires that we engage with the what and how of representation and meaning in the practice of tourism as a necessary complement to other more descriptive concerns. My purpose is then to explore some of the implications of a 'cultural' focus.

I have already indicated that approaching tourism 'as a cultural practice' means that one is concerned with the meaning of tourist locales, thus generating questions such as: What is going on there? Why is it attractive? What is the significance of the time spent there for visitors? How does the specific tourist site relate to broader frameworks of

representation of social identity and change available in mass entertainment? It is, however, immediately clear from these questions that
meaning is not self-evident, nor is it likely to be uncontested. What and
how a place represents will differ between visitors and locals, but then
neither of these categories will be homogeneous, so that meaning is
dispersed, existing on a number of dimensions simultaneously, and
subject to change through succeeding waves of expectations.[3] The
problem of meaning in tourism is part of a broader change in popular
culture towards industries of mass entertainment in which commercially provided culture has become more important in everyday life,
and yet, almost paradoxically, 'culture' has lost its unity and coherence
and become more problematic (Chaney 1999).

In this paper I will explore some aspects of a cultural analysis of
tourism and, in an inevitable reflexive move, touch on what this contributes to an understanding of mass culture. I begin from an assumption that cultural analysis necessarily trades upon the use of
metaphors. The power of metaphors in cultural analysis is that they
are uniquely able to signify complexities of representation and meaning. Metaphors work through an impossible conjunction of referents
to create an association that is illuminating.[4] An example is neatly
provided by the continuation of the paragraph quoted above when
Rojek and Urry suggest that a notion of 'escape' is inadequate (but presumably relevant) to the practice of tourism. Two pages earlier, when
talking about 'unpacking the orientations' of tourism (itself of course
a metaphor of analysis), they say they will be: 'tracing some of the
mythologies of escape involved when people go touring or dream of
touring' (1997: 3).

The point about the metaphor of escape is that while it cannot be
literally true (What is the nature of confinement? Who sustains it?),
it brings out some of the privileged licence of a temporary phase
when normality is 'relaxed' by actors changing places. Metaphors are
therefore essential because they say concisely what can otherwise
only be put elaborately and with difficulty, if at all. I have already said
that cultural practices in mass society are complex because they are
dispersed across a number of settings, but it has also been traditionally accepted that metaphors are essential for the interpretation of
cultural representations because, however realistic, representations
are not literal – they go beyond the here-and-now to ambiguous levels of association and meaning. This can most easily be seen in
relation to works of art such as paintings, novels and theatrical performances, but if we are saying that the practice of tourism is cultural
then it, too, will share these qualities of ambiguous representation.
The meaning of tourism will not be self-evident but will require
'unpacking' through some form of hermeneutic analysis articulated
through crucial metaphors.

We begin then from an appreciation that tourist attractions are rep-resentations that appeal to different audiences in a variety of ways, indicating in this phrasing that they are in important respects designed constructions. It seems to me natural therefore that the dominant metaphor in tourism studies has been the idea that the tourist setting should be imagined as a form of performance or staging. The dramaturgical metaphor in social theory (the idea that social life is best understood as a form of dramatic performance) has a long his-tory and has generated many widely used analytic metaphors such as role and actor. Although generally unfashionable in social theory, the drama metaphor has persisted as dominant – one might say the root metaphor (Turner 1974) – in tourist studies. Since MacCannell (1976 – as admittedly one of a number of analytic perspectives) first provided it, the idea of a tourist site as a staged performance has worked well at indicating the artifice of the site. However 'natural' the attraction, for the tourist to get there, to know what to look at, and to sustain the visit, all involve associated metaphors of performance such as practice and rehearsal, scripting and staging etc. This complex of metaphors deals with what makes somewhere visit-able, how the place is articu-lated (how the story is told), and how the constitutive features of any-where are framed in order to make them recognisable and distinctive.

It is important to stress that the metaphors help us to recognise and disentangle the social construction of place; they do not address why tourists go. The latter question is concerned with motives and we will need different, although possibly related metaphors (such as 'mythologies of escape') to deal with them. I should also indicate that one of the central weaknesses of imagining social life as a form of per-formance is that it can encourage too static a view of social settings. By this I mean that settings (places, sites) can be divorced from the flow of historical change that I have already noted. The point of emphasis-ing an historical perspective is to ensure that due attention is paid to the contests and conflicts that crosscut cultural meanings. Although it is important to emphasise that meaning is the product of practical activity, these activities utilise vocabularies and perspectives that have their own histories and significance.

I do not, however, intend to use this paper to mount a critical assault on the validity of the dramatic metaphor in tourist studies.[5] It is clearly a powerful and productive metaphor that directs our atten-tion to the constitutive practices of the organisation of spaces and places rather than treating them as self-evident givens. I have, though, already noted that a core metaphor will generate associated ideas – further implied metaphors – that help to fill out a perspective and make it into a theoretical current. Although these might seem to grow organically from the 'root', I think it is always necessary to engage reflexively with our rhetoric. Therefore, in the rest of this paper I will look more carefully at how we might most effectively use two further associated themes of the dramatic metaphor – notions of participation and authenticity. Before going on to do so I should note quickly that, in a way that is typical of the layering of metaphors, the notion of the tourist has itself been used as a metaphor for a distinctive way of being-in-the-world.

To say that tourism is cultural means that it is concerned with representation and meaning; but processes of signification do not just happen – they require structures to be comprehensible. So, in practice, cultures are institutionalised through forms which provide distinctive strategies for the articulation of representation and meaning. I have previously suggested (for example 1983 and 1990) that in order to differentiate between cultural forms we need to attend to at least three dimensions – relations of production, characteristic narratives and typical modes of participation. If tourism is to be treated as a cultural form (and clearly the form will vary between national cultures and crucially between whether the emphasis is on the perspective of visitor or visited), then all three dimensions have to be considered. I suggest that the third dimension of how visitors typically participate in the places they visit (in terms of the dramatic metaphor I can say how audiences consume or appropriate a tourist site), has been relatively underdeveloped in tourist studies. The main resource presented in recent years as a metaphoric representation of the practice of consumption has been John Urry's notion of 'the tourist gaze' (1990 and see also 1995).[6]

While the gaze is clearly a visual interrogation, signalling Urry's contention that the primary mode of appropriation is visual and thereby emblematic of a broader theme in a culture of mass consumption, it is not uniform. Urry primarily distinguishes between a collective and a romantic gaze although he also mentions, in other places, ironic and spectatorial gazes.[7] The main distinction between collective and romantic closely parallels characteristics of the traditional distinction between popular and high cultural forms, or what I have previously described as contrasting aesthetics of representation and realism (1994 Chap. 5). In this way, Urry indicates that in his view different modes of gaze are socially located (perhaps each characteristic of a distinctive habitus?) and are associated with distinctive strategies of appropriation. I will go on to suggest that, although this metaphor of gaze has been useful, it has unattractive connotations, but first I need to briefly indicate why the other association of dramaturgy – authenticity – is significant.

At first glance the dramaturgical metaphor should make the issue of authenticity (that is whether some tourist sites are more authentic than others) superfluous. If the idea of performance directs attention to the constructed, what I called earlier the necessarily artificial, character of social settings, then nowhere, certainly no tourist site, could be really authentic. One can go further and strengthen a connection between tourism and inauthenticity. The cultural form of tourism is a form of mass culture; by this I mean it is a way of producing culture for mass audiences in which the performance (the narrative) is marketed as a commodity. The distinctiveness of mass culture is displayed in a set of values and associated institutional forms called consumerism. These values are often criticised because they are seen to promote inauthenticity – by which I think the critics mean the drive by agencies or institutions of consumerism to promote false needs. That is, needs, desires and wants that are not as authentic or as appropriate as real needs.

An illustration of such a situation might be the study Miller (1995) has cited, where the researcher found that Afghan tribesmen were uninterested in the authenticity or not of locally-made rugs, but that they had quickly got caught up in the intricacies of Western fashion so that they sought prized instances of American jeans. (Miller has also recounted the anecdote of a tribe who delayed their annual migration in order not to miss the end of a series of Dallas [1992: 163], which, as he says, raises considerable issues: 'over concepts of authenticity' [ibid.].) This example of new consumer demands snags the attention because it initially seems 'wrong'. Jeans are alien to Afghan culture, and certainly jeans as fashion choice is a novel idea in this setting, and therefore to find they are taken seriously suggests something inauthentic.

It follows that inauthenticity is introduced when something is adapted or changed in order to meet expectations that would not have been influential in an original state. A particularly forceful version of essentialism in an unlikely sphere has been aptly provided by a recent article in The Guardian (Gray 1997). In the article Georgina Born is quoted as referring to authentic music as 'undisturbed music', an approach she expands by saying that the notion of authenticity is a 'way of understanding an artefact that is untainted by the market or the need to make concessions. In fact, autonomy is the only thing that guarantees a thing's authenticity'. I think she is stating most starkly here her perception of the irreconcilability between consumerism and authenticity. Similarly, in the same piece Charlie Gillett is quoted as saying that: 'Popular music is actually anti-authentic. . . Anything that develops or changes has to be anti-authentic. How could it be otherwise?'

The conclusion of this perspective is inescapable. A combination of a concern with change and a use of design to meet commercial ends means that tourist sites are deeply inauthentic. The place to be visited has been changed to accommodate tourists and must thereby be locked into the false values and concerns of consumer culture. I do not have the space to consider the broader issue of consumerism, but I do find such a blanket conclusion troubling for two reasons. First, it seems to reserve travel for an élite, either social or intellectual, who can appreciate the exotic in other cultures without polluting it. Secondly, it condemns popular audiences to unremitting false consciousness because a great deal of tourism – from the search for the sublime and the picturesque in romanticism to the contemporary popularity of safari parks – has been motivated by a quest for authentic experiences. The broader issue is then about the quality of popular culture in mass society. MacCannell's clever account of the staging of authenticity previously cited was not only concerned with the laminations of reality, but also with the tragic consciousness of modernity. Reflexively aware of the staging of place, indeed of culture more generally, the modern traveller in MacCannell's terms is endlessly but fruitlessly spurred by a quest for untrammelled meaning, for appearance that is true to itself (see also MacCannell 1992).

The related questions of whether some places or activities as tourist entertainments can be more authentic than others, and what it is that consumers are concerned with when they seek greater authenticity, are therefore both aspects of the possibility of meaningful experience in mass culture. Authenticity in tourism theory retains its power as a metaphor through representing a significant dimension of the ethics and aesthetics of participation/appropriation. The number of times the theme of a dominant quest for authenticity amongst tourists is mentioned in different papers in the Rojek and Urry collection previously cited is an indication of the metaphor's significance. It is true that the quest is usually dismissed as no longer really relevant. The reasons given for detecting a change are varied, but can be summarised by saying that the tragic quest of modernity is no longer troubling.

Thus, in their introduction, Rojek and Urry argue that too many places are gleefully inauthentic; in part because the dramaturgy of place is now so elaborate that nobody could imagine there could be a 'real' backstage, and in any case cultures are dispersed heterogeneously through space rather than located on distinctive sites. Similarly, in his single-authored contribution, Chris Rojek argues that a concern with authenticity is now irrelevant because there are no real places anymore; and in contrast to the sort of aesthetic appreciation possible in high culture: 'mass culture reduces the ordinary consumer to the position of an addicted consumer of reproduced objects, packaged events and other manipulated stimulants' (1997: 60). Post the modern era then, our consciousness has ceased to be tragic because we, as ordinary consumers, are no longer aware of, or no longer care about, the artifice of dramaturgy.

One way of understanding these arguments is to say that a quest for authenticity should be more typically associated with a romantic gaze.

If authenticity is no longer sought this may be due to a more general collapse of cultural distinctions and an indiscriminate pursuit of experiences characteristic of consumerism. Such an analysis would be unattractive to me both because it does not adequately represent trends in the fragmentation of tourist markets (Munt 1994) and because it is a continuation of the mass culture critique that it is impossible to sustain sophisticated cultural appreciation amongst mass audiences (Strinati 1995 Chap. 1; and Milner 1994 Chap. 2). In any case, even in these arguments there is an implicit recognition that the issue of authenticity is used as a point of reference for how we understand the meaning of tourist experiences. I will propose that the dismissal of authenticity as no longer relevant is too hasty and is based upon a particular understanding of the meaning of authenticity. Before I can outline an alternative, however, I have to return to the appropriateness of gaze as a metaphor for participation or consumption.

The main reason for being unhappy about the metaphor of gaze is that it seems to be based in a very theatrical conception of the dramaturgical metaphor. In gazing, the audience is contemplating from outside, they are looking at something in a way that commands. Extending the theatrical metaphor one could say that the gaze is through an implicit proscenium arch, for example, the staging practices of those who have made the tourist visit possible, or, more generally, the interpretive frame provided by the visitors' culture, at the spectacle of the place being visited. Despite, then, the frequently reiterated theme taken from Benjamin (1970) that the aura of the unique work of art has been subverted by the duplication of experiences in mass culture, the idea of gaze retrieves auratic appropriation. The audience of tourist visitors becomes the implicit author of the collectively staged spectacular site, replacing an author of scripted performances. Through their appropriation the work of others is completed, legitimated, and thus the tourist visit is understood as a form of annexation. The gaze in its untroubled authority is masculine in the presupposition that it articulates normality, and imperialist in the way it appropriates other cultures.[8]

It seems to me inevitable that this metaphor of gaze for the mode of appropriation of a tourist site should imply a concern with the authenticity, the right-ness, the real-ness of that being visited. Even the ironic gaze of the postmodern post-tourist, while savouring the impossibility of authentic engagement, still assumes that 'his' gaze commands the fabrications of others. It is his connoisseurship that discriminates between spectacles, presumably on grounds of fashion and style alone. This way of understanding tourist experiences cannot be accepted. It makes all tourism intrinsically and irretrievably morally repugnant, and surely it is inadequate in an era of mass tourism when the everyday life of the metropolis as well as rural idyll is as likely to be the objective for travel as national monuments or specialised pleasure zones. While there may be much to criticise in many aspects of the global tourist industry, the fact that it is a cultural form means that it is a form of engagement in everyday life that has to be respected. It is for these reasons that I want to suggest that the metaphor of tourist gaze be supplanted by another mode of visual engagement – the glance.

Glancing is more attractive as a metaphoric summary for a number of reasons. It suggests that the viewer is not so much seeking to command as fleetingly note. Crucially, glancing is a form of interaction through an exchange of glances – the participants are, in principle, on an equal footing and in some sort of dialogue. The visitor who glancingly notes the many features of their environment is also acknowledging that they are simultaneously being seen. The visitor is therefore reflexively engaging with the specificity of local spaces rather than appropriating them for their own purposes. Glancing also suggests that the site is robbed of its aura; instead the ephemerality of appearance is celebrated and the objects of tourist environments are easily allowed to be unfinished – to be what John Fiske has called producer-ly texts (1989). By this he means cultural objects that are not treated as closed or complete, but rather open to constant reinterpretation and thus themselves produce new meanings, new forms of engagement and participation. Finally, I think one can say that the stress on locality and intimacy in the process of glancing implies a less rational, masculine public sphere – the public spaces of touristic environments are effectively privatised and feminised.

Tourists are consumers of the public places of other cultures, but, as so often in the privatisation of public culture in mass society, their consumption is unpredictable, uncontrollable by public authorities. Their haphazard consumption can be described as a form of play in public spaces.[9] In all these ways then, the metaphor of glancing as a summary of a mode of participation seems more consistent with the pervasiveness of mass tourism and the dispersion of cultural environments. Glancing seems more consistent with the idea that global citizens increasingly inhabit mobile spaces, that the boundaries between environments are more fluid and unstable. Above all, glancing enables us to move away from a theatrical interpretation of the dramatic metaphor. While recognising that tourist sites are staged and fabricated spectacles, the sociality of performers and audiences is more like that of the civilised play of manners of the eighteenth- and early nineteenth-century pleasure garden. If, then, we have begun to rethink the ramifications of the dramatic metaphor this should enable us to return to the significance of authenticity and reconsider quite what is being sought in the use of this value.

I have suggested that the necessary artifice of tourist entertainments, allied to a broader context of the perceived deceptions of consumer culture, has generally been taken to deny any possibility of authenticity in tourist entertainments. I think these judgements both express a negative view of the distractions of mass entertainment and retain a positive sense of an implied assumption of a deeply constitutive relationship between real culture and authenticity. It is because authenticity is closely bound in with related notions of nature, truth, tradition, originality and integrity that an intrinsic authenticity has been a root metaphor for the traditional notion of culture employed in the human sciences; functioning as a normative focus in relation to which specific practices can be judged to be more or less appropriate. The reason for this is, I suggest, that it allows the notion of authenticity to function as an appeal to a self-evident essence.

These attitudes derive from the fact that the notion of culture was becoming central to social theory at the same time as the idea of nationhood was beginning to dominate the politics of modernisation. The connection is that nationalism is an ideology that famously denies its own contingency; for any group of nationalists the nation they cherish is natural and self-evident – one can easily say that it has an authentic identity. Apostles of national identity have shunned the arbitrariness of their creation, nationalist histories preferring to stress the charismatic role of leaders and theorists in the realisation of dormant destiny.[10] The notion of culture in one of its uses has functioned as a complementary analogue to that of national identity, and it is therefore unsurprising to find that cultures have also usually been treated as self-evident givens – the 'natural' foundations of social life.

Haskell (1993) has elegantly illustrated how in the new 'national' museums of the early nineteenth century, artefacts and images were sought that would clearly display the intrinsic continuity – the authenticity – of national history. Preziosi has subsequently more forcefully argued that since the invention of the museum some two hundred years ago it has become: 'an indispensable feature of the modern bourgeois nation-state' (1996: 100). The significance of the museum for Preziosi in part stems from the way it displays and thereby authenticates the cultural discourses governing its constituent sections, but more substantially because the museum came to provide an implicit frame within which the individuality of any displayed object – work of art – could be located. The museum, and its related form the public art gallery, came therefore to represent both physically and metaphorically the relationship between culture and its citizens: 'The work of art that came to be sited in the new historically organised museums of the early nineteenth century was in fact staged as a model of the new bourgeois social subject' (1996: 105). Citizenship in a liberal democracy in this account presupposed an authenticating frame, a culture, within which individual actors could take both their own autonomy and their interconnectedness for granted.

It is relevant in this respect that one of the key dictionary definitions of authenticity is as being true to the self (and thus I think the etymological link to authorship as something that is a direct result of personal creativity). This meaning has been nicely illustrated by Potter, writing of a study that sought to explain shifts in musical taste. Rather than talking of succumbing to fashion (consumerism again), Potter writes of members of sub-cultures having 'problems in displaying authenticity – that is, showing that they are making considered choices' (1996: 126). Without pressing etymological connections too far there is of course a common root of self-ness to aura, author and authenticity, so that we are forced to recognise a recurrent connection here between the authenticity of the object and a presumed individuality within a governing discourse (culture). I should note in passing that Celia Lury has argued that punk was the 'last' authentic music because its aesthetic of random agglomeration of discarded items and trash imagery denied the possibility of authenticity offering only 'a black hole of cynicism from which there could be no [way] back to the future' (Lury 1996: 198). It seems that in this view, to imagine a radically incoherent discourse is to deny both authenticity and individuality.

If culture is a discursive frame, it is likely to be used in very different ways when being used as a narrative resource in social theory (from 'outside') than when being used as a practical resource (from 'inside') (Clifford and Marcus 1986). In this respect it is helpful to note an example of a type of innovation in cultural production that has naturally led to uses of a value of authenticity that are themselves dependent upon outsiders' theorisations of culture (and one which has interesting resonances for the acquisition of artefacts by tourist visitors). The innovation has been the implementation of policies for new forms of object and image-making being introduced to local cultures. Examples here are the Inuit in northern Canada and Aborigines in Australia, where state agencies have sponsored new forms of craft production, often to replace threatened or destroyed traditional ways of life (more generally on 'native' art see Karp et al. 1992 and Hiller 1991). Judgements of authenticity in these circumstances become inevitably more complex. Here, native objects and images are being incorporated in another regime of value oriented towards the discourses of folk culture, which treats the notion of tradition very differently. Museum curators, representatives of state cultural agencies and nationalist intellectuals will combine to collect instances of native art and craftsmanship. These are held to authentically represent a traditional way of life – because they exemplify a culture. It is in this respect that Clifford has dissected what he has called the 'art-culture system' which he sees as functioning as a machine for the production of authenticity (1988).

It seems, then, that authenticity as a quality of cultural 'objects' is intrinsically ideological. I have so far accepted the idea that authenticity is a root metaphor for culture without question, and yet the metaphor is puzzling because it is paradoxical. We are also well aware that culture has traditionally been used in opposition to nature (thus the deep connection between culture and cultivation). Culture in this second sense is necessarily artificial – it is a complex set of practices employing human fabrication, it is a shaping of nature to designed ends. It follows then that the generalised idea of human culture common in the human sciences involves a combination of, first, a unified set of distinctive customs and attitudes (with an implied normative consciousness of how these practices should be performed), that is, something that is primarily traditional; and, second, an appreciation that this combination has been designed and is continually being redesigned – so that traditions are always changing. It is this second element that is frequently neglected (for example by Born and Gillett cited above) when appeals are made to the value of authenticity.

To begin to see the value of this second approach let me turn to a very different example which should lead us to ask what social interests actions or objects serve. My example here is Featherstone's discussion of sexual interaction in virtual reality (1995). I suspect that many would instinctively feel that seeking sexual gratification with the phantasmagoria of cyberspace is inherently inauthentic. Featherstone, however, makes a strong case that: 'For those who have bodies which do not match up to the cultural ideals, or are disabled or old, entering into a virtual reality 'teledildonic' network may offer a new range of opportunity structures, forms of intimacy and emotional attachments' (ibid.: 239). This example raises a number of complex issues because the sexual experience made electronically available is not a staged experience in the sense of a spectacular show. It is also hard to make a conventional distinction between performer and audience as the 'performers' are the figments of the audience's imagination. Yet, of course, the spectacle is a representation commercially developed as an opportunity to cater for others' leisure (it is perhaps not too far-fetched to see it as a form of tourism.)

The sexual experience generated does not have the messiness of 'reality' but may be at least as rewarding in certain respects. In order for these experiences to be seen as authentic or even more authentic than physical intercourse, then, authenticity supposedly resides in the creative intensity of commitment rather than the conventional criteria of more directly sensual experiences. This argument is politically tenable if cybersex is not restricted to the disabled or the elderly, that is that its not a surrogate for the second class. Even so I am still sceptical because I suspect that the depth of sexual experience is not orgasmic release alone. It is, rather, dependent upon an intimation of emotional fragility or the imminence of loss; in other words that authenticity in this area at least requires its own reflexive consciousness. It is import-ant to note that what I am doing here is shifting the notion of auth-enticity from consistency with a cultural template, to being a characteristic of actions or objects as they are being used.

I want to suggest, then, that authenticity should be understood as a quality of a process rather than an object. Authenticity is a cultural value because when it is invoked people are talking about how some-thing is being done rather than the what it is (that is being done). Authenticity concerns representation and performance. Although the presupposed truth of authenticity may mean that it might be taken to be 'the real', it should not be confused with reality and the terms treated as synonymous. It follows that any judgement of authenticity or not is an interpretation; although the naturalness of the authentic state might seem to be self-evident, in practice, appeals to, or invoca-tions of, authenticity depend upon judgements of appropriateness that are essentially contestable.

I hope it will now be apparent why I believe that this sense of auth-enticity is consistent with the use of a glance or glancing as more apposite metaphors for the practice of tourism. They enable us to think of how the audiences for tourist places interact with the presen-tations staged for their entertainment as forms of production – not as passive dupes, nor as pilgrims, or as colonialists commanding a view.[11] Emphasising interaction with presentations does not mean, however, that we lose the ability to make critical judgements, particularly ethi-cal and aesthetic judgements. I do not believe we are condemned to the infinite relativism of accepting whatever happens as all having equivalent desirability. While I do not have the space now to set out the grounds for different types of judgement, an indication of how they might go and a starting point is provided by the notion of kitsch. Typically, many of the entertainments patronised by tourists, and par-ticularly the souvenirs they purchase, have seemed to exemplify all that is tasteless about kitsch. If re-thinking the quality of authenticity meant that we could no longer use a notion of kitsch then I think it would be self-evident that we would be following the wrong trail, but Gronow's recent book on taste (1997: 42) suggests that kitsch be understood as 'a cheap, mass-produced copy of some original object or model which was considered elegant'. It is in the imperfections of copying that we detect kitsch and surely many tourist presentations do offer only ersatz imitations.

I also have to recognise that the practice of glancing as I have devel-oped it here is akin to Rojek's notion of the audience seeking distrac-tions, but I am not making this connection as part of an implied mass cultural critique saying that this is all they are fit for. It is rather that 'distractions' is a good term for the heterogeneous jumble of experience in tourists' practice. I want to argue that a value of authenticity should be used discursively to invoke the distinctiveness of local interactions. It is the contrast between the local and mass anonymity that gives meaning to authentic features, but 'the local' is an intrinsic element in the eclecticism of mass culture. There is, in this view, no necessary dissonance between eclecticism and authenticity in contemporary cultural discourse, and neither is authenticity precluded by the fragmentation of cultures in postmodernism.

Locality is a point of reference that will be constituted in an infinite multiplicity of ways to meet particular contextual concerns. Locality is not a place that can be mapped as either authorised or institutionalised social order. It is rather a pragmatic, reflexive space that is constituted in what de Certeau has called the walking of social action (de Certeau 1984).[12] In this respect I note that, towards the end of his paper on collecting art and culture, when referring to a book by Ralph Coe on native American art, James Clifford asserts that 'authenticity is something produced not salvaged' (1988: 250). To quote Daniel Miller again: 'Authenticity has increasingly to be judged a posteriori not a priori, according to local consequences not local origins' (1992: 181). What is being produced is a distinctive inflection of social forms – a form of production that is creative and undeniably cultural.

Notes

1. I have been worrying at the issue of authenticity in contemporary culture for some time now; it has previously surfaced in presentations given at the History of the Human Sciences Conference in 1997 and a Departmental seminar at the University of Durham. I am grateful to the participants of these sessions for their helpful comments.

2. In my collection of essays on the significance of culture for contemporary social theory grouped under this heading (1994), I explore some aspects of the phenomenology of tourism in the fourth chapter.

3. See for example a history of battles over appropriate identity and social location of a British resort such as Blackpool (Walton 1983; Walvin 1978; see also Urry 1990 Chap. 2).

4. There is of course a very substantial literature on metaphors in social theory; my own thinking has been greatly influenced by Brown 1977.

5. It would be particularly inappropriate to do so as I have used the idea of changing modes of staging (fictions) as a central metaphor for the social (1993) – discussing as one such fiction the staging of tourist visits (Chap. 5).

6. Although there is clearly a literal core to the role of gaze in tourist consumption, I think the broader way in which Urry uses the idea indicates it is, even so, a metaphor.

7. I know that the nature of the 'gaze' has been of critical concern in French social theory in the twentieth century (Jay 1994), but neither Urry, nor I in the criticisms I go on to make of this concept, are drawing upon this theoretical tradition.

8. In a paper that is explicitly oriented to another set of problems in how we

conceptualise different modes of visual appropriation (1997) I have explored an alternative way of seeing that is analogous to the alternative I present in this paper.

9. I think it is worth noting in this context an analogous shift in studies of television audiences in which commentators are now less likely to see the intermittent attention of television viewers as evidence of triviality and more as a distinctive type of consumption with its own values (Morley 1992; Silverstone 1995).

10. An apposite illustration of this usage came in celebrations of fifty years of Indian and Pakistani statehood when several commentators referred to these years as 'this phase of Indian national identity' as though there had ever been another.

11. In general my approach encourages us to think of the drama metaphor in relation to tourism as a form of play and not restrict it to theatrical 'plays'.

12. In this idea of strolling as a critical practice I am both nodding to the theme of the flâneur in modernity (Tester 1994), and picking up again an idea I mentioned earlier of the tourist as a metaphor for a way of being-in-the-world.

Surrounded by Place

Embodied Encounters

David Crouch

Introduction

In this chapter I seek to articulate tourism as an encounter with space and as something that is made through space. Tourism is a practice and is made in the process. In making these claims I challenge familiar representations of tourism as product, destination, consumption. A central feature in making an interpretation of tourism as encounter is the importance of mediation. In encountering place in tourism our bodies are important mediators of what happens and of what we comprehend to be 'there'. I present tourism as mediated by our bodies in an animation of space that combines feeling, imagination and sensuous and expressive qualities. Doreen Massey has argued that space, contextualised, becomes enlivened and endowed with meaning through the practices that people make in their lives, and tourism is one of those human practices (1993). Space is a prevailing component of tourism and a ubiquitous medium which the subject encounters. Tourism is part of lived practice. In considering encounter as part of human life it is necessary to embrace the notion of human practice. Tourism becomes validated in human practice in relation to knowledge. Knowledge is constructed through encounters, and space is important in informing this knowledge.

Prevailing reflections on tourism represent space as an inert medium prescribed by inscriptions *upon it*. The subject is rendered an object, object of interest, object of a consumption process. The body is similarly represented as object; object of interest in decorating tourism representations, object of 'othering' and so on (Selwyn 1996, Rojek and Urry 1997). That approach has prioritised vision as detached, separated, over-emphasising the object of the gaze and the decentralised observer, relegating the body to the object of representation (Selwyn

1996). Tourism is often represented as a key contemporary example of such detached vision, which is then demonstrated in exemplification of postmodern conditions (Urry 1990). The argument is reasonable, but relies upon a peculiar understanding of what tourism in space amongst people is.

The individual doing tourism tends to be theorised as decoder of products, production and their representation. This approach readily becomes part of a wider discussion of consumption that has been dominated until recent years by understanding particular relations between context, representations and consumption (Miller 1997). There are important spatial dimensions to this relation and what is understood to be tourism.

To recover the argument, the space in which tourism happens is an inert field of action predicated by its representation. The experience and 'practice' of tourism is itself represented as operating on an inscribed surface. The surface is already inscribed and provides the 'material' on which the tourist operates. The space 'between' the subject and this surface is inert, and it is across this space that the reading of representations and their inscription occurs. This is perhaps an unfairly mechanistic reading as Benjaminian imagination and some collision of desires is always acknowledged. However, this representation of tourism's space is essentially a metaphorical process where the metaphor and meanings are read as text. At most, the text may also be a stage, less enlivened by tourism activity, but across which the tourist's imagination plays. Too often the content of that 'playing' is ignored, in an assumption of direct textual analysis.

Another way to approach this problem is by acknowledging that the essential character of space in tourism practice is its combination of the material and the metaphorical. Once we acknowledge the subject as embodied and tourism as practice it is evident that our body does encounter space in its materiality; concrete components that effectively surround the body are literally 'felt'. However, that space and its contents are also apprehended imaginatively, in series and combinations of signs. Furthermore, those signs are constructed through our own engagement, imaginative enactment, and are embodied through our encounter in space and with space. There is a surprising lack in tourism geographies of the content of doing tourism. Instead of considering the 'doing' of tourism the tourist is enumerated, 'located', assumed simply to 'read' texts of abstractions labelled 'tourism' (Selwyn 1996). In order to make sense of the subject doing tourism, it is necessary to challenge the idea of tourism spaces as inert and having their limits as spaces with meanings inscribed upon them. This approach requires an analysis that utilises concepts of embodied knowledge. Thus I argue that without paying careful attention to the embodied practice of space any understanding of tourism remains abstracted from human experience. In consequence, our abstractions consist of ranges of idealised 'choices', inert spaces and surfaces constituted by inscriptions and across which a detached observation plays.

Knowing and Doing

Embodiment is important in the mediation of space in human practice. In this section I draw upon recent work on the embodied subject and practice. I explore and articulate ways in which space as a mediation of embodied subjectivity may be understood in terms of tourism. This includes an attention to tourism practices that may be considered typical of everyday life in many ways: speech, movement, sensuality and sensuousness, imagination, human relatedness and social interactions, feeling, turning, touching and 'doing'.

It is through practices such as these that we may consider tourism as a practice of space. Every tourism 'event', activity and practice takes place in and through space, even if that space is momentarily hyper-real or cybernetic. In the latter, the subject appears from a space, her body is situated in space during mental abstractions and then returns to another apprehended space afterwards. Much recent literature that has considered embodiment has done so in terms of the body as object (Featherstone 1991; Frank 1991). Here I pursue arguments that are surrounded by notions of the body as subject, doing rather than acted and gazed upon. Of course, these two categories of object and subject are not separate but mutually engaged. The individual emerges as subject, as an active (but not free) agent 'doing tourism'.

There has been a recent emergence of recognition of the body in tourism as complexly sensual. Cloke and Perkins acknowledge the general lack of attention to practice and body-practice in tourism discourse (1998). This is a very informative and a welcome enlargement of analysis beyond the familiar two-dimensional detachment of the gaze onto inscripted surfaces by a non-involved bystander. However this reading emerges from a consideration of particularly 'adventurous', active, sport tourism such as white water rafting and bungee jumping. In these activities the body is explicit in the process. In this chapter my concern is to provide a framework through which to rewrite all tourism in terms of embodied practice, not only those kinds of tourism that more self-evidently demonstrate the extreme movement and disruption of the body. By making recognition only in terms of extreme physical involvement one renders the greater part of tourism once again detached in an inert space.

Embodiment presented as only a physical phenomenon is incomplete. It is necessary to relate that physicality to imagination, to social contexts and to a 'making sense' of practice and of space. I intend to step beyond the familiar limits of embodiment to include brief consideration of the body engaged in an embodied poetics. It is strange that the poetic quality of tourism is polarised. It is commonplace that dreams are conjured up and played with in tourism literature directed at the 'customer'/potential tourist. Moreover this poetic content is especially inscribed on the landscapes, the buildings, the spaces that provide the content of tourism. Heritage and shopping tourism, for example, are represented with bodies as subjects of poetic inscription. Across these different examples the body itself, situated in a landscape, is used as a poetic surface – as can be seen in adverts for sticks of chocolate. It is self-evident, as Rojek has argued, that the poetics is the content of much touristic representation, and especially in representations of space (1995). However the poetic content of practice has been under studied (Rojek ibid.).

Of course the active subject is not free, and the significance of contexts and socialisation are considered below. Moreover, in practising tourism the subject is a social subject as well as a socialised one. This would require a consideration not only of the social contexts in which practices are made, but also of how, at any particular moment, practices in specific spaces relate and are related by the subject's life, and are socially constructed through practice, friendships and other human relations. Once again these social practices are spatialised and embodied. They happen in particular spaces where we may conceptualise the subject as having an awareness of content and meaning, spaces that are apprehended and mediated through the body, engaged, realised through practice in everyday actions. We may conceptualise not only space as practised, but also the body surrounded by and practised in and through space.

Developments in what is called 'non-representational geography' are supportive of this effort to embody and spatialise tourism practice (Thrift 1997). This includes an acknowledgement of the subject, practice and embodiment and reintroduces the material from what has become an often dematerialised geography of representations (Philo 2000). However, this nonrepresentational geography seeks an engagement of the material and the immaterial and metaphorical, rather than seeking to displace one with the other (Thrift 1996). A necessary focus of nonrepresentational geography is on knowledge as lay knowledge, the subject through practice grasping the world in an embodied way. There are two particular dimensions of this that I discuss in order to provide a basis for considering tourism as nonrepresentational practice. One of these is an interpretation of how lay geographical knowledge is made with particular reference to an active process of practice. The other specifically addresses the idea that in such a process there is a 'feeling of doing', and therefore focuses on embodiment. Both of these approaches are valuable in terms of understanding space.

John Shotter has explored such a practical knowledge in his work on people operating a particular social situation through which they develop a grasp of the world around them (1993). Thus he understands a popular or lay knowledge, developed in and through practice, which is different from expert and learnt knowledge. He calls this 'ontological knowledge'. Rom Harré uses another social constructionist approach in his consideration of how we engage the world around us and how that direct engagement is mediated through the body. He uses the term 'the feeling of doing' (1993).

Tourism is a practice of ontological knowledge, an encounter with space that is both social and incorporates an embodied 'feeling of doing'.

Story

When we are doing tourism we find ourselves in a place. This place might be a beach, a historic site, a park, mountain range, the inside of a club, on a raft in a river valley, a pub. We may be aware of people around us. We feel the ground, recall the brochure, the advertisements, the reports of what people do in places like this. We talk over what happened the previous day. We turn round, touch a friend, sit on the ground. There is an atmosphere in the place. There may be effort felt in what we are doing in the way we move our body, work out a friendly encounter. We pretend, imagine, discover a sensuality and a texture in ourselves we had forgotten or hoped for, or we may feel frustrated. We think over where we have come from and how far we have come and where else we desire to go. We negotiate an awkward slope. We make little judgements, reflexively we talk things over, mixing and re-mixing all of these impulses and desires. There are particular things in this place, another encounter, recent memories of similar places and what we did there. We bend to adjust our clothing and notice that the view has changed, the cliff, the water surface, the group standing nearby, the edges of the caravan site have changed.

This brief story includes a number of components of embodiment that I develop below. In this story there are at least two spaces. We may call these spaces of practice. Close-up there is a surrounding space that we see, touch, smell and in which we meet people. There may be a distant view. Nearby there may be a foreshortened space in terms of a spectacle. However there is almost always, the 'close-up' space where we sit, shuffle to view an event, mingle amongst people, share a story, move through. In the 'far off' there may be a view through a window; spaces reached only in vision.

Of course the space grasped immediately around the body and the one reached only in vision are not separate. They interact; we acknowledge them together and in relation. The individual in body and thought turns, momentarily makes another grasp of what is around and moves on. Through this process we construct a kaleidoscope of events and artefacts in a subjective way, through points of reference and desire that collide reference and desire, conveyed and made meaningful by a feeling and an imagination. Materiality and metaphor collide, as Radley puts it:

> these memories are part of culture and depend, in various ways, upon the physical setting for how people remember the course of events leading up to the present. It is not just that individuals remember specific things, or are reminded of the past by particular objects figured against a background of a shared discussion of the past. Artefacts and the fabricated environment are also there as a tangible expression of the basis from which one remembers, the material aspect of the setting which justifies the memories so constructed (1990).

Memory and meaning merge. Practice informs the way we negotiate meaning (Crouch D. 1997, Crouch D. 1998).

Aspects of embodied practice

Harré addressed his idea of 'the feeling of doing' through the work of Merleau-Ponty who paid meticulous attention to the sensing of space amongst, for example, people with seriously impaired vision (1962). Merleau-Ponty also explored the awareness of space in multiple dimensions. In terms of senses he alerts us to the collective, combinative way in which space is practised: touching, smelling, hearing, tasting and seeing. Vision is not sensed and made sense of separately from other senses but in interrelation and tension with them. Even vision becomes more complex than the gaze would suggest. Gazing at particular 'sights' (sic) is inflected by all sorts of other visual, as well as multisensual, awarenesses. In this complex and multiple engagement with the world a more multilayered semiotics may be imagined. Places and their contents are seen from numerous angles and are apprehended as fractured but recomposed in mental processes. However, they are not recomposed as 'set pieces', as theatre in relation to horizon and ordered importance, but understood in more complex and unsettled and energetic ways and in combinations and associated with complexities of feelings (Crouch and Toogood 1999). In tourism it is through rather than 'in front of' spaces that we experience where we are. There may be momentary limited-focus observation but this is short-lived, and such limited scoping is accompanied by bouts of much greater diversity and engagement of multisensuality and multidimensionality.

In thinking of the subject as embodied we are necessarily taken beyond a one-dimensional reading of texts and representations across an inert space. Tourist places, unlike paintings and posters with which they are too often elided in analysis, are multidimensional (Crouch and Toogood 1999). We discover and encounter the world in tourism 'with both feet' and figure sensual and mental and imaginative evidence together. Of course this 'evidence' is not taken in isolation. The metaphorical information that informs 'countryside', for example, is inter-cut and mutually worked in numerous senses made in the practice, both now and on previous occasions (MacNaghten and Urry 1998). Metaphors are not only stimulated, but constituted through practice itself in the collision of influences and events.

It is wrong to abstract staged semiotics from the world, since there are limits of the stage-set and the imitative representation. The fragments of vision that are collected in photographs themselves produce prompts that rework memory, relations and lay knowledge. Mike Crang examines the use of photographs not only as objects of gaze and of a popular desire to circulate programmed tourist representations, but also as the embodied artefacts of memory and objects of social interaction (1997). The sensation of space is one of engulfing, surrounding volume. In the familiar emphasis, perhaps overemphasis, on vision, we have neglected other bodily senses. It was necessary to acknowledge vision in the wake of an over concentration on the purely mental processes of knowledge (Jay 1993), but this is not enough. Rather than adding different senses in our existing schemas to include embodiment, it is important to comprehend the interaction of the multiplicity of senses acting together. In Merleau-Ponty's terms, this is an awareness of surrounding volume; the subject is aware of space all round her, a sensation and knowledge of being engulfed in space.

A feeling of doing does not come only through receiving feelings, but in animating them ourselves. The subject expressively encounters space.

> The expressive form of display in general, as with metaphors in particular, works not only to carry meaning of the whole but, in being reflected through the features that it takes up, infuses these with a new significance (Radley 1995: 11)

The way that Radley identifies the link between the expressive self and its influence on how we work significance in the space around us is inevitably connected with the social character of body-space.

Sociality is often overlooked in tourism practices. However from holiday camps to Club Mediterranne, trekking and skiing holidays and the youth lager culture caricatured in Southern Spain there is a profound sociality and practice of body-space. Maffesoli calls this tribal practice, and identifies the significance of space in such processes (1996). In spaces, people practise their rituals and relations and express themselves through their bodies. Making particular dance movements, acknowledging the shared value (rather than only 'cultural capital') in particular kinds of beers and modes of body-touching are part of a repertoire of social engagement and friendship. The space is practised through these embodied actions. Knowledge of the space is constituted through social encounter (Malbon 1998). Practices such as these include lay artistic production, ritualist practices (Finnegan 1997) and a range of human feelings including love, care and friendship (Gorz 1992). The fuller consideration of embodied spatial and social practices enables us to enlarge the acknowledgement given by both MacCannell and also Wearing and Wearing's 'human interactions' of a social nature (1992: 7, 1996).

Shared spaces, as body-space, are transformed by the presence and practice of bodies (Kayser Nielsen 1995). This constitutes a combining of sensed and social encountering. The subject doing tourism makes lay knowledge through a complexity of awareness that is immediate, diffuse and interactive and far more complex than a detached vision and sign-reading. We 'know' places bodily and through an active intersubjectivity. Tourism has a sensual component of abutting a surrounding world and of engaging that world. This sensuous component combines with the social engagement in that surrounding space and people are mentally embedded and needs drawing out through the metaphors that we develop of these spaces and practices.

Working metaphors

Whilst the initial prompt to visit a particular place may be from a TV programme, that prompt itself is engaged with feelings and desires already present in the individual. The visit to the place in question is likely to transform the TV semiotics once the place is encountered, embodied and practised. It is this complex feeling that confronts the materiality and combinations of metaphor in spaces around the subject. This engagement is neither wholly instrumental nor wholly subjective. The imaginative and embodied sociality used to negotiate another highly orchestrated semiotics was the subject of earlier work by Ley and Olds. In their analysis of the symbolism people took home from their visit to a World's Fair they discovered 'sharing time' and 'being together' to be the most prevailing (1988). It is easy without ethnographic evidence like this to construe the power of the semiotics rather than consider the practice (Warren 1993).

The ability to engage all the senses is, as Merleau-Ponty reasoned in terms of differing abilities, uneven (1962). Numerous other contexts of the practising subject may make particular combinations of practice work in different and distinctive ways, and here both the notion of habitus as class (Bourdieu 1984) and the socialised genderd subject provide important dimensions (Young 1990). Body-movements, what happens in embodiment itself, can be 'learnt' and inhibit or liberate, influencing and eliciting different responses. However, these contexts are neither total nor complete. Young acknowledges that the gendered subject encounters, practices, interprets and negotiates (1990: 11, Lamaison 1990). Of course, each culture accumulates its own 'baggage' of cultural meanings that influence what practice achieves (Thrift 1996). In distinguishing tourism as productive and subjective we acknowledge additional ground through which to understand its workings. In the contemporary period the possibility of being reflexive subjects unsettles a strict relation of context and critical negotiation of the self. The world toured and the world of the tourist are not hermetically sealed, but in part these processes of embodiment are mutually interleaved and overlapping, influenced through this complex series of practices.

Recent analyses of shopping provide further argument for deconstructing semiotic power transmitted in the vision of consumption. Gregson and Crewe demonstrate that consumption includes considerable social negotiation and networking and spatial knowledge (1997). Spending time at shops in tourism, as Miller has recently demonstrated in terms of everyday shopping, includes much more than consumption and it becomes possible to speak of engaged and expressive body space, human interaction and so on (Miller et al. 1998). The goods sought in tourism shopping, in beach malls, city shops and historic sites may serve similar roles to the photographs that Crang problematises. The 'goods' as artefacts may be passed around amongst friends. They are also part of processes of human encounter, of sensual experiencing and ritualistic practices that serve to connect and to remind. The act of purchase can be one amongst a number of aspects in the practice called shopping. In each of these aspects the spaces in which shopping happens is embodied. The area crossed, the surrounding volume informing and informed by our movements and the awareness of others and the engagement with them across space all constituting the practice. These places provide sensuous experience. They may be used to punctuate other experiences during tourism. In each case the shopping artefacts and doing shopping may be theorised as components of being away, of separation, ritual, anchoring the self and of liminality.

Rather than focus on the abstracted semiotics on display in tourism it is possible to consider a much more complex semiotic process. The meaning of tourism, of tourism spaces, encounters and engagements is constructed through these very practices, negotiating in the process the semiotics constituted through brochures and other contexts of tourism. It is possible to think in terms of meaning constructed through the complexity of practice, not simply from material features, but as Radley argues, through the practice that makes sense of artefacts. In her work on a sociology of embodiment, Anne Game calls this a 'materialist semiotics' (1991). She arrives at this idea of materialist semiotics through a wide-ranging exploration of feminist psychology across considerations of the body, power and time. For her, meaning is developed from the individual outwards, engaging a myriad of influences in the process. In order to illustrate this and to explore the way it may work she provides an account of her own visits to two very different 'tourism' spaces, Bondi Beach in Australia and the Haworth area of the Pennines in northern England. She 'knows' these two places in different ways, but develops very similar processes through which her own lay knowledge emerges. She knows Bondi from time spent over many years where she has 'a way of being on the beach' that she calls 'a drifting of the body' through which she makes an embodied knowledge and with which she counters the representations of this place in tourism promotion and its own corporate and institutionalised mythology. She visits England infrequently and is again aware of the inscriptions in the spaces she visits around Haworth, a place mythologised in English literature. Her account of Haworth is informed by making sense of these codes, but through a process of embodying the place and directing her attention to herself and what she does as subject.

> In Haworth my desire has been to know the place, to be able to read the codes of, for example, public footpaths and bridle ways; to have a competence with respect to this landscape, as I do body-surfing at Bondi; to be local and party to local stories. In a sense this is a desire to 'know' what cannot be seen (Game 1991: 184).

Her 'competence' is more like Shotter's ontological knowledge (made in the doing) than an expert competence.

Game acknowledges the contributory grounding borne from travel material. However, the subject behaves subjectively rather than rationally to these and is involved in a practice whose bounds are much more widely set, as we have discussed, and involves individual desires. The human subject is also poetic, and Game draws upon de Certeau's work on the creative and poetic manipulation of space (1984). The poetic comes in the creative and emotional space between the embodied 'feeling' that grasps the sensuous and sensual space of the body and does so expressively, and the imaginative and reflexive mental process. When Bachelard sees a particular hill he is awakened to a feeling of walking and a feeling of space triggered in imagination that reads the hill as 'muscular'. He is speaking of the poetics where the memory of space is informed directly from practice and practice that is embodied (1994).

Touristic representations matter and are part of the numerous influences and contexts through which we practise tourism. However they are no more than that:

The museum, the trail, the pamphlet are structured spaces, texts (the trail perhaps more open than the pamphlet); but it is possible that the constructed order of these is punched and torn open. (Game 1991: 166)

The pamphlet may be less open than the site because it cannot be engaged, encountered, practised, felt, embodied, and must remain more detached.

Conclusions

Embodied knowledge of space would suggest an ongoing patina of flows occurring through the complexity of human activity. This is profoundly different from the knowledge that is implicit in the gaze, and the processes of which the gaze is composed. Moreover it goes beyond the merely mentally constructed knowledge of, to a 'knowledge through'. We may call the process one of lay knowledge. Applying this interpretation to tourism would deliberately avoid a notion of knowledge as product or end point, but informed, informing, and continuing to inform, unstable, fragmented, and valued.

In each of the aspects considered there is recognition of the human subject doing things in the passage of life, through events, relations and spaces. This is not a chapter about a physical materialist privileging of space in tourism. However, these are always inflected by, and always inflect, thinking, learned knowledge, particular expertise. In another way they are each inflected by and inflect memory and friendships in terms of love, care and other human capacities and emotions noted by Gorz (1992). In imaginative practice they also become involved in a two-way frisson with poetics. All of these can be drawn on in their expressive capacity in reaching kinds of artistic practice where the borders with the élite, the professional and the amateur are blurred. This territory is often ignored and its reach into subjectivities is difficult. Yet subjectivities would seem to be crucial in making sense of what the touring subject does.

The world is grasped through the body and the world is mediated through the body. Our bodies are important in the ways in which we grasp and make sense of the world. Tourism is a practice through which we make this grasp. In building a more complex understanding of tourism as practising spaces it will be necessary to investigate components of embodiment and sociality. This will begin to fill out the notion of reflexivity into practice and a much more complex process of understanding, coping, playing with, the body bending and turning, and so on.

The ideas of liminality and of reflexivity offer useful material for further investigation, although as yet they have tended to work more semiotically (Shields 1991, Lash and Urry 1994). Rojek recently suggested that 'indexing' and 'dragging', as with computer interfaces, express the epistemological action of tourism (1997). Whilst acknowledging the active process of practice these suggest an all too clinical way of knowledge that occurs in a much more chaotic way. Selwyn has pointed to a much more complex desire in tourism that may include much less disruption and more intention towards seeking wholeness, largely unexplored in contemporary writing (1996). It may be possible to develop the idea of the 'other/ed' if we consider the mutual and shared complexity through which we know space and make encounters that are also social. This possibility becomes more approachable when we include the embodied and imaginative components of practising space in tourism (Crouch 1997; Crouch and McCabe 2002).

All of these ideas expand the possibilities of the expressive subject, imagination, and the capacity for fuller dimensions of reflexivity. This means that when we 'tour' and/or spend time at and/or practise our lives in a space, that may include an encounter with an 'other' culture, something more complex and nuanced occurs than is usually comprehended. The consumer arrives at this moment of encounter bearing knowledge, expectation, influenced by representations and other dimensions of life embodied and socialised, worked in imagination and friendships, from which she may seek to be dislodged or, through liminality, to readjust or to be steadied. With this kaleidoscope and patina of meanings and references she also practises space in tourism in embodied and social ways, and still the imagination works. Through this practice she encounters more representations, spaces, peoples, cultures and individuals, but her body already knows aspects of practising space that can be used again as familiar in this different context (again, tourism is still in her life, not outside it).

The critical teasing out and critical interpretation of these minutiae provide the greatest multidisciplinary intellectual challenge for making sense of practising space in the immediate future.

References

Abbeele, G. van den, 'Sightseers: Tourist as Theorist', *Diacritics* 10 (1980): 2–14.
———, *Travel as metaphor: from Montaigne to Rousseau*. University of Minnesota Press, Minneapolis, 1991.
Abram, S., 'Reactions to Tourism: A View from the Deep Green Heart of France', in *Coping With Tourists*, ed. J. Boissevain, Oxford: Berghahn, 1996.
Abram, S., Waldren, J. and Macleod, D., (eds) *Tourists and Tourism: Identifying People with Places*, Berg, Oxford, 1997.
Adam, R. and Kenneth J. H., 'Nature conservation in Scotland and furth of Scotland', *Scottish Geographical Magazine*, 60 2 (1944): 45–50.
Albrow, M.,'Travelling beyond Local Cultures: Socioscapes in a Global City', in *Living the Global City: Globalization as Local Process*, ed. J. Eade, London and New York: Routledge, 1996.
Albrow, M., *The Global Age*, Cambridge: Polity Press, 1996.
Albrow, M., Eade, J., Durrschmidt, J. and Washbourne, N., (1997) 'The Impact of Globalization on Sociological Concepts', in *Living the Global City: Globalization as Local Process*, ed. J. Eade, London and New York: Routledge, 1996.
Allison, A., *Nightwork: Sexuality, Pleasure, and Corporate Masculinity in a Tokyo Hostess Club*. Chicago, University of Chicago Press, 1994.
Ames, M., *Cannibal Tours and Glass Boxes: The Anthropology of Museums*. Vancouver, UBC Press, 1992.
Amino, Y., *Nihon Chûsei No Minshûzô: Heimin to Shokunin* (Portrait of the Folk in Medieval Japan: The Common People and the "Professionals"). Tokyo, Iwanami Shoten, 1980.
Anderson, D.G., 'Property as a Way of Knowing on Evenki Lands in Arctic Siberia', in C. Hann (ed.): 64–84, 1988.
Andrews, D., 'The (Trans)National Basketball Association: American Commodity-Sign Culture and Global-Local Conjuncturalism', in *Articulating the Global and the Local: Globalization and Cultural Studies*, eds A. Cvetkovich and D. Kellner, Boulder, CO, Westview Press, 1997, 72–101
Angelopoulos, Y. (ed.), *Athens Today*. Athens: Info Editions, 1997.Anon, *The Grand Canyon of Arizona: Through the Stereoscope*. New York: Underwood and Underwood, 1904.
Appadurai, A. and Breckenridge, C., 'Museums are Good to Think: Heritage on View in India', in *Museums and Communities: The Politics of Public Culture*, eds I. Karp, C. Kreamer, and S. Lavine, Washington, DC., Smithsonian Press, 1992, 34–55.

Appadurai, A., 'Disjuncture and Difference in the Global Cultural Economy' *Theory, Culture and Society* 7 (1990): 295–310.

Appadurai, A., 'Global Ethnoscapes: Notes and Queries for a Transnational Anthropology', in *Recapturing Anthropology: Working in the Present*, ed. R. Fox, Santa Fe, New Mexico: School of American Research Press, 1991a, 191–210.

——, 'The Production of Locality', in *Counterworks: Managing the Diversity of Knowledge*, ed. R. Fardon London and New York: Routledge, 1995.

Ashworth, G. and Tunbridge, J., *The Tourist – Historic City*. Aldershot, Belhaven, 1990.

Augé, M., *Non-Places; Introduction to an Anthropology of Supermodernity*. London, Verso, 1995.

Augé, M., *Nonluoghi*. Milano, Eleuthera 1993.

Babcock, B.,'Too Many, Too Few: Ritual Modes of Signification' *Semiotica* 23 (1978): 291–301.

Bachelard, G., *The Poetics of Space* Beacon Press, Massachusets, 1994.

Back, L., *New Ethnicities and Urban Cultures*, London, UCL Press, 1995.

Bagnasco, A. and Trigilia, C., *Societa' e Politica nelle Aree di Piccola Impresa* Venezia: Arsenale 1984.

Bakhtin, M.M., *Rabelais and his World*. Cambridge (Mass.), MIT Press, 1968.

Barthes, R., *Mythologies*. Paris: Editions Seuil, 1957.

Barthes, R., *The Eiffel Tower and Other Mythologies*. New York, Hill and Wang, 1979.

Barthes, R., *The Empire of Signs*. New York, Hill and Wang, 1987.

Basch, S., *Le Voyage Imaginaire: Les Ecrivains Français en Grèce au XX Siècle*. Paris, Hatier, 1991.

Baudrillard, J., *America*, Verso, London, 1988.

Baudrillard, J., *For a Critique of the Economy of the Sign*. St.Lewis, Telos, 1981.

Baudrillard, J., *Simulations,* New York, Semiotext, 1983.

Bauman, R., Sawin, P. and Carpenter I., *Reflections on the Folklife Festival: An Ethnograph into Participant Experience*. Bloomington, IN., Special Publications of the Folklore Institute 2, 1992.

Belich, J., *Making Peoples* Penguin, New Zealand, 1996.

Bell, C., *Rural Way of Life in New Zealand. Myths to Live By*. Ph.D thesis University of Auckland, 1993.

Bell, C., *Inventing New Zealand. Everyday Myths of Pakeha Identity*. New Zealand, Penguin, 1996.

Bellotti, E., *Davanti a un'Ombra* Bassano: Tassotti, 1983.

Bellotti, E. and Parolin, G., *Le Arti per Via* Bassano, Ghedina e Tassotti, 1985.

Benjamin, W., *Illuminations*. London: Fontana, 1969.

Benjamin, W., 'On the Mimetic Faculty', in *One Way Street and Other Writings*. London, Verso, 1979, 160–163.

Berengo, M., *L'Agricoltura Veneta dalla Caduta della Repubblica all'Unita'* Milano: Banca Commerciale Italiana, 1963.

Bernardi, U., *Paese Veneto* Firenze: Edizioni del Riccio, 1986.

Berti, G., *Storia di Bassano* Padova: Il Poligrafo, 1993.

Best, S. and Kellner, D., *Postmodern Theory: Critical Interrogations*. Macmillan, London, 1991.

Bhabha, H.K., 'Of Mimicry and Man: The Ambivalence of Colonial Discourse', in *Politics and Ideology*, eds J. Donald and S. Hall, Milton Keynes, Open University Press, 1986, 198–205.

Bhabha, H., *Nation and Narration*. London, Routledge, 1994.

Bhattacharyya, D.P., 'Mediating India: An Analysis of a Guidebook', *Annals of Tourism Research,* 24(2) (1997): 371–389.

Bicknell P.C., *Guidebook of the Grand Canyon of Arizona: With the Only Correct Maps in Print.* Kansas City, Fred Harvey, 1901.

Biorcio, R., *La Padania Promessa* Milano, Il Saggiatore, 1997.

Bishop, P., *The Myth of Shangri-la: Tibet, Travel Writing and the Western Creation of Sacred Landscape.* London, Athlone Press, 1989.

Bloch, M. 'Symbols, Song, Dance and Features of Articulation', *Archives Europeenees de Sociologie* 15 (1974): 55–81.

Boissevain, J. (ed.), *Coping with Tourists: European Reactions to Mass Tourism.* Oxford, Berghahn, 1996.

—— (ed.), *Revitalising European Rituals.* London, Routledge, 1992.

Bonnett, A., 'Situationism, Geography and Poststructuralism', *Environment and Planning D: Society and Space* 7, (1989): 131–146.

Boorstin, D., *The Image: A Guide to Pseudo-Events in America.* New York, Harper and Row, 1961.

Bourdieu, P., *Distinction: A Social Critique of the Judgement of Taste.* Cambridge, Harvard Univ. Press, 1984.

Bowman, G., 'Passion, Power and Politics in a Palestinian Tourist Market', in *The Tourist Image: Myths and Myth Making in Tourism*, ed. T. Selwyn, London, Wiley, 1996, 83–103.

Boyes, G., *The Imagined Village: Culture, Ideology and the English Folk Revival.* Manchester University Press, Manchester, 1995.

Boyle, M. and Hughes, G., 'The Politics of the Representation of 'The Real': Discourses from the Left on Glasgow's Role as European City of Culture, 1990', *Area* 23 (1991): 217–228.

Briguglio, L. et al. (eds), *Sustainable Tourism in Islands and Small States: Case Studies.* London, Pinter, 1996.

Britton, S., 'Tourism, Capital and Place: Towards a Critical Geography of Tourism', *Environment and Planning D: Society and Space*, 9, (1991): 451–478.

Brown R.H., *A Poetic for Sociology: Toward a logic of Discovery for the Human Sciences.* London, Cambridge University Press, 1977.

Brown, G., 'The Queer Spaces of Tower Hamlets: Gay Men and the Regeneration of an East London Borough', *Rising East* 2 (1998): 72–92.

Bruner, J., 'Transformation of Self in Tourism', *Annals of Tourism Research*, 18 (1991): 238–50.

Bruschi, E., Pagnini, E. and Pinzuati P., *Cultura Turistica.* Milano, Hoepli, 1987.

Burgin, V. (ed), *Thinking Photography.* London: Macmillan, 1982.

Burke, P., *Popular Culture in Early Modern Europe* London, Temple Smith, 1978.

——, *The Historical Anthropology of Early Modern Italy* Cambridge, CUP, 1987.

Burton Williamson, M., 'A Visit To The Grand Canyon', *Historical Society of Southern California* vol. 4 (1899): 203.

Butler, J., *Bodies that Matter.* New York and London, Routledge, 1993.

Calvino, I., *Invisible Cities*, New York, Harcourt, Brace and Co., 1974.

Cantwell R., *Ethnomimesis: Folklife and the Representation of Culture.* Chapel Hill, University of North Carolina Press, 1993.

——, 'Feasts of Unnaming: Folk Festivals and the Representation of Folklife', in *Public Folklore* eds R. Baron, and N. Spitzer, Washington DC, Smithsonian Institute Press, 1992, 263–305.

Caro Baroja, J., *El Carnaval* Madrid, Taurus, 1979.

Casey, E.S.,*Getting Back into Place.* Bloomington and Indianapolis: Indiana University Press, 1993.

Castells, M., *The Rise of the Network Society.* Oxford: Blackwell, 1996.

——, *The Informational City: Information Technology, Economic Restructuring, and the Urban-Regional Process*, Oxford and Cambridge, Mass., Blackwell, 1989.

————, *The Power of Identity: Economy, Society and Culture* (Vol. 2), Oxford, UK and Cambridge, Mass., Blackwell, 1997.

Catling, C., *AA Explorer London*. Basingstoke: AA Publishing, 1996.

Cazes, G., *Les Nouvelles Colonies de Vacances? Le Tourisme International (la Conquete du Tiers-Monde*. Paris, L' Harmattan, 1989.

CCS 'Proposta di regolamentazione della circolazione viaria all'interno del centrol storico di Bassano del Grappa', *Comitato del Centro Storico*, mimeograph, 1992.

Centre for Bangladesh Studies, *Roots and Beyond: Voices from 'Educationally Successful' Bangladeshis*. Roehampton Institute London, 1994.

Certeau, M. de, *The Practice of Everyday Life*, University of California Press, Berkeley, 1984.

————, *Heterologies: Discourses on the Other*. Manchester University Press: Manchester, 1986.

Chaney D., 'The Department Store as a Cultural Form', *Theory, Culture and Society* Vol. 3(1) (1983): 22–31.

————, 'Subtopia in Gateshead: the MetroCentre as Cultural Form', *Theory, Culture and Society* Vol. 7(4) (1990): 49–68

————, *Fictions of Collective Life: Public drama in Late Modern Culture*, Routledge, London, 1993.

————, *The Cultural Turn: Scene-Setting Essays in Contemporary Cultural History*, London, Routledge, 1994.

————, ' "Ways of Seeing" Reconsidered: Representation and Construction in Mass Culture', *History of the Human Sciences* Vol.9(2) (1997): 39–50.

————, 'Re-thinking Culture as Ideology and Sensibility', in *Culture in the Communication Age*, ed. J. Lull, Thousand Oaks, Sage, 1999.

Chapman, M., *The Gaelic Vision in Scottish Culture*. Croom Helm, London, 1978.

Chateaubriand, R., *Itinéraire de Paris (Jerusalem*. Paris, Julliard, 1964.

Clark, N., 'The Occluded Vision of the European Voyager', in *Art Now* Exhibition Catalogue, Museum of New Zealand, Te Papa Tongarewa. Wellington, New Zealand, 1994.

Clark, N., *Prospects of Enchantment, Dreamworlds of Nature*, Ph.D Thesis, University of Auckland, 1994.

Clifford, J., *The Predicament of Culture: Twentieth-Century Ethnography, Literature and Art*. Cambridge Mass., Harvard University Press, 1988.

————, 'Notes on Theory and Travel', *Inscriptions* 5 (1989): 177–188.

————, 'Traveling Cultures', in *Cultural Studies*, eds L. Grossberg, C. Nelson, and P. Treichler, New York: Routledge, 1991, 96–116.

Clifford, J. and Marcus G.E. (eds), *Writing Culture: The Poetics and Politics of Ethnography*, Berkeley, University of California Press, 1986.

Cloke, P. and Perkins, H., ' "Cracking the Canyon with the Awesome Foursome": Representations of Adventure in New Zealand', *Environment and Planning D: Society and Space* 16 (1998).

Clyde, R., *From Rebel to Hero: The Image of the Highlander, 1745–1830*. Tuckwell Press, Edinburgh, 1995.

Cohen, A., 'A Polyethnic London Carnival as a Contested Cultural Performance', *Ethnic and Racial Studies* 5 (1982): 23–41.

————, *The Symbolic Construction of Communit.y*. London, Ellis Horwood and Tavistock, 1985.

Cohen, E., 'Rethinking the Sociology of Tourism', *Annals of Tourism Research* 6 (1979): 18–35.

————, 'Contemporary Tourism – Trends and Challenges: Sustainable

Authenticity or Contrived Post-Modernity?', in *Change in Tourism – People, Places, Processes,* eds R. Butler and D. Pearce, London: Routledge, 1995.
——, 'Toward a Sociology of International Tourism', *Social Research* 39 (1972): 164–82.
Collins, G. N. M., *The Diary of James Morrison,* G N M Collins, Edinburgh, 1984.
Connerton, P.,*How Societies Remembe.r* Cambridge: Cambridge University Press, 1989.
Cosgrove, D. and Daniels, S. (eds), *The Iconography of Landscape.* Cambridge: Cambridge University Press, 1988.
Counihan, C.M., 'Transvestism and Gender in a Sardinian Carnival', *Anthropology* Vol. IX (1–2) (1985): 11–4.
Crang, M., 'Picturing Practices: Research Through the Tourist Gaze', *Progress in Human Geography* 21, 3 (1997): 359–373.
Crang, P., 'Performing the Tourist Product', in *Touring Cultures: Transformation of Travel and Theory,* eds C. Rojek and J. Urry, London, Routledge, 1997, 37–54.
Crary, J., 'Unbinding Vision: Manet and the Attentive Observer in the Late Nineteenth Century', in *Cinema and the Invention of Modern Life,* eds L. Charney and V. Schwartz, Berkeley: University of California Press, 1995.
——, *Techniques of the Observer: On Vision and Modernity in the Nineteenth Century.* Cambridge, MA, MIT Press, 1990.
——,'Eclipse of the Spectacle', in *Art After Modernism: Rethinking Representation* ed B. Wallis, New York, New Museum of Contemporary Art, 1984.
Crick, M., 'Representations of International Tourism in the Social Sciences: Sun, Sex, Sights, Savings and Servility', *Annual Review of Anthropology* 22 (1989): 461–81.
Crossley, N., 'Body-Subject/Body-Power: Agency, Inscription and Control in Foucault and Merleau-Ponty', *Body and Society* 2.2 (1996): 99–116.
Crouch, D. and Toogood, M. (1999)Crouch, D., 'Others in the Rural: Leisure Practices and Geographical Knowledge', in *Revealing Rural Others,* ed P. Milbourne, London, Cassell, 1997.
——, 'The Street in the Making of Geographical Knowledge', in *Images of the Street,* ed N. Fyfe, London, Routledge, 1998.
——, ed., *Leisure/Tourism Geographies: Leisure Practices and Geographical Knowledge,* Routledge London, 1999.
Crouch D. and Toogood M. 'Everyday Abstraction: Geographical Knowledge in the Art of Peter Lanyon', *Ecumene* 6(1) (1999): 72–89
Crouch D. and McCabe S. 'Culture, Consumption and Eco-Tourism' in *Eco-Tourism and Eco-Tourism Policies* ed. D. Fennell, Routledge London.
Culler, J. 'The Semiotics of Tourism', *American Journal of Semiotics* 1, no. 1–2 (1981): 127–140.
Curtis, B. and Pajaczkowska, C., 'Getting There: Travel, Time and Narrative', in *Travellers' Tales,* eds Robertson et al., London: Routledge, 1994, 199–215.
Da Matta, R., 'Carnival in Multiple Planes', in McAloon ed. 1984, 220–41.
Dahles, J., 'The Social Construction of Mokum: Tourism and the Quest for Local Identity in Amsterdam', in *Coping with Tourists: European Reactions to Mass Tourism,* ed. J.Boissevain, Oxford, Berghahn, 1996.
Dann, G., 'The Tourist as Child. Some Reflections', in *Cahiers du Tourisme,* Serie C, (1989): 135.
——,'Writing out the Tourist in Space and Time' in *Annals of Tourism Research,* 26 (1) (1999): 159–187.
De Grazia, V., *The Culture of Consent.* Cambridge: Cambridge University Press, 1981.

Debord, G. *Society of the Spectacle*, Black and Red, Detroit, 1977, also *The Society of the Spectacle*, translated by Donald Nicolson-Smith, Zone Books, New York, 1994.

——, 'Untitled Text 28.1.71', in *Situationist International Antholog*, ed. K. Knabb, Berkeley, CA, Bureau of Public Secrets, 1981.

——, *Panegyric*, Verso, London, 1991.

Debord, G. and Sanguinetti, G., *The Veritable Split in the International, Public Circular of the Situationist International*, London, B M Piranha, 1974.

Debord, G. and Wolman G., 'Methods of Detournement' in *Situationist International Anthology* ed. K Knabb, Berkeley, CA, Bureau of Public Secrets, 1981.

Delillo, D., *The Names*. London, Picador, 1983.

Diamanti, I., 'The Northern League', in *The New Italian Republic*, eds S. Gundle and S. Parker, London, Routledge, 1995a.

Diamanti, I., *La Lega*, Roma, Donzelli, 1995b.

Downs, R.M. and Stea, D., *Maps in Mind: Reflections on Cognitive Mapping*. New York, Harper and Row Publishers, 1972.

Duncan, J. and Duncan, N., '(Re)reading the Landscape', *Environment and Planning D: Society and Space*, 6 (1988): 117–126.

Dundes, A., 'Nationalistic Inferiority Complexes and the Fabrication of Fakelore: A Reconciliation of *Ossian*, the *Kinder-und Hausmurchen*, the *Kalevala*, and Paul Bunyan', *Journal of Folklore Research* 22 (1) (1985): 5–18.

Dutton, C. E., *The Tertiary History of the Grand Canyon District, with Atlas*. Washington: Government Printing Office, 1882.

Eade, J., *The Politics of Community: The Bangladeshi Community in East London*. Aldershot, Avebury, 1989.

Eade, J., 'Nationalism, Community and the Islamization of Space in London' in *Making Space for Islam in North America and Europe*, ed. B. Metcalf, Berkeley, University of California Press, 1996.

Eade, J., 'Reconstructing Places: Changing Images of Locality in Docklands and Spitalfields' in *Living the Global City: Globalization as Local Process*, ed. J. Eade, London and New York, Routledge, 1997.

Eagleton, T., *Ideology: An Introduction*. Verso, London, 1991.

Eagleton, T., *The Illusions of Postmodernism*. Blackwell, Oxford, 1996.

Eagleton, T., 'Marxist Literary Theory', in *The Eagleton Reader*, ed. S. Reagan, Blackwell, Oxford, 1998.

Eames, A., ed., *Insight Guides London*, Singapore, Hofer Press, 1995.

Eco, U., *Travels in Hyper-Reality*, London, Picador, 1987.

Edensor, T., *Tourists at the Taj.: Performance and Meaning at a Symbolic Site*. London, Routledge, 1998.

Edwards, E., 'Postcards: Greetings from Another World', in *The Tourist Image: Myths and Myth Making in Tourism*, ed T. Selwyn, London, Wiley, 1996, 197–221.

Eisenstadt, S.N. and Roniger, L., *Patrons, Clients and Friends*. Cambridge, CUP, 1984.

Ekholm Friedman, K. and Friedman, J., 'Global Complexity and the Simplicity of Everyday Life', in *Worlds Apart*, ed. D. Miller, London, Routledge, 1995, 134–68.

Elissalde, B., 'Guides, mode d' emploi', in *Espaces – Temps, Reflechir les Sciences Sociales: Edition Special 'Voyage au Centre de la Ville'* 33 (1986): 27–30.

Entrikin, J.N.,*The Betweenness of Place*. Baltimore, Johns Hopkins University Press, 1991.

Fairburn, M., *The Ideal Society and its Enemies*. Auckland, Auckland University Press, 1989.

Fardon, R. (ed.), *Counterworks*. London, Routledge, 1995.

Faubion, J.D., *Modern Greek Lessons: A Primer in Historical Constructivism*. New Jersey, Princeton University Press, 1993.

Featherstone M., 'Post-Bodies, Ageing and Virtual Reality', in *Images of Ageing*, eds M. Featherstone and A. Wernick, London, Routledge, 1995.

Featherstone M. et al., eds, *The Body: Social Processes and Cultural Theory*, London, Sage, 1991.

Featherstone, M., *Undoing Culture – Globalization, Postmodernism and Identity*. London, Sage, 95.

Featherstone, M. 'Local and Global Culture', in *Mapping the Futures: Local Cultures, Global Change*, eds J. Bird et al., London and New York, Routledge, 1993.

Featherstone, M., 'The Body in Consumer Culture', in *The Body: Social Processes and Cultural Theory*, eds M. Featherstone et al., London, Sage, 1991, 170–96.

Federal Writers' Project, Works Progress Administration, *A South Dakota Guide*, American Guide Series, Pierre, SD: State of South Dakota, 1938.

Federal Writers' Project, Works Progress Administration, *South Dakota: A Guide to the State*, ed. M. Lisle Reese, 2d ed., New York: Hastings House, 1958.

Feifer, N., *Going Places*, London: Macmillan, 1985.Feldman, D. and Stedman Jones, G., eds., *Metropolis – London: Histories and Representations*, London and New York, Routledge, 1989.

Fieldings, *Travel Guide to Europe*. New York, William Sloane Associates, 1965.

Filippucci, P., 'Tradition in Action: The Carnevale of Bassano 1824–1989', *Journal of Mediterranean Studies* 2 (1) (1992): 55–68.

———, 'Landscape, Locality and Nation: The Case of Bassano', *Paragraph* 20 (1) (1997): 42–58.

Filippucci, P., Grasseni, C. and J. Stacul, *'Knowing the Territory'*, paper presented at Association for the Study of Modern Italy annual conference, London, November 1997.

Finnegan R., *The Hidden Musicians: Music Making in an English Town*. Open University Press, Buckingham, 1989.

———,'Music, Performance and Enactment', in *Consumption and Everyday Life*, ed. G. Mackay, Sage, London, 1997.Fishman, W., *East End 1888*. London: Duckworth, 1988.

Fiske J., *Understanding Popular Culture*. Unwin Hyman, London, 1989.

———, *Television Culture*. London: Routledge, 1987.

Forman, C., *Spitalfields: A Battle for Land*. London, Hilary Shipman, 1989.

Fowler, P., 'Heritage: a Post-Modernist Perspective', in *Interpreting Heritage: The Built and Natural Environment*, ed D. Uzzell, Hampshire, Belhaven, 1989, 57–63.

———, *The Past in Contemporary Society: Then, Now*. Routledge: London, 1992.

Frank, A.W., 'For a Sociology of the Body: An Analytical Review', in *The Body* eds M. Featherstone, M. Hepworth and B.S. Turner, 1991, 36–102.

Franzina, E., 'Dopo il '76: una regione all'estero', in *Il Veneto* ed. S. Lanaro, Torino, Einaudi, 1984, 469–575.

Frommers, *Europe on 5 Dollars a Day*. London, Frommers Guides, 1968.

Frow, J., 'Tourism and the Semiotics of Nostalgia', *October* 57 (1991): 123–151.

Fsadni, C. and Selwyn, T., eds, *Tourism, Culture and Regional Development in the Mediterranean*, Malta, University of Malta Press, 1997.

Fussell, P., *Abroad, British Literary Traveling Between the Wars*, New York, Oxford University Press, 1980.

Galt, A.N., 'Carnival on the Island of Pantelleria' *Ethnology* 12 (1973): 325–41.

Game, A., *Undoing the Social: Towards a Deconstructive Sociology*. Open University Press, Milton Keynes, 1991.

Gardner, K., *Global Migrants, Local Lives: Travel and Transformation in Rural Bangladesh,*. Oxford, Clarendon Press, 1995.

Gardner, K. and Shukur, A., ' "I'm Bengali, I'm Asian and I'm Living Here"', in *Desh Pardesh: The South Asian Presence in Britain*, ed, R. Ballard, London, Hurst and Co., 1994.

Gennep, A. Van, *The Rites of Passage*, London, Routledge, [First Published 1909] 1960.

Giddens, A., *The Consequences of Modernity*. Cambridge, Polity/Blackwell, 1990.

Gilloch, G., *Myth and Metropolis: Walter Benjamin and the City*. Cambridge, Polity Press, 1996.

Gilmore, D.,'Friendship in Fuenmayor',*Ethnology* 14 (1974): 310–24.

——, 'Carnival in Fuenmayor', *Journal of Anthropological Research* 31 (1975): 331–49.

——, *Aggression and Communit*, New Haven and London, Yale University Press, 1987.

Gilroy, P., *The Black Atlantic: Modernity and Double Consciousness*. Cambridge MA., Harvard University Press, 1993.

Ginzburg, C. 'Folklore, Magia, Religione', in *Storia d'Italia: I Caratteri Originali*, Torino, 1972, 602–76.

Gluck, C., *Japan's Modern Myths: Ideology in the Late Meiji Period*. Princeton, NJ, Princeton University Press, 1985.

Gold, J.R. and Ward, S.V. (eds), *Place Promotion: The Use of Publicity and Marketing to Sell Towns and Regions*, Chichester, John Wiley and Sons, 1994.

Goodman, R., *Japan's 'International Youth': The Emergence of a New Class of Schoolchildren*. Oxford, Clarendon Press, 1993.

Gordon, B., 'The Souvenir: Messenger of the Extraordinary', *Journal of Popular Culture* 20 (3) (1986): 135–46.

Gorz A., *Paths to Paradise*. Pluto, London, 1982.

Gourgouris, S., *Dream Nation: Enlightenment, Colonization and the Institution of Modern Greece*. California: Stanford University Press, 1996.

Graburn, N., 'The Anthropology of Tourism', *Annals of Tourism Research*, 10 (1983): 9–31.

——, 'Tourism: The Sacred Journey', in *Hosts and Guests*, ed. V. Smith, USA: University of Pennsylvania Press, 1989.

Greenwood, D., 'Culture by the Pound: An Anthropological Perspective on Tourism as Cultural Commoditization', in *Hosts and Guests: The Anthropology of Tourism*, ed., V. Smith, Philadelphia, University of Pennsylvania Press, 1989, 129–138.

Gregory, D., 'Between the Book and the Lamp: Imaginative Geographies of Egypt, 1849–50', in *Transactions of the Institute of British Geographers*, 20 (1995): 29–57.

Gregson N. and Crewe L., 'The Bargain, the Knowledge and the Spectacle: Making Sense of Consumption in the Space of the Car-Boot Fair', *Environment and Planning D: Society and Space* 15 (1997): 87–112.

Gritti, J., 'Les contenus culturels du Guide Bleu: monuments et sites "(voir"' *Communications* Vol.10 (1967): 51–64.

Gronow J., *The Sociology of Taste*. London, Routledge, 1997.

Guide Bleu *Grèce*. Paris, Librairie Hachette, 1932.

Guizzardi, G., 'The Rural Civilization: The Structure of an Ideology of Consent', *Social Compass* XXII (2–3) (1976): 197–220.

Hall, S., 'New Ethnicities', in *'Race', Culture and Difference*, eds, J. Donald and A. Rattansi, London, Sage, 1992b.

———, 'The Question of Cultural Identity', in *Modernity and Its Futures*, eds S. Hall, D. Held, and A. McGrew, Cambridge, Polity and Milton Keynes, Open University Press, 1992a.

Hampton, M. P., 'Backpacker Tourism and Economic Development', in *Annals of Tourism Research*, 25 (1998): 639–660.

Handler, R. and Gable, E., *The New History in an Old Museum: Creating the Past at Colonial Williamsburg*. Durham, Duke University Press, 1997.

Handler, R. and Linnekin, J., 'Tradition, Genuine or Spurious', *Journal of American Folklore* 97 (385) (1984): 273–290.

Hannerz, U., 'Cosmopolitans and Locals in World Culture', *Theory, Culture and Society* 7 (1990): 237–251.

Harré R., *The Discursive Mind*, Blackwell, Oxford, 1993.

Harris, R., 'Interpreting Teenage Inter-Ethnic Violence', in *International Journal on Minority and Group Rights*, 1996–7.

Harvey, D., *The Condition of Postmodernity*, Blackwell, Oxford, 1989.

———, 'The Nature of the Environment: The Dialectics of Social and Environmental Change', in *The Socialist Register*, eds R. Miliband, and C. Panitch, Merlin Press, London, 1993.

———, *Justice, Nature and the Geography of Difference*, Blackwell, Oxford, 1996.

Haskell, F., *History and its Images: Art and the Interpretation of the Past*. New Haven, Yale University Press, 1993.

Hayden, D., *The Power of Place: Urban Landscapes as Public History*, Cambridge, Mass., MIT Press, 1996.

Helms, M., *Ulysses Sail: Travel, Knowledge and Power*. Princeton, Princeton University Press, 1989.

Herzfeld, M., *Anthropology Through the Looking Glass*. Cambridge, Cambridge University Press, 1987.

———, *Cultural Intimacy: Social Poetics and the Nation-State*. New York, Routledge, 1997.

Hetherington K., *The Badlands of Modernity: Heterotopia and Social Ordering*, London, Routledge, 1997.

Higgins, C. et al. (eds), *Grand Canyon on the Colorado River, Arizona*, Chicago, Santa Fe Railway Passenger Department, 1892, republished as *Titan of Chasms: The Grand Canyon of Arizona*, Chicago, Santa Fe, var. dates.

Hiller S. (ed), *The Myth of Primitivism: Perspectives on Art*, London, Routledge, 1991.

Hirsch, E. and O'Hanlon, M. (eds), *The Anthropology of Landscape: Perspectives on Place and Space*, Oxford, Clarendon, 1995.

Hobsbawm, E. and Ranger, T. (eds.), *The Invention of Tradition*, Cambridge University Press, Cambridge, 1989.

Hoelscher, S., 'Tourism, Ethnic Memory and the Other Directed Place', *Ecumene* 5 (4) (1998): 369–98.

Horne, D., *The Great Museum*. London: Pluto, 1981.

Hughes G., 'Tourism and the Semiological Realization of Space', in *Destinations: Cultural Landscapes of Tourism* ed., G. Ringer, London, Routledge, 1998, 17–32.

Hughes-Freeland, F. (ed.), *Ritual, Performance, Media*, London, Routledge, 1998.
Humboldt, W. Von, *Humanist Without Portofolio: An Anthology*. Detroit, Wayne State University Press, 1963.
Hungerford, E., 'A Study in Consistent Railroad Advertising,', *The Santa Fe Magazine* 19 (March) (1923): 44.
Hunter, J., *The Making of the Crofting Community*. John Donald, Edinburgh, 1976.
Hutnyk, J., *The Rumour of Calcutta: Tourism, Charity and the Poverty of Representation*. London, Zed Books, 1996.
Hutt, M., 'Looking for Shangri-la: From Hilton to Lāmichhāne', in *The Tourist Image: Myths and Myth Making in Tourism*, ed, T. Selwyn, London, Wiley, 1996, 50–60.
Huyssen, A., *Twilight Memories; Making Time in a Culture of Amnesia*. London, Routledge, 1997.
Imrie, M., 'Shattering of the Spectacle', Obituary: Guy Debord, *The Guardian* 5 Dec. 1994, 94.
Jackson, M., 'Knowledge of the Body', *Man* N.S. (1983): 327–45.
James, G. W., *In and Around The Grand Canyon: The Grand Canyon of the Colorado River in Arizona*, Boston, Little, Brown, and Co., 1900.
Jameson, F., 'Postmodernism and Consumer Society', in *The Anti-Aesthetic: Essays on Postmodern Culture*, ed, H. Foster, Port Townsend, WA: Bay Press, 1983, 111–125.
Jay M., *Downcast Eyes: The Denigration of Vision in Twentieth Century French Thought*. Berkeley, University of California Press, 1994.
Kabbani, R. *Europe's Myths of Orient*. Bloomington, Indiana University Press, 1986.
Karp, I. and Lavine, S. (eds.), *Exhibiting Cultures: The Poetics and Politics of Museum Display*, Smithsonian Press: Washington, DC, 1991.
Karp, I., Kreamer, C.M., and Lavine S.D. (eds), *Museums and Communities: The Politics of Public Culture*, Washington, Smithsonian Institution Press, 1992.
Karpodini-Dimitriadi, E., 'The Promotion of the Cultural Identity Through the Tourist Guidebooks', in *The Technical Chronicles: Tourism and Monuments – Cultural Tourism*, Athens, Technical Chamber of Greece (in Greek), 1995, 109–113.
Kayser N., 'The Stadium in the City: a Modern Story', in *The Stadium and the City*, ed. J. Bale, Keele, Keele University Press, 1995.
Kazantzakis, N., *Zorba the Greek*. Oxford: Bruno Cassirer, 1952.
Keith, M., 'Making the Street Visible: Placing Racial Violence in Context', *New Community* 21, 4 (1995): 551–65.
Kenneth, M. and Davis, R., *Athens and Attica*. Athens, Kauffmann, 1934.
Kirshenblatt-Gimblett, B., 'Objects of Ethnography', in *Exhibiting Cultures: The Poetics and Politics of Museum Displays*, eds, I. Karp and S. Lavine, Washington, DC., Smithsonian Press, 1991, 386–443.
———, *Destination Culture: Tourism, Museums, and Heritage*. Berkeley, University of California Press, 1998.
———, 'Folklore's Crisis', *Journal. of American Folklore* 111 (441) (1998): 281–327.
Kohn, T., 'Incomers and Fieldworkers: A Comparative Study of Social Experience', in *Social Experience and Anthropological Knowledge*, eds K. Hastrup and P. Hervik, London, Routledge, 1994.
———, 'Island Involvement and the Evolving Tourist', in *Tourists and Tourism: Identifying People with Places*, eds S. Abram, J. Waldren, and D. Macleod, Oxford, Berg, 1997.

Konidaris, I. (ed.), *Fun Time: The Athens Magazine,* no.6, Athens, Konidaris Publications and Co., 1998.

Lacan, J., *Ecrits: A Selection.* New York and London, Norton, 1977.

Lamaison P., 'From Rules to Strategies: An Interview with Pierre Bourdieu', *Cultural Anthropology* 1,1 (1990): 110–120.

Lash, S. and Urry J., *The End of Organized Capitalism.* Madison, University of Wisconsin Press, 1987.

Lash, S. and Urry, J., *Economies of Signs and Space,* London, Sage, 1994.Law, C. ed., *Tourism in Major Cities,* London: International Thompson Business Press, 1996.

Lee, M. J., *Consumer Culture Reborn: The Cultural Politics of Consumption.* London, Routledge, 1993.

Lee, S., 'Traveling the Sunshine State: The Growth of Tourism in South Dakota, 1914–1939', *South Dakota History* 19, no. 2 (summer) (1989): 219, 222–223.

Lefebvre, H., *The Production of Space.* Blackwell, Oxford, 1991.

Let's Go, *The Budget Guide to Europe.* New York: St. Martin's Press, 1991.

Levine, L., *Highbrow/Lowbrow: The Emergence of Cultural Hierarchy in America.* Cambridge, MA., Harvard University Press, 1988.

Ley D. and Olds K., 'Landscape as Spectacle: World's Fairs and the Culture of Heroic Consumption', *Environment and Planning D: Society and Space* 6 (1988): 191–212.

Life World Library, *Greece.* New York, Time Incorporated, 1963.

Löfgren, O., 'The Nationalization of Culture', *Ethnologia Europaea, 19,* (1989): 5–23.

———, 'Learning to be a Tourist', *Ethnologia Scandinavica,* 24, (1994): 12–125.

Lonely Planet, *Travel Survival Kit to Turkey* (3rd edition), Victoria and Berkeley: Lonely Planet Publications, 1996.

Lonely Planet, *Destination Greece.* Web Site, Lonely Planet, 1997.

Lowenthal, D., *The Past is a Foreign Country.* Cambridge, Cambridge University Press, 1985.

Lury C., *Consumer Culture.* Cambridge, Polity Press, 1996.

Lury, C., 'The Objects of Tourism', in *Touring Cultures: Transformation of Travel and Theory,* eds C. Rojek, and J. Urry, London, Routledge. 1997, 75–95.

Lynch, K., *The Image of the City.* Cambridge, The Technology Press and Harvard University Press, 1960.

Macaulay, P., 'Proposals would "Put Culture in Time Capsule"', *West Highland Free Press,* 9 Nov 1990.

MacCannell, D., *The Tourist. A New Theory of the Leisure Class.* New York, Shocken Books, 1976.

MacCannell D., *Empty Meeting Grounds: The Tourist Papers.* London, Routledge, 1992.

MacCannell, D., 'Cannibal Tours', in *Visualising Theory: Selected Essays from V.A.R. 1990–1994,* ed, L. Taylor, Routledge: London, 1994, 99–114.

MacDonald, F., 'Viewing Highland Scotland: Ideology, Representation and the 'Natural Heritage"', *Area* 30.3 (1998).

Macdonald, S., *Reimagining Culture: Histories,Identities and the Gaelic Renaissance,* Berg, Oxford, 1997a.

Macdonald, S., 'A People's Story: Heritage, Identity and Authenticity', in *Touring Cultures: Transformation of Travel and Theory,* eds C. Rojek, and J. Urry, London, Routledge, 1997b, 155–75.

MacKinnon, I., 'Gaelic Arts Survey Reveals Split', *West Highland Free Press,* 6 March 1998.

MacNaghten P. and Urry J., *Contested Natures*. London, Routledge, 1998.

Maffesoli, M., *Times of Tribes*. London, Sage, 1996.

Malbon, B., 'The Club: Clubbing: Consumption, Identity and the Spatial Practices of Every-Night Life', in *Cool Places: Geographies of Youth Culture*, eds, T. Skelton and G. Valentine, Routledge London, 1998.

Mannari, H. and Harumi B. (eds), *The Challenge of Japan's Internationalization: Organization and Culture*, Tokyo, Kwansei Gakuin University and Kodansha International Ltd., 1983.

Marcus, G., *The Dustbin of History*. Cambridge MA, Harvard University Press, 1995.

Marcus, J., *A World of Difference – Islam and Gender Hierarchy in Turkey*. London, Zed, 1992.

Marling, K., *The Colossus of Roads: Myth and Symbol along the American Highway*. Minneapolis, University of Minnesota Press, 1984.

Marx, K., *Capital*. vol 1, London, Penguin, 1976.

Massey D., 'A Global Sense of Place', *Marxism Today* Jun (1991): 24–29.

———, 'The Politics of Spatiality', *New Left Review* 196 (1992): 65–84.

———, 'Power-Geometry and a Progressive Sense of Place', in *Mapping the Futures: Local Cultures, Global Change*, eds J. Bird, et al., London and New York, Routledge, 1993.

McCutcheon, J. T., *Doing the Grand Canyon*. Chicago, The Fred Harvey Company, 1909.

Meethan, K., 'Consuming (in) the Civilized City', *Annals of Tourism Research* 23 (2) (1996): 322–40.

Mentzos, B., *Lamartine, Nerval, Gautier: Three French Romantics in Greece*. Athens, Olkos (in Greek), 1989.

Merleau-Ponty M., *The Phenomenology of Perception*. London, Routledge, 1962.

Metz, C., *The Imaginary Signifier: Psychoanalysis and the Cinema*. Bloomington, Indiana University Press, 1982.

Meyrowitz, J., *No Sense of Place*. Oxford University Press, Oxford, 1985.

Miller D., 'The Young and the Restless in Trinidad: A Case of the Local and the Global in Mass Consumption', in *Consuming Technologies: Media and Information in Domestic Spaces*, eds R. Silverstone and E. Hirsch, London, Routledge, 1992.

———, 'Consumption as the Vanguard of History', in *Acknowledging Consumption: A review of New Studies*, ed. D. Miller, London, Routledge, 1995a.

———, 'Introduction', in *Worlds Apart* London, Routledge, 1995b, 1–22.

———, 'Consumption and its Consequences', in *Consumption and Everyday Life*, ed. G. Mackay, London, Sage, 1997, 13–64.

Miller D. et al., *Shopping, Place and Identity*, London, Routledge, 1998.

Miller, H., *The Colossus of Maroussi*. London, Secker and Warburg, 1942.

Miller, J. H., *Topographies*. Stanford CA., Stanford University Press, 1995.

Milner A., *Contemporary Cultural Theory: An Introduction* London, University College of London Press, 1994.

Mitchell, W. T. J., *Landscape and Power*. Chicago and London, University of Chicago Press, 1994.

Monroe, H., 'The Grand Canyon of the Colorado' *The Atlantic Monthly*, vol. 84, no. 506, December, (1899): 818–819.

Moran, T., *The Grand Canyon of Arizona: Being a Book of Words from Many Pens, About the Grand Canyon of the Colorado River in Arizona*, Chicago, Passenger Department of the Santa Fe Railway, 1902.

Morley D., *Television, Audiences and Cultural Studies*. Routledge, London, 1992.

Morris, M., 'At Henry Parkes Motel', *Cultural Studies* 2 (1) (1988a): 1–16.

———, 'Banality in Cultural Studies', *Discourse* 10 (2) (1988b): 3–29.

———, 'Things to Do with Shopping Centres', in *Grafts: Feminist Cultural Criticism*, ed. S. Sheridan, London, Verso, 1988c, 193–224.

———, 'The Man in the Mirror: David Harvey's "Condition" of Postmodernity', *Theory, Culture and Society* 9 (1992): 253–279.

Moscardo, G. and Pearce, P., 'Historic Theme Parks: An Australian Experience in Authenticity,' *Annals of Tourism Research* 13 (3) (1986): 467–79.

Muir, E., *Civic Ritual in Renaissance Venice*. Princeton, Princeton University Press, 1980.

Muir, J., 'The Wild Parks and Forest Reservations of the West', *The Atlantic Monthly* vol. 81, no. 483 (January) (1898): 28.

Munt, I., 'The 'Other' Postmodern Tourism: Culture, Travel and the New Middle Classes' *Theory, Culture and Society* Vol. (11) 3 (1994): 101–124.

Murray, J., *A Handbook for the Travellers in the East*. London, John Murray, 1845.

Murray, J., *A Handbook for the Travellers in Greece*. London, John Murray, 1854.

Nash, D., 'Tourism as a Form of Imperialism', in *Hosts and Guests*, ed. V.L. Smith, Philadelphia PA, University of Pennsylvania Press, 1977, 37–52.

Nash, R., *Wilderness and the American Mind*. New Haven and London, Yale University Press, 1968.

Nelson, P., *After the West Was Won: Homesteaders and Town-Builders in Western South Dakota, 1900–1917*. Iowa City: University of Iowa Press, 1986.

Neumann, M., *On The Rim: Looking for the Grand Canyon*. Minneapolis: University of Minnesota Press, forthcoming.

Nisanyan, S., *Athens and the Classical Sites*. London, American Express Travel Guides, 1994.

Nora, P., 'Between Memory and History: Les Lieux de Memoire', *Representations* 26 (1989): 7–25.

Oakes, T., 'Eating the Food of the Ancestors: Place, Tradition and Tourism in a Chinese Frontier River Town', *Ecumene* 6 (2) (1999): 123–45.

Odermatt, P., 'A Case of Neglect? The Politics of (Re)presentation: A Sardinia Case', in *Coping With Tourists*, ed. J. Boissevain, Oxford: Berghahn, 1996.

Ohnuki-Tierney, E., *Rice as Self: Japanese Identities Through Time*. Princeton, NJ: Princeton University Press, 1993.

Olmstead, F.L., 'Preservation for All' in *Mirror of America: Literary Encounters with the National Parks*, ed. D. Harmon, Boulder, CO., Roberts Rinehart, 1865/1989.

Olwig, K. and Hastrup, K., *Siting Culture: The Shifting Anthropological Object*. London, Routledge, 1997.

Palumbo-Liu, D., 'Introduction: Unhabituated Habituses', in *Streams of Cultural Capital: Transnational Cultural Studies*, eds D. Palumbo-Liu and H.U. Gumbracht, Stanford: Stanford University Press, 1997, 1–21.

Papataxiarchis, E., 'Friends of the Heart' in *Contested Identities*, eds, P. Loizos and E. Papataxiarchis, Princeton, Princeton University Press, 1991, 156–79.

Passin, H., *Japanese and the Japanese: Language and Culture Change*. Tokyo, Kinseido, 1980.Payne, R., *The Splendour of Greece*. London, Pan Books Ltd., 1961.

Perfecture of Athens, *Athens: History and Civilization*. Athens, Athens County Council Department of Tourism, 1998.

Petoello, G. and Rigon, F., 'Sviluppo urbanistico dal secolo X ai nostri giorni', in *Storia di Bassano* Vicenza: Rumor, 1980, 389–432.

Phillips, J., *A Man's Country?* New Zealand; Penguin, 1996.

Philo, C., More Words, More Worlds: Reflections on the 'Cultural Turn' and Social Geography, in *Cultural Turns*, eds I. Cook, D. Crouch, D. S. Naylor and J. Ryan, London, Longman, 2000.

Plant, S., *The Most Radical Gesture: The Situationist International in a Postmodern Age*. London, Routledge, 1992.

Plath, D., *Long Engagements: Maturity in Modern Japan*. Stanford, CA., Stanford University Press, 1980.

———, 'My-car-isma: Motorizing the Showa Self', *Daedalus 119*(3) (1990): 229–243.

Pocock, D.C.D., 'City of the Mind: A Review of Mental Maps of Urban Areas', *Scottish Geographical Magazine* 88(2) (1972): 115–124.

Poppi, C., *We Are Mountain People*, Ph.D. Thesis, University of Cambridge, 1983.

———, 'Building Differences: The Political Economy of Tradition in the Ladin Carnival of the Val di Fassa', in *Revitalising European Rituals*, ed. J. Boissevain, London, Routledge, 1992, 113–136.

Potter J., *Representing Reality: Discourse, Rhetoric and Social Construction*. London, Sage, 1996.

Pound, F., *Frames on the Land. Early Landscape Painting in New Zealand*. New Zealand, Collins, 1984.

Pratt, M.L., *Imperial Eyes: Travel Writing and Transculturation*. London, Routledge, 1992.

Pretes, M., 'Postmodern Tourism', *Annals of Tourism Research*, 22 (1995): 1–9.

Preziosi D., 'Brain of the Earth's Body: Museums and the Framing of Modernity', in *The Rhetoric of the Frame: Essays on the Boundaries of the Artwork*, ed, P. Duro, London, Cambridge University Press, 1996.

Radley A., 'Artefacts, Memory and a Sense of the Past', in *Collective Remembering*, eds D. Middleton and D. Edwards, London, Sage, 1990.

Radley A. 'The Elusory Body and Social Constructionist Theory', *Body and Society* 1 (2) (1995): 3–24.

Rawlins, C.L., *Greece, Culture Shock: A Guide to Customs and Etiquette*. London, Kuperard, 1997.

Redfoot, D., 'Touristic Authenticity, Touristic Angst and Modern Reality', *Qualitative Sociology* 7 (4) (1984): 291–309.

Relph, E., *Place and Placelessness*. London, Pion, 1976.

Relph, E., *Rational Landscape and Humanistic Geography*. London, Croom Helm, 1981.

Rhodes, C. and Nabi, N., 'Brick Lane: A Village Economy in the Shadow of the City?', in *Global Finance and Urban Living: A Study of Metropolitan Change*, eds L. Budd, and S. Whimster, London, Routledge, 1992.

Ringer, G., 'Introduction' in *Destinations: Cultural Landscapes of Tourism*. Ed. G. Ringer, London, Routledge, 1998, 1–13.

Ritzer, G., *The McDonaldization of Society: An Investigation into the Changing Character of Contemporary Social Life*. Thousand Oaks: Pine Forge Press, 1993.

Robertson, J., *Native and Newcomer: Making and Remaking a Japanese City*. Berkeley, University of California Press, 1991.

Robertson, R., *Globalization*, London: Sage, 1992.Rodman, M., 'Empowering Place: Multilocality and Multivocality', *American Anthropologist* 94 (1992): 640–56.

Roemer, M., *Telling Stories: Postmodernism and the Invalidation of Traditional Narrative*. Maryland, USA, Rowman and Littlefield Publishers, 1995.

Rojek, C., *Ways of Escape: Modern Transformations in Leisure and Travel*. London, Macmillan, 1993.
———, *De-centring Leisure*. London, Sage, 1995.
———, 'Indexing, Dragging and the Social Construction of Tourist Sights', in *Touring Cultures: Transformations of Travel and Theory*, eds C. Rojek and J. Urry, London, Routledge, 1997, 52–74.
Rojek C. and Urry J. eds, *Touring Cultures: Transformations of Travel and Theory*. London, Routledge, 1997.
Rosaldo, R., 'Imperialist Nostalgia', *Representations* 26 Spr (1989): 107–122.
Rough Guide, *Greece*. London, Rough Guide Publications, 1996.
Saarinen, J., 'The Social Construction of Tourist Destinations: The Process of Transformation of the Saariskelkä Tourism Region in Finnish Lapland', in *Destinations: Cultural Landscapes of Tourism*, ed. G. Ringer, London, Routledge, 1998, 154–73.
Sack, R. D., *Place, Modernity, and the Consumer's World*. London, John Hopkins, 1992.
Said, E.,*Orientalism*. New York, Pantheon, 1978.
Samad, Y., 'Book Burning and Race Relations: Political Mobilisation of Bradford Muslims', *New Community* 18, 4, (1992): 507–19.
Samuel, R., *Theatres of Memory Vol. 1: Past and Present in Contemporary Culture*. London, Verso, 1994.
Santa Fe Railway, *Grand Canyon Outings*. Chicago, Santa Fe Railway, 1915.
Sasaki, K., *Insaku Izen* (Before Rice Cultivation). Tokyo, Nihon Hôsô Shuppan Kyôkai, 1983.
Sassen, S., *The Global City*, Princeton, Princeton University Press, 1991.
Schmidt, S.W. et al. eds, *Friends, Followers and Factions*. Berkeley, University of California Press, 1977.
Scottish Council for National Parks, *National Parks for Scotland*, (leaflet) Edinburgh, SCNP, 1944.
Scottish Natural Heritage, *National Parks for Scotland: A Consultation Paper*, Battleby, SNH, 1998.
Seamon, D., *A Geography of the Lifeworld*. London, Croom Helm, 1979.
Sears, J., *Sacred Places: American Tourist Attractions in the Nineteenth Century*. Amherst, University of Massachusetts Press, 1989.
Selwyn T. ed., *The Tourist Image: Myths and Myth Making in Tourism*, London, Wiley, 1996.
———, 'The Anthropology of Tourism – The State of the Art', in *Tourism – The State of the Art*, ed. A.V. Seaton, Chichester, John Whiley, 1994.
———, 'Introduction', in *The Tourist Image: Myths and Myth Making in Tourism*, ed. T. Selwyn, London, Wiley, 1996, 1–32.
Sheehy, D. 'Crossover Dreams: The Folklorist and Folk Arrival', in *Public Folklore*, eds R. Baron and N. Spitzer, Washington DC, Smithsonian Institute Press, 1992, 217–30.
Sheldon, G., *American Painters*, New York, D. Appleton and Co., 1881.
Shields, R., 'Social Spatialisation and the Built Environment: The West Edmonton Mall', *Society and Space* 7 (1989): 147–164.
———, *Places on the Margin: Alternative Geographies of Modernity*. London, Routledge, 1991.
———, *Lifestyle Shopping*. London, Routledge, 1992.
Shotter J., *Cultural Politics in Everyday Life: Social Constructionism, Rhetoric and Knowing of the Third Kind*. Buckingham, Open University Press, 1993.

Shriver, J., 'Kitschy Coup: When it Comes to Corniness, South Dakota Leads the Field', *USA Today*, 18 Aug. (1995), final ed.: D4+.

Silverman, S., 'Patronage and Community-Nation Relationships in Central Italy', in *Friends, Followers and Factions*, eds Schmidt, S.W. et al., Berkeley, University of California Press, 1977, 293–304.

Silverstone R., *Television and Everyday Life*. London, Routledge, 1994.

Simmel, G., 'Sociability', in *The Sociology of Georg Simmel*, New York: The Free Press, 1950, 40–57.

Simon, R. 'The Formal Garden in the Age of Consumer Culture: A Reading of the Twentieth Century Shopping Mall', in *Mapping American Culture*, eds W. Franklin, and M. Steiner, Iowa City, University of Iowa Press, 1992, 231–50.

Skopetea, E., *The 'Model Kingdom' and the Grand Idea: Views of the National Problem in Greece (1830–1880)*. Athens, Polytypo (in Greek), 1988.

Slater, D., 'Photography and Modern Vision: The Spectacle of "Natural" Magic', in *Visual Culture*, ed. C. Jenks, London, Routledge, 1995, 218–37.

Smith, I. C., *Towards the Human*. Edinburgh, Macdonald, 1986.

Smith, P., *Japan: A Reinterpretation*. New York: Pantheon Books, 1997.

Smith, V. ed., *Hosts and Guests. The Anthropology of Tourism*. Philadelphia, University of Pennsylvania Press, 1977.

Snow, S., *Performing the Pilgrims: A Study of Ethnohistorical Role-Playing at Plimoth Plantation*. Jackson, University Press of Mississippi, 1993.

Sontag, S., *On Photography*. London, Penguin, 1979.

Soper, K., *What is Nature? Culture, Politics and the Non-Human*. Oxford UK and Cambridge USA, Blackwell, 1995.

Springwood, C. F. 'Space, Time, and Hardware Individualism in Japanese Baseball: Non-Western Dimensions of Personhood', *Play and Culture 5* (1992): 280–294.

———, *Cooperstown to Dyersville: A Geography of Baseball Nostalgia*. Boulder, CO: Westview Press, 1996.

Spurr, D., *The Rhetoric of Empire: Colonial Discourse in Journalism, Travel Writing and Imperial Administration*. Durham, Duke University Press, 1993.

Squire, S., 'Rewriting Languages of Geography and Tourism: Cultural Discourses of Destinations, Gender and Tourism History in the Canadian Rockies', in *Destinations: Cultural Landscapes of Tourism*, ed. G. Ringer, London, Routledge, 1998, 80–100.

Stallabrass, J., *Gargantua: Manufactured Mass Culture*. London, Verso, 1996.

Stegner, W., 'C.E. Dutton – Explorer, Geologist, Nature Writer', *The Scientific Monthly* vol. 45 (July) (1937): 82–85.

Stewart, S., *On Longing: Narratives of the Miniature, the Gigantic, the Souvenir and the Collection*. Baltimore, Johns Hopkins University Press, 1984.

Stirling, P., *Turkish Village*. London, Weidenfeld and Nicolson, 1965.

Stirling, P. ed., *Culture and Economy – Changes in Turkish Villages*. Huntingdon, Eothen Press, 1993.

Storace, P., *Dinner with Persephone*. London, Granta Books, 1996.

Strinati D., *An Introduction to Theories of Popular Culture*. London, Routledge, 1995.

Suran, W. C., *The Kolb Brothers of Grand Canyon*. Grand Canyon Natural History Association, 1991.

Swyngedouw, E., 'Responses to Fordist and Post-Fordist Accumulation and Regulation', *Papers of the Regional Science Association*, Vol. 64, (1988): 11–23.

Taussig, M., *Mimesis and Alterity: A Particular History of the Senses*. London, Routledge, 1993.

Tester K. ed., *The Flâneur*. London, Routledge, 1994.

The American Legion Auxiliary, Carrol McDonald Unit, *Eastern Pennington County Memories*. Wall, SD: The American Legion Auxiliary, c.1965.

Thrift N., *Spatial Formations*. London, Sage, 1996.

———, 'The Still Point', in *Geographies of Resistance*, eds S. Pile and M. Keith, London, Routledge, 1997.

Tilley, C. *A Phenomenology of Landscape: Places, Paths and Monuments*. Oxford, Berg, 1994.

Todorov, T., *Nous et les Autres. La Réflexion Française sur la Diversit(Humaine*. Paris, Seuil, 1989.

Tolei, T., *'La Banda Communale: Brani di Storia'*, *Il Garzone* n.4. (Luglio) (1992): 35.

Tsuboi, H., *Ine o Eranda Nihonjin* ('The Japanese who Chose the Rice Plant'), Tokyo, Miraihsa, 1984 [1982].Tuan, Y-F., *Topophilia*. Englewood Cliffs: Prentice-Hall, 1974.

Tucker, H., 'The Ideal Village: Interactions Through Tourism in Central Anatolia', in *Tourists and Tourism – Identifying With People and Places*, eds S. Abram, D. Macleod and J. Waldren, Oxford: Berg Press, 1997.

Turner V., *Dramas, Fields and Metaphors: Symbolic Action in Human Society*. Ithaca, Cornell University Press, 1974.

———, *The Forest of Symbols*. Ithaca, Cornell University Press, 1967.

Urbain, J.D., *L' Idiot du Voyage: Histoires de Touristes*. Paris, Plon, 1991.

Urry J. *Consuming Places* London, Routledge, 1995.

Urry, J., *The Tourist Gaze: Leisure and Travel in Contemporary Society*. London, Sage, 1990.

Waldren, J., *Insiders and Outsiders – Paradise and Reality in Mallorca*, Oxford, Berghahn Books, 1996.

———, 'We Are Not Tourists – We Live Here', in *Tourists and Tourism – Identifying With People and Places*, eds S. Abram, D. Macleod and J. Waldren, Oxford, Berg Press, 1997.

Walle, A. H., 'Pursuing Risk or Insight – Marketing Adventures' *Annals of Tourism Research*, Vol 24, No 2, (1997): 265–282

Walton J.K., *The English Seaside Resort: A Social History 1750–1914*. Leicester, Leicester University Press, 1983.

Walton, K.R.L., *Mimesis as Make-Believe: On the Foundations of the Representational Arts*. Cambridge, Mass., Harvard University Press, 1990.

Walvin J., *Beside the Seaside: A Social History of the Popular Seaside Holiday*. London, Allen Lane, 1978.

Warner, C.D., *Our Italy*. New York, Harper and Brothers, 1891.

Warren, S., ' "This Heaven Gives Me Migraines": The Problems and Promise of Landscapes and Leisure', in *Place, Culture, and Representation*, eds J. Duncan and D. Ley, London, Routledge, 1993, 173–186.

Wearing, B. and Wearing, S., 'Refocusing the Tourist Experience: The Flaneur and the Choraster', *Leisure Studies* 15(1996): 229–243.

Webb, W. P., *The Great Plains*, New York: Grosset and Dunlap, 1931.

Weinberg, D. 'Bands and Clans: Political Functions of Voluntary Associations in the Swiss Alps', *American Ethnologist*, 2, (1976): 175–189.

West Highland Free Press (1.8.75) Letter, untitled, 3.

West Highland Free Press (11.7.80) Letter, "Tourist Attractions", 3.*West Highland Free Press* (18.7.75) Letter, untitled, 3.

West Highland Free Press (18.7.80a) Letter, "A Good Laugh", 3.*West Highland Free Press* (18.7.80b) Letter, "I Won't Be Back", 3.

Weyeneth, R., *Moral Spaces: Reforming the Landscape of Leisure in Urban America, 1850–1920.* Ph.D., University of California, Berkeley, 1984.

Wheeler, V., 'Travelers' Tales: Observations on the Travel Book and Ethnography', *Anthropological Quarterly*, 59(2) (1986): 52–63.

Wilk, R., 'Learning to be Local in Belize: Global Systems of Common Difference', in *Worlds Apart*, ed. D. Miller, London, Routledge, 1995b, 110–33.

Williams, W. and Papamichael, E. M., 'Tourism and Tradition: Local Control Versus Outside Interests in Greece', in *International Tourism – Identity and Change*, eds M. Lanfant, J. Allcock and E. Bruner, London, Sage, 1995.

Wilson, A., *The Culture of Nature.* Cambridge MA and Oxford UK, Blackwells, 1992.

Wilson, D. 'Paradoxes of Tourism in Goa', *Annals of Tourism Research*, 24(1997): 52–75.

Withers, C., 'The Historical Creation of the Scottish Highlands', in *The Manufacture of Scottish History*, eds, I. Donnachie and C. Whatley, Edinburgh, Polygon, 1992.

Withers, C., 'Picturing Highland Landscapes: George Washington Wilson and the Photography of the Scottish Highlands', *Landscape Research* 19, 2 (1994).

Wolf, E., *Europe and the People without History*, Berkeley, University of California Press, 1982.

Womack, P., *Improvement and Romance: Constructing the Myth of the Highlands.* London, Macmillan, 1989.

Yatsuki, J., 'Osaka "Old Kids": Yakyu no seichi de yume no enseishiai' ('A Dream Game in Baseball's Holy Land'). *Semba* (September 1) (1990): 13–18.

Yoshimoto, M., 'Images of Empire: Tokyo Disneyland and Japanese Cultural Imperialism', in *Disney Discourse: Producing the Magic Kingdom*, ed. E. Smoodin, New York, Routledge, 1994, 181–199.

Young I.M., *Throwing Like a Girl and other Essays in Feminist Philosophy and Social Theory.* Indiana, Indiana University Press, 1990.

Zizek, S., *The Sublime Object of Ideology.* London, Verso, 1989.

———, *For They Know Not What They Do: Enjoyment as a Political Factor.* London, Verso, 1991a.

———, *Looking Awry: An Introduction to Jacques Lacan through Popular Culture.* Cambridge, MA, MIT Press, 1991b.

Index